Trusting the Word and Nothing Else at All

Trusting the Word and Nothing Else at All

Luther's Design for Evangelical Preaching

Perry Toso

FOREWORD BY
Roy A. Harrisville

WIPF & STOCK · Eugene, Oregon

TRUSTING THE WORD AND NOTHING ELSE AT ALL
Luther's Design for Evangelical Preaching

Copyright © 2018 Perry Toso. All rights reserved. Except for brief quotations in critical publications or reviews, no part of this book may be reproduced in any manner without prior written permission from the publisher. Write: Permissions, Wipf and Stock Publishers, 199 W. 8th Ave., Suite 3, Eugene, OR 97401.

Wipf & Stock
An Imprint of Wipf and Stock Publishers
199 W. 8th Ave., Suite 3
Eugene, OR 97401

www.wipfandstock.com

PAPERBACK ISBN: 978-1-5326-6076-4
HARDCOVER ISBN: 978-1-5326-6077-1
EBOOK ISBN: 978-1-5326-6078-8

Manufactured in the U.S.A.

This book is dedicated to Gerhard Forde, faithful proclaimer of the Gospel as a matter of death and life.

Contents

Foreword by Roy A. Harrisville | ix

Introduction | 1

CHAPTER ONE — Two Worlds Collide | 8

CHAPTER TWO — The Word of God as Event | 15

CHAPTER THREE — A Brief History of "Free Will" | 20

CHAPTER FOUR — The Objective of Christian Preaching: Certainty of Faith | 26

CHAPTER FIVE — The Reformation Discovery | 43

CHAPTER SIX — Preaching as the Prosecution of God's Election | 74

CHAPTER SEVEN — Preaching the "Non-Asterisk Absolution" | 87

CHAPTER EIGHT — Luther's Preaching Model—Conscience as "Man Addressed" | 109

CHAPTER NINE — Toward a "Proper Confidence" | 129

CHAPTER TEN — Distinguishing Law and Gospel | 152

CHAPTER ELEVEN — On the Work of the Holy Spirit | 168

Epilogue: Bearing Witness | 193

Bibliography | 197

Foreword

Perry Toso has been known to me for years, first as student, now as pastor. While a student he consistently, persistently, perennially, and with a bit of ferocity engaged me in debate over the question of the fruits that "faith should bear." I insisted that he pay attention to the imperatives attendant upon the gospel, and he insisted that I attend to the indicatives at its heart. As I remember, we both agreed that while there was a specific, discrete, and particular Christian faith, there was not a specific, discrete, and particular Christian ethic. But it was the question respecting the emphasis on the arms and legs which Christian faith must take over which we broke our lances.

Now that Perry has served as my pastor for the better part of two years, I suspect him of locating the doctrine of predestination and election in every blessed word of the Bible. In other words, my student, now my pastor, has not altered his preoccupation with the sovereignty of God. And that preoccupation was bound to have its consequence in this volume devoted to the sole authority of the scriptures for Christian faith and life, thus for their enunciation in proclamation, in preaching.

If the one-sidedness I thought to detect in Perry's papers written for my class should strike the reader as repeated in this volume, I happily celebrate it. In a land a-swarm with imperatives, with demands attaching to every aspect of human life and conduct, to the point where freedom of speech and expression is in thrall to the do's and don'ts concocted by countless, unnumbered litigants and do-gooders, all in a frenzy, and all of it without linkage to an engine of promise and hope able to draw and drive it—the "exclusive particle" respecting "the Word alone" needs shouting from the housetops. For behind that "Word alone" there stands "Christ alone," no doubt "with a face like all men's faces," but the only one able to deliver on the promise that the good, the true, and the beautiful we hope for are possible, provided they are anchored in him.

This accent on the divine sovereignty may be as distant from pulpits of the mainline denominations as heaven from earth. The urge to avoid it has been a huge mistake. The accent on that God who alone bears the promise and hope able to bring about a new humanity has been imagined to be exclusivistic, imperialistic, parochial, intolerant. It is as if a blind beggar refused ministrations from the sole physician able to offer him sight. And the mistake has been multiplied in the substitution of an oblong, amorphous spirituality, coupled with concentration on the self of the one in the pulpit. I leave it to the reader to reflect whether or not that great old portrait of Matthias Grünewald, with the Baptist pointing an elongated finger at the crucified One and saying: "He must increase, but I must decrease," has been exchanged for a self-portrait. At any rate, I invite the reader to follow this accent on the "Word alone," on this royal intolerance, to allow for the possibility that a return to it and "Nothing Else At All" may be the one chance left to redeem a Church once more near collapse.

—Roy A. Harrisville

Introduction

It was Holy Thursday, 1985. I was 38 years old, and had made the emergency flight from my church in San Diego to St. Paul, because the previous Sunday we had received the news that Dad could not last much longer. That afternoon, our whole family was gathered in a circle around Dad's bed. He was so near death that he could not even speak. So we sang hymns and prayed together. Then, as families do, without permission, they assign you your role within the family structure, and there is no discussion about it. So, the mantle that had been Dad's authority and office was passed wordlessly to me, as they looked in my direction. I was a pastor, after all. But what was I supposed to do? Part of the dishonoring and insulting nature of Death is that it renders us all so helpless! As missionary kids we had learned the liturgy by heart, along with whole chunks of scripture. Then the words presented themselves to me from the liturgical song Lutherans used to sing at the end of communion, the words of Simeon, as he held and looked in amazement at the baby Jesus as the fulfillment of a promise waited upon for years. So I laid my hand on Dad's head and said Simeon's words, now new, now living: "Lord, now lettest thou thy servant depart in peace, according to your word. For mine eyes have seen thy salvation, which thou hast prepared in the presence of all peoples, a light for revelation to the Gentiles, and for the glory of thy people Israel." (The old King James was how we sang it, and how I said it.)

Something *happened* in those words. It felt as if the entire room was changed—held up and embraced by the utterance of those words. The benediction of those words *happened* to us! God's Peace came, right in the midst of our crushing sorrow and pain. Never before in my life had I experienced anything nearly so dramatic, so real, or so clear. For the first time in my memory, I became convinced as never before, that God's Word really did have the power to perform—to perform what it said.

This book about preaching flows from that event and from that conviction. But it is about something far more fundamental than preaching. It is an attempt, after more than thirty years of wrestling to get ready to preach, to come to personal terms with how the Word has affected me, changed my mind and the very way I think. It is my attempt to honestly express my bafflement over why the God, who reveals His love for sinners in the sending of His own Son, would insist that all our knowing of Him must flow most centrally from the cross, whose purpose is to mortally wound all human wisdom or intellect. My Dad would ask, after a life time of preaching, "Why is the Gospel so hidden?"

It is shocking to say, but the Bible does say that God hides. He must reveal himself to sinners. This revelation is not in our control. We cannot make it happen. Preachers, themselves, struggle with the helplessness of standing empty before a word which they are called to preach. But we do have this assured context: that if God wanted so much to reveal himself that he devised the miracle of becoming incarnate in the person of his very own Son, who, as God's definitive Word is sent not only to redeem but to reveal, then all who are interested in hearing God's Word will never be disappointed. God will always faithfully come and do what he promised through the means He chose –through His Word.

- In Jeremiah we hear, "If with all your heart you truly seek me, you shall ever surely find me. Thus says your God."
- In John 1 we hear, "The light shines on in the darkness and the darkness has not overcome it."
- In Romans 10 we hear that God sends preachers so we can rightly hear that Word in a living fashion.

So God ordains the office of preaching and sends preachers to reveal himself to whomever will listen to His Word.

This book is shaped by the unshakeable conviction that we do not read God's Word so much as God's Word "reads us," recreating our minds, our thoughts, and our beliefs. We are not the masters who "understand" (think of the power that we confer upon ourselves by the word-picture that we "under-stand" something!); rather, the Word shines its light into our darkened minds, so that we can rightly see for the first time. In the Luther-Erasmus debate which resulted in what Luther esteemed as one of best works, "The Bondage of the Will," Erasmus was complaining that obscure doctrines like God's election should not be preached so as to avoid making believers anxious. Luther's rejoinder began by asserting that it is not scripture that is obscure, but rather, our minds which are darkened, and that nothing in the Bible should be hidden from hearers of God's Word. From this exchange grew a hermeneutical (interpretive) principle that Luther forcefully espoused ever after—the clarity of scripture. This assertion is not only about scripture's clarity. It also asserts that our sin-impaired minds need an agent, called the Holy Spirit, to make scriptural revelation clear to us.

. . .

The preachers of the Old Testament were definitely not "three points and a poem" kind of men (a sermon structure which we mocked as seminary students). First, they did not speak unless they were spoken to. Then, when that happened, they began their utterance with the awesome and formal introduction: "Thus says the LORD." They were universally feared, never popular, never keepers of the status quo like the priests, and certainly not on the A-list for anyone's party. Anybody who said, "Thus says the LORD" without proper warrant or revelation was subject to death, whether by humans or by God Himself. (See the story of Hananiah, the priest, in Jeremiah 28, especially 15-17). In contrast to the priests, who would be more the caregivers, prophets always seemed to be more like porcupines than teddy bears. That is, through their preaching God exposed that God and His people were related fundamentally by contradiction and not by congruence.

An additional trial for the bearers of their office was that prophecy, by its very function, could have nothing to do with measurement by the standards of "effectiveness" or "success." God says to Jeremiah, "So you shall speak all these words to them, but they will not listen to you. You shall call to them, but they will not answer you." He says to Isaiah, "Go tell these people, 'Be ever hearing, but never understanding, be ever seeing, but never perceiving.' Make the heart of the people calloused, make their ears dull and close their eyes." Isaiah understandably asks, "How long O Lord?" These prophets shared our own bafflement over God's strange ways, and the unpredictable results of their preaching.

Still, proclamation was never an option to them. Jeremiah bitterly complains to God that he can't win no matter what he does. He says to God in effect, "When I preach what you tell me to, everybody hates me; but when I try to hold it in, I cannot because there is in my heart, as it were, a burning fire shut up in my bones, and I am weary with holding it in, and I cannot." (Jer. 20:7ff)

For Old Testament prophets, proclamation, if not always "successful", was always performative. It always did something. When the Word was proclaimed, it rendered God's judgment. Part of God's performing of the judgment occurred *in the hearing of the proclaimed Word itself*.

History bent to the utterance. Neighbors, just because they were neighboring lands, got to hear God's working prediction. Sometimes proclamation literally caused things to happen in the very process of utterance. The most famous is Ezekiel 37 with the valley of dry bones. The valid argument that Ezekiel 37 was a vision, and therefore merely a metaphor and not actual, does not change or alter the fundamental point—God's Word is the agent, and preaching God's Word invokes the Holy Spirit. The Word, alone, via the Holy Spirit which it invokes, creates resurrection from what was dead. God's Word does the deed, both metaphorically and actually. Another example of proclamation literally causing things to happen in the very process of utterance is when Jesus begins his first sermon at Nazareth with this: "Today, this word became reality as you heard it spoken." While no one would characterize the electric effect of those words as "a success" (not a single person was a candidate for an altar call that day) no one will deny the nuclear explosion that ensued!

Why, then, do the majority of Americans, even among many church goers, instead of experiencing the sermon time as a momentous (not to say dangerous) encounter, seem to regard preaching as innocuous, tame, irrelevant, embarrassingly boring, something to be timed and endured for as short a time as possible? Why is there such a yawning chasm between the current assessment of preaching and what we see in the Gospels? Jesus held proclamation in such high esteem that he refused to let *anything* take priority over this salient activity of his ministry—not healing, not exorcism, not controversy with religious leaders, not even time with his disciples. Jesus says, already in the first chapter of Mark, "Let us go on to the next towns, that I may preach there also; for that is why I came out." (Mark 1:38)

When we contrast Jesus' enthusiasm and estimation concerning the vital nature and place of preaching with our own, it raises questions—questions that baffle us—over the reason for the apparent extreme variance in effect when we proclaim. Why is there such difference in both expectation and effect, between us and Jesus, when we preach? Although we try other activities or methods to augment preaching, fashioning it from the perspective of more therapy-oriented disciplines such as counseling or clinical pastoral education or adorning it with surrounding beautiful worship—it never quite captures what we see happening in the Bible's narrative. We find some consolation in the amazing crowds that flock to churches who *redefine* preaching, by making it into an emotionally manipulative hour built upon the attention span of our entertainments, or a self-esteem hour that never confronts but leaves you feeling good about yourself, or an educational hour that is focused on how you, too, can achieve some spiritual objective.

INTRODUCTION 5

...

A mighty comet streaked across the horizon of world history exactly 500 years ago in the person and work of Martin Luther, through whom 1500 years of scriptural interpretation was overturned, solely by strenuously attending to the Word. The Reformation cannot be understood fundamentally until one understands that it was rigorously focused upon the Word of God, and nothing else at all. It owed its staying power and triumph to the power of the proclaimed Word, and nothing else at all. When Luther (then hidden at Wartburg Castle to protect him from the public warrant for his capture dead or alive) learned of the riots taking place in Wittenberg, which included tearing down statues and beautiful church adornments, he disregarded his personal safety, returned to Wittenberg, and relying only on preaching God's Word from the local pulpit, brought calm to the anarchic crowd. He trusted that God's powerful Word, let loose in that situation by preaching, was the only thing that could or would bring peace to the situation. Again, during the Peasants Revolt, when Luther was asked to make the Reformation movement into a political thing, he refused the power of the sword, and trusted in the proclaimed Word, and nothing else at all. When, in desperate straits during the meeting at Augsburg of 1530, considering the hopeless prospects of the little Reformation movement against the overwhelming panoply of papal power gathered together with the leadership of the Holy Roman Empire, he trusted not in stratagem or wiles, but in the Word of God, and nothing else at all. Unable to be personally at the gathering of all the continental powers, because he was under an international warrant seeking his death, he put verses from God's word up on the walls all around him to support him and keep him from despair. He literally leaned on God's visible word. He needed to see the word. He needed to hear the word, present tense. What he proclaimed, he expected to work, in all its power, for himself.

Because he strictly submitted utterly everything to the power of the Word, he was driven to attack the authority structure of the existing church, to redefine what made a valid sacrament, to redefine Christian vocation, to take on the settled doctrinal decisions of church councils, to redefine Sin, Grace, Faith, and Justification as well as to utterly redefine every current method of interpreting God's Word.

I have read through Luther's published sermons in English, some several times. At first blush, they don't seem that different from other collections of sermons. What, then, gave them their power, which both transformed preaching from then on, and gave the vital force to prevail against the panoply of power represented by counter-reformation which was mounted against it? Why is it that Luther seems to get to the heart of the matter better than most moderns with all their new array of scientific tools, making him in the considered opinion of many theologians the finest expositor of scripture the world has ever known? Surely some of the answer lies in the fact that all of Luther's proclamation was rooted and shaped in the hot forge of his own encounter with the Word. These intensely existential, sometimes terrifying encounters created abiding, unshakeable convictions, which fundamentally transformed the way he preached—convictions so sure, that he took on a whole monolithic establishment bent on killing him for his words. This proclamation, born out of the heat of awful temptation and crisis (which he referred to as his Anfechtungen) everywhere demonstrates the following unique convictions, which have since been either largely abandoned or never properly acknowledged:

- that God's Word operates at the level of effect, always performing what it says;
- that preaching is intimately defined and flows from an encounter with God, arising in turn from the preacher's personal wrestling with God—this encounter aspect making preaching distinct in function from a teaching hour;
- that God's proclaimed Word is an event, creating personal encounter best in its active, here and now, I-you, oral form (Luther called the church a 'mouth-house');
- that God sends the preachers of His Word to *do* two things in this encounter—to kill their hearers, in order to then resurrect them, to make them truly alive;
- that God's Word, rightly proclaimed, thus must *without fail* exhibit the two more abstract forms, which correspond to their two active functions—Law to kill, and Gospel to resurrect (*and in that order*: "God must first be your devil before He can be your Savior."[1]);
- that the Word encounters us as "dead people", unable to respond, in whom the Word must even create the power to believe;
- following from that, proclamation must be addressed not to some imagined human capacity such as free *will*, but must have as its target

1. LW 14:31 The English translation of Luther's works, the American edition will be used in the presentation. References from Weimar Ausgabe, the original language version will be cited where helpful. Abbreviations used in this book: LW, for Luther's Works; WA, for D. Martin Luthers Werke: Kristische Gesamtausgabe; BR, for D. Martin Luthers Werke: Kristische Gesamtausgabe. Birefweschsel; WA TR, for D. Martin Luthers Werke: Kristische Gesamtausgabe. Trischreden.

and goal the freeing from fear and assuring the bound *conscience* that God loves *sinners*;

- God's preached Word, alone, can perform the pastoral office (and miracle) of establishing the hearer's conscience unshakably confident in God's grace and favor. This is the pastoral goal of all preaching and all theology;

- Additionally, any theology done abstractly or directed toward any other final purpose than proclamation is pure poison.

. . .

A professor at Luther Seminary for over thirty years, Gerhard Forde, made it his central effort, working in the department of systematics, to recall the church to the task of vital evangelical preaching. His emphasis on the proclaimed Word understood as a performative power, rather than understood and dealt with merely at the level of signification, required a whole new assessment of what the vocation of preaching actually entailed. He was my mentor, and I owe much of my argument to him. However, Forde was never comfortable with the component, so vital to Luther, which Luther called "conscience." The reason for this, I surmise from conversations with him, is that, in his estimation, the term conscience has been so degraded and warped by modern definition as to raise more problems than it was worth to resurrect it to usability again. The chapter on "conscience" seeks to address that issue.

In summary, one could make the argument, that when one compares prophetic preaching and Jesus' preaching with preaching heard during the Luther's Reformation, that Jesus' enthusiasm for proclamation and His estimation of preaching were there proved and confirmed. In the absence of similar vitality in our churches today, it is very evident that we have lost something central along the way. Obviously, the fault does not lie in the Word. We have the same performative, life-giving, faith-breathing Word given to us. Preachers who are rooted in Luther's passion to be fearlessly subject to the encountering Word, and who then preach that Word, trusting that Word, and nothing else at all, I am convinced, can and will renew that same vitality to our proclamation today. This book seeks to flesh out some of the necessary correlates to the list above, to re-orient our minds to a Biblical world view in contrast to the current world view's hold on our minds, and, from that, to see the release of some of the same life-breathing power which, flowing through Luther in his words, changed a whole world. Why not expect that the God, by His Spirit, will use His Word to do the same again through us?

CHAPTER ONE

Two Worlds Collide

Dr. Martin Luther testified twenty years after the fact, "I, Doctor Martin, was called and forced to become a doctor, against my will, from pure obedience, and had to accept a doctor's teaching post, and promise and vow on my beloved holy scriptures to preach and teach them faithfully and sincerely."[1] "In the course of this teaching, the papacy slipped away from me."[2] Not only did his whole world fall apart, but two worlds had collided, and he was the ground of their collision. The collision resulted in almost unbearable terrors and anguish for him, the combination of which he called his "*Anfechtungen*." (his terrors, his temptations, his spiritual anxieties)

There was a rupture of the times going on with Luther, says Oswald Bayer. It was a rupture located by the cross of Jesus Christ, whose cross called the old age to a absolute end, while ushering in the new. But when the new age is proclaimed, the old age rears its ugly head most violently. "Therefore, we learn from the gospel to know the devil rightly." Says Luther[3] "Luther's understanding of evil provided him with the lens to perceive the world realistically. This realistic perspective distinguishes Luther sharply from the harmlessness of modern theologians of love . . . Luther's life and work, contrary to what modern theologians of love think, is determined throughout by the trials and temptations (*Anfechtungen*) suffered and the hands of these enemies and by the fight against them."[4]

The direct positive result of the way in which he had had his vocation forced upon him, as lecturer of the Bible and preacher of the scripture, was the *decisive certainty* that it created in his utterance. First, he felt that the command of his superior in the Augustinian order to become a lecturer of divine scripture was God's own calling, and that call required of him the

---

1. WA 30, 386, 14-17 (1531).
2. WA 30, 3; 386, 17 (1531).
3. WA 41:3:26.
4. Bayer, *Luther's Relevance for Today's Rupture of Times*, 38.

duty to speak clearly and boldly what he himself found in scripture—even if it was against his monastic vows, or against the hierarchy of the church, or, in the most extreme case, against the received tradition of Church Councils. Second, his arduous labors to speak the word truthfully brought him to trust the warrant of that Word, alone. He was convinced that he had no other calling than to give proper utterance to the Word, as truthfully and candidly as he could. These two convictions shaped the very way he spoke. The decisive certainty with which he spoke was unprecedented, immediately felt, and powerful. This utterance brought upon him the accusation of immense hubris (who did he think he was, the only one in the history of the church who had received revelation?)[5] and the undying enmity of the most awesome power of his day including the threat of death.

What brought him to this juncture, to this collision with received tradition? It all began with his original spiritual terror/crisis/temptation—what he called his *Anfechtungen*. He experienced a direct confrontation with imminent death and judgment in a frightening thunderstorm, during a trip home from school through open country. This led him to cry out to God (actually to Saint Anne) in terror, that if he were spared, he would become a monk. He summed it up later, "I wanted to escape hell by becoming a monk."[6] This vow he proceeded to fulfill with sober determination, against all the objections of both father and friends.

During his early years at the monastery he became familiar with the texts of scripture, memorizing virtually the entire psalm book. Additionally, he read most of Augustine's work, and became familiar with mystical devotional literature. However, years of work on these things did nothing toward achieving his original goal of either peace of conscience or certainty of faith. The holier his way of life was in outward appearance, the more he despaired within himself. Instead of finding any certainty of salvation through increased personal and moral rigor, the reverse was happening. Now, he was not only tormented by uncertainty, but also by a growing anger toward God. And that exponentially compounded the guilt of his situation. He found no reason in himself not to despair at the thought of judgment.

The cause for this lay in the received teaching of the whole thought world of scholasticism, in which he had been led to trust. This received scholastic teaching included at least three axioms: that the Fall had left some parts of human heart still operative and unaffected including the will; that grace was a supposed possession imparted to the believer; and that the infusion of this grace was supposed to engender renewed human righteousness.

5. LW 54:18.
6. WA 47; 90, 35, (1538).

Crucially, however, the relation of this righteousness to God's final judgment upon a person was not open to our knowledge. Further, it was impious to inquire about it. A century earlier, the faculty of Paris had tried to trap Joan of Arc into answering the question about her certainty of salvation in the affirmative. But she gave the doctrinally correct answer to them, that one did not know these things. One simply was required to live in darkness about God's judgment concerning it, trusting in the mercy of God. Mounting evidence, from Luther's conscience, was bearing witness in him that the judgment was not going to be in his favor.

More than thirty years later, shortly before his death, Luther describes the in-breaking of a whole new world of belief and thought, which contested all the axioms just listed, and which originated from a rigorous examination of the *scriptural* warrant.

> "A strange burning desire had seized me to understand Paul in the Epistle to the Romans; it was not coldness of heart which had stood in my way until then, but a single phrase in chapter 1: 'For in it the righteousness of God is revealed.' (Romans 1:17) For I hated this phrase, "the righteousness of God", which I had been taught to understand philosophically, from its normal usage by all who teach doctrine, as referring to the so-called formal or active righteousness, by means of which God is righteous and punishes sinners and the unrighteous. But I, who, however blamelessly I lived as a monk, felt myself to be a sinner before God, with a deeply troubled conscience, and could not rely on being reconciled through the satisfaction I could carry out myself. I did not love—no, I hated—the just God who punishes sinners; and I silently rebelled against God, if not with blasphemy, at least with dreadful murmuring: Was it not enough that poor sinners, eternally lost as the result of original sin, should be cast down in pure wickedness through the Law of the Decalogue, but that God would add one torment to another through the Gospel, and even through the Gospel should threaten us with his righteousness and his anger? So I raved on with a wild and confused conscience; and yet I returned time and again to the very passage in Paul, burning with thirst to know what St. Paul meant. Finally, thanks to the mercy of God, and thinking ceaselessly of this matter, one night, I recalled the context in which the words occur, namely: "In it the righteousness of God is revealed . . . as it is written, 'The righteous shall live by faith.'" Then I began to understand the righteousness of God as that through which by God's gift, the righteous lives, that is by faith, and that this is the meaning

of the passage: through the gospel the righteousness of God is revealed, that is, passive righteousness, through which the merciful God makes us righteous through faith, as it is written: "The righteous shall live by faith." Then I had the feeling that straight away I was born again, and had entered through open doors in paradise itself. The whole scripture revealed a different countenance to me. I then went through the whole scripture in my memory and compared analogies in other expressions: for example, the work of God, that is, what God works in us; the power of God, through which he makes us powerful, the wisdom of God, through which he make us wise, the strength of God, the salvation of God, the glory of God. As I had hated the phrase "the righteousness of God" before, I now valued it with equal love, as the word which was sweetest to me. Thus in truth this passage of Paul was the gate of paradise for me . . . [7]

Several things should be noted here. First, the release from his accusing conscience, which Luther had finally received after all these years of searching, had come from the word of Biblical revelation alone. In fact, it had come in spite of, and in direct opposition to the whole received scholastic world of theological interpretation. This would necessarily almost immediately lead to a direct and fundamental challenge to the current method of biblical hermeneutics. By itself, this would be a momentous collision. I will argue later, that what we now call the Law-Gospel hermeneutic, new with Luther, constitutes the most fundamental Reformation discovery.

A second significance arises from how Luther chose to narrate to us how the collision played out, alerting us to pay close attention to his use of the term "conscience". Though our current usage has reduced the term "conscience" to a discredited and hopelessly subjective psychological phenomenon (commonly discarded as some Freudian psycho-babble), it was for Luther a non-negotiable, critical expression to denote a huge theological reality. For him, conscience described *the venue* of our human awareness that, whether we deny it or not, we live "in the presence of God," before His face, "*coram deo.*" This entails the affirmation that the verdict over our lives rests not with us, but with another. But that verdict has already been revealed for those who believe that the death and resurrection of Jesus Christ was for them. And so, *the experience* which Luther described here, of receiving the verdict "righteous" from God's own lips, declared in His Word, became for Luther *the central description of the pastoral office* which he felt himself called to perform. Preaching delivers the verdict anew to each hearer of the Gospel. Preaching gives the gift. That is, it became his duty, and the duty of

---

7. WA 54; 185, 14-186, 16 (1545).

all preachers of the Gospel to utter clearly and distinctly this news which delivers our conscience.

The introduction to the 1535 Galatians commentary is as succinct as Luther gets regarding his understanding of the vocation of preaching.

> The righteousness of faith, which God imputes to us through Christ without works, is neither political nor ceremonial nor legal nor work-righteousness but it quite the opposite; it is a merely passive righteousness, while all the others are active ... this is a righteousness hidden in a mystery, which the world does not understand. In fact, Christians themselves do not adequately understand it or grasp it in the midst of their temptations. Therefore it must always be taught and continually exercised. And anyone who does not grasp or take hold of it in afflictions and terrors of conscience cannot stand. For there is no comfort of conscience so solid and certain as is this passive righteousness ... A bad dialectician does not properly distinguish, but confuses these two righteousnesses, the active and the passive. But when I go beyond the old man, I also go beyond the Law. For the flesh or the old man, the Law and works, are all joined together. In the same way the spirit or the new man is joined to the promise and to grace. Therefore when I see that a man is sufficiently contrite, oppressed by the Law, terrified by sin, and thirsting for comfort, then it is time for me to take the Law and active righteousness from his sight and to set forth before him, through the Gospel, the passive righteousness of Christ, who came for the afflicted and for sinners. Here a man is raised up again and gains hope. *Therefore I admonish you, especially those of you who are to become instructors of consciences, as well as each of you individually, that you exercise yourselves by study, by reading, by meditation, and by prayer, so that in temptation you will be able to instruct consciences, both your own and others, console them and take them from the Law to grace, from active righteousness to passive righteousness, in short, from Moses to Christ* ... In my conscience not the Law will reign, that hard tyrant and cruel disciplinarian, but Christ, the Son of God, the King of peace and righteousness, the sweet savior and Mediator. He will preserve my conscience happy and peaceful in the sound and pure doctrine of the Gospel and in the knowledge of this passive righteousness.[8] (my italics)

Third, the collision described by Luther has been succinctly described by Dr. Gerhard Forde in a seminal essay he wrote in 1980 for the

---

8. LW 26:4, 7, 10, 11.

Interpretation quarterly entitled *"The Exodus from Virtue to Grace: Justification by Faith Today"* whose theme was the Reformation and its interpretation of the book of Romans. It was an essay that characterized and shaped his whole subsequent theological effort. Taking the story of the Exodus of the children of Israel from Egypt, Forde expanded upon the compelling line in the first page of Luther's commentary, that our Christian life is not *"an exodus from vice to virtue,"* (a phrase which succinctly summarizes Scholastic doctrine, and the conviction of most modern theology) but conversely, it is *"an exodus from virtue* (!) *to grace."*[9] The contrast between these two thought worlds is so immense as to contain the whole Reformation effort. In short, what resulted from the collision that took place in Luther's belief and thought (in what is now popularly called a complete paradigm shift) required a comprehensive polemical confrontation and refutation of how received theology was done, as well as a reformulation of the entire purpose of theology, redirecting it now solely to proclamation.

Finally, the collision described here involves and portends a continuing *Anfechtung* for every Christian—not just Luther. The terror of being accused by the Law never ends, but the art of resting our conscience in the Gospel is learned ever anew by hearing the Gospel. Preaching, thus understood, becomes the living, present tense, spiritual contest for the hearer's conscience, against every spiritual power and against every accusing word of the evil one. True preaching produces the collision, each time, between our old thought world and the world of the Gospel. This always creates anxiety, if not terror, within us. But that very collision is required to produce the only true certainty, which is now based upon a new foundation—the completed work and faithfulness of Another. *Through death to life* is how a Reformation Christian experiences this encounter with God's Word. Or, it is as the great English preacher, P.T. Forsythe had inscribed on his gravestone, *per crucem ad lucem.* (through the cross to light) Certainty ("Proper Confidence", as Leslie Newbigin calls it in his book by that name) is never a static thing but a living dynamic won through to in mortal combat with temptation and doubt. This certainty inheres in the fact that the whole enterprise of deliverance of the sinner through the death-resurrection of the person, is conducted by God alone. In consequence, the whole category of righteousness has been removed from being defined as the uncertain calculus of a joint endeavor between humans and God (*partum partum*), to being an absolute, total, categorical assault and rescue by God—something which is complete and not yet to do. God's work of justifying the sinner has to be a total assault on the old man, for the new to arise.

9. Forde, *Exodus From Virtue to Grace*, 32.

This whole construct is imputed by faith alone—imputed because we continue to be sinners, and we will never by our five senses apprehend that we are actually righteous, in this old age. So our righteousness needs to be imputed. It needs to be apprehended by faith alone. Additionally it needs to be an alien righteousness—outside of ourselves. It needs to be total, absolute, and already completed. This biblical formulation of righteousness is so non-intuitive, that it has to be believed. It has to be proclaimed.

CHAPTER TWO

The Word of God as Event

WHEN LUTHER FIRST BEGAN to teach and preach at Wittenberg it was miniscule compared to the imposing campuses of Vienna, Heidelberg, Cologne, Erfurt, and Leipzig. Yet by 1518 Melanchthon's Greek class had 400 students and two years later, almost 600! By 1520 Wittenberg far surpassed every other German university. The number of students was rising like a flood and, according to Luther's letters, many had to be turned away since the town was unable to accommodate them. For several decades Wittenberg became, by far, the leading university in Germany.[1]

Here is a small profile of what was creating this explosion: university reform, reorganization of academic instruction, and the awakening of a new academic spirit. Luther wrote, "Our theology and St. Augustine's are making good progress, and are dominant in our university, thanks to what God has done. Aristotle is gradually declining, and is approaching his imminent and final demise. To an astonishing extent, lectures on the *Sententiae* (a medieval book of systematic theology) are disdained, and the only people who can expect anyone to attend their lectures are those who have resolved to deal with this theology, that is the Bible, or St. Augustine, or one of the other neglected Fathers of the Church."[2] Not only were the *Sententiae* disdained by Luther as one example of an attempt to systematize theology, he completely disdained the normal enterprise of pressing on from exposition of scripture to the creation of dogmatic teaching. In fact he made no attempt at all to systematize his reflection upon God's revelation. Although the *Smalcald Articles*, his very condensed theological summary for the Reformation churches, failed at Augsburg in 1530 to head off final conflict with the Roman Catholic Church, they continue to serve as guideposts for Reformation churches. Yet they hardly represent a system. In fact, Luther's exclusive concern with scripture should be contrasted with all preceding Scholastic

1. Ebeling, *Luther: An Introduction To His Thought*, 18.
2. Ebeling, *Luther: An Introduction To His Thought*, 19.

theological convention which sought to root all things in a system. It also contrasts with the more modern humanist attempt at systematization under Melanchthon's hand in his *Loci Theologici*. Luther's remarkable and unique rejection of both scholastic and modern humanist efforts at systematization flowed from his perception of the Word as a living Word—something that could not and should not be tamed or controlled by human agents via a system. Although system serves to make any study more logical and accessible, in attempting to do so with God's revelation, while serving to make things more predictable and safe, systematization essentially distorts and living nature of God's revelation by "canning" it. System always serves man's agency or control. But the living Word can never be controlled, predicted, or tamed no matter how strenuous the human effort to do so.

In 1518, the year after the whole controversy broke loose over the 95 theses, Luther wrote to his former teacher in Erfurt, Professor Jodokus Trutfetter: "I am firmly convinced that it is impossible to reform the Church unless the canons, the decretals, scholastic theology, philosophy and logic, as they are now taught, are completely uprooted, and other subjects are taught. And I go so far in this conviction, as to beg the Lord every day that the study of the Bible and the holy Fathers may at once be restored in all its purity." [3] At least three things should be noted here:

- That the villain in this letter is the Church, together with its whole tradition;
- That the study of the Bible is driving Luther into unavoidable, categorical warfare with these entities; and
- That although Luther never set out to take on the entire Church, his study of the Word inevitably and ineluctably drove him to it.

Although we can designate Luther first as a professor, he moved constantly between the lecture hall and the pulpit. In both he was involved with the very same issue—the strenuous effort to clearly exposit and articulate the Word of God. The two forms of the Word, preaching and teaching, were very close to one another. Luther saw both forms as fundamentally oral, present tense, uttered I-you, here and now. Thus, he made little effort to preserve the spoken word in writing. The vast sea of Luther's works in the Weimar edition far exceeds 70,000 pages, not because Luther wrote so much, but because we have the valuable benefit of faithful transcribers of his lectures and sermons—most notably Georg Roehrer.

---

3. Ebeling, *Luther: An Introduction To His Thought*, 19.

Students can tell when something real is going on. The word spread like wildfire about the new phenomenon at Wittenberg. Here was a professor and a preacher who, in contrast to the usual professors opining carefully and boringly about dusty books and received theory, electrified his hearers with the power of his words. His research on God's Word evidently affected and flowed through his very person, giving his lectures and sermons unprecedented warrant and believability. When they described Luther, people remarked about his compelling eyes. One who overheard him in prayer was awestruck by the way Luther "just leaned into it." Gerhard Ebeling writes, (without any qualification!) "Never in the history of the university has the work of a scholar, in the study and in the lecture room, had so direct and so extensive an influence upon the world, and changed it so much. If we ask what is the utmost that can be expected from a university, Luther provides the answer."[4]

So what was the source which created the person who merits such unprecedented praise? One could make a very good case that all this excitement and vitality arose from a fundamental discovery arising from Luther's own experience with God's Word. His characteristically decisive utterance, so lively, so immediate in its impact, had to have an origin in the redefinition of language itself. This redefinition of language involved God's speech, God's Word, God's language.

Our language, and our words operate at the level of signification. The famous poetic phrase, "a jug of wine, a loaf of bread, and thou" conveys powerfully and suggestively a beautiful experience which we each fill full of meaning. Yet the poetic words only signify or symbolize a shared and communally agreed upon meaning. It brings to mind in hearers some mental picture of the phenomenon we have seen with our eyes or experienced with our senses. Our human word, however, remains merely a symbol. It evokes but does not perform. It symbolizes, but does not effect what it says.

God's Word, in contrast, while operating also on the level of signification, operates most fundamentally at the level of effect. God's Word, alone, and most characteristically, *performs* what it says. When God speaks His Word, "Let there be light", it produces light. Jesus' spoken Word, "Be still", quiets both the wind and the waves. The declared Word of God, "Your sins are forgiven you", sends them all away. The Word, "Little girl, I say to you, arise", brings her back from the dead.

Gerhard Ebeling treats Luther's discovery of this phenomenon by considering *Luther als Sprachereignis* (Luther as linguisitic innovator.) But *Sprachereignis* can also be translated "speech event", something closer to the foregoing paragraph. While he cites praise from Goethe and others for

---

4. Ebeling, *Luther: An Introduction To His Thought*, 17.

giving Germans their language, for almost bringing Latin literature to an end in the universities, and for the peculiar force of Luther's words—in my view, he only suggests but does not get to the heart of the issue. The issue is that Luther insisted upon dealing with God's Word as personal address and never as "text" or an abstraction. The encounter which God's Word engenders is succinctly and accurately described by Schlegel: "Everywhere in (Luther's) writings there is a struggle between light and darkness, between a firm and unshakable faith and his equally wild and unrestrained passion, between God and himself."[5] This struggle made its way out into the lecture hall and the pulpit in the form of personal testimony, in the form of decisive declarations, in the form of revelation that had obviously been experienced and which flowed from the declarer himself. The drama was not contrived. It was the real thing. It was life and death in mortal combat, light and darkness struggling for supremacy within the person himself. The students knew that declarations concerning the truth had a new warrant in the way Luther confessed his encounter with the Word, and so did the congregation at Wittenberg.

Now, remember, Luther taught only one subject his entire life—the holy scriptures, primarily the Old Testament. It was during the time when theology was still regarded as the queen of the university subjects. Luther was called to exposit God's Word, both in lecture and in sermon. And, whether the venue was the lecture hall or the pulpit, the treatment he gave his subject was remarkably the same. That is all he did his whole life.

And for him, that Word had two fundamental effects that needed to be testified to in all exposition: it was a Word that killed, and it was a Word that made alive again. He gradually sharpened and grew more decisive in his definition of those two effects, which he gradually came to call the Law and the Gospel. By the time he presented his new theology to the Augustinian brothers in 1517, a formal presentation in the form of 28 carefully constructed theses for debate now known as the Heidelberg Disputation, he had solidified his basic hermeneutical position for the entire future of the Reformation.

This hermeneutic involved rightly distinguishing between Law and Gospel, something Luther called an art. Failure to rightly distinguish between the two, or failure to recognize the proper place and time for each application resulted in the direct opposite of salvation. For instance, preaching comfort to the comfortable, or condemnation to the despairing accomplished, in each case, only the personal destruction which the devil seeks to accomplish—the exact opposite of salvation. Such is the power and the

---

5. Schlegel, *Geschichte der alten un neuen Literatur.* 2, 178.

danger inherent in proclaiming God's Word. While it may be difficult for us, who have tamed those terms, Law and Gospel, into mere philosophical abstractions, to imagine the electricity generated when those two effects of God's Word were newly proclaimed, the unprecedented transformation of a whole world in such a short time, beginning in Wittenberg, bears witness that the power there let loose, could only belong to God Himself. It was a Word that newly established printing houses could not publish fast enough, for the public hunger. Here was a Word which did what it said.

The argument can be rightly made that Luther's power also derived from how effectively he brought to expression a whole complex of seething societal issues. He clearly addressed long simmering religious longing and unrest, frustration of abuses in church practice, public disgust over clergy behavior. He gave voice to emerging German nationalism and pride, and concisely defined the underlying causes to social upheaval and discontent. All these confused voices were unified into a whole, in the three remarkable treatises from his hand in 1520—*"The Freedom of a Christian"*, *"To the Christian Nobility of the German Nation,"* and the *"Babylonish Captivity of the Church"*. Yet neither the phenomena of this whole complex, considered singly or jointly, adequately explain the power that carried the day. In each instance Luther's speech was decisive, amazingly confident, always flowing somehow from God's revelation, and nothing else at all. It always flowed from his one and only vocation, to articulate the Word of God clearly for his hearers.

I have become convinced that when humans encounter God's truth, it is not so much the logic of the argument or the persuasiveness of the presentation that wins the day, though these are important, as is every detail of the person who incarnates and delivers the Word. Otherwise one could just mimeograph the Word and distribute the papers to the congregation. Obviously, that is not what the Word has in mind when he sends preachers. Good news delivered in a listless fashion will certainly have a negative effect upon the news itself. Yet for all our careful qualifications, it is still the case that when we meet the Truth, it is the Truth itself that does the deed. The Spirit bears witness with our spirit, that it is so. That is what carries the day. We cannot explain how that happens. To seek elsewhere for Luther's amazing effect is to look in vain. At the very least, any other explanation for how the world history literally swung on its hinges, with the pins located at this single point, remains unconvincing.

CHAPTER THREE

A Very Abbreviated History of the Concept "Free Will"

The notion of "free will" has served for so many centuries as the nexus which has structured the whole debate regarding man's relation to God, that it comes as shock to learn that the early Greek philosophers, who thought carefully about such things, worked completely without such a concept. The original Greek cosmology was inhabited by capricious gods, while human life was understood to be ruled by deterministic Fate. The gods themselves were even subject to inscrutable Fate. Horoscopes were popular, because while not giving one absolute predictions, they at least gave one some inkling regarding the basic contours of personal Fate.

Virgil often reminds us that Fate rules all in the *Aeneid*. "By changeless law each man's day stands fixed" (X.467) and, "if thou canst break the harsh bonds of Fate." (VI.882) The whole point of Virgil's effort is to show that the destruction of Troy together with the rise of Rome was not due to efforts of men but controlled rather by the determination of Fate. The effort of mere mortals was thus reduced to getting whatever inside information on fate that was available through the horoscope' twelve signs, and thus to be somewhat fore-armed. Augustine, in the 4th century, ridicules the illogic of this popular conviction, by showing that the sign under which you were born has completely unpredictable results in the people thus described.

This conviction that dark Fate ruled all gradually gave way to a new cosmology which understood the universe as an ordered rational place, in which a rational mind could discover both congruence and virtue through rational thought. Socrates emphasized the rationality of the soul. Plato, his student, founded the school of idealism, asserting that behind all observable reality there existed a universe of controlling, transcendent "ideals". The goal of philosophy then became to comprehend and understand the ideal through the rational exercise of the soul. Aristotle developed Plato's philosophy by distinguishing between human emotion (*pathe*) and action (*praxeis*), subdividing the latter into voluntary and involuntary action. "Voluntary" action depended upon our human ability and rested in our power. "Involuntary" action comprised that which was imposed by necessity or fate or some other power beyond human control. So, at the end of this very long train of development, we have finally arrived at the vital importance of human voluntary action—what became the foundation for the concept "free will."

Gospel proclamation addressed a world informed by the ruling Greek worldview. When the New Testament themes of law, righteousness, faith, good works, and salvation were heard by Greek ears, a transformation happened. Prophecy which was subsequently fulfilled was heard by them as dark fate. "Good works" easily became the Gnostic doctrine of salvation by nature. Early Eastern Fathers of the church emphasized that man was created in the image of God. Therefore, salvation included restoring that image. For Valentinians, to deny that humans had free choice was to deny the very definition of what a human being was. "Thus, appeal was made to the idea that man was created with a rational nature and was able to choose right or wrong. Therefore, referencing Greek ethical thought and terminology, it was proven that man is responsible for his actions and not subject to a natural or fatal necessity unto salvation or destruction. This argument is found already in Justin and Irenaeus. Origen argued in the same way in Book 3 of his *De Prinicipiis*.[1] However, right along side such theological positions, church liturgy presented grace and the absolute necessity of God's action for our salvation. The contrast produced and uneasy, unresolved tension that could be articulated in the shape of the following question: *Is salvation the result of God's sovereignty (election) or the result of human responsibility (free choice), or both?*

In the west, Augustine articulated a mediate position, which became foundational for all subsequent Christian theology. He argued against the theological position proposed by Pelagius, who fiercely defended the centrality of human free will in salvation. Like any respectable theologian, Augustine sought to assert the central biblical tenet of God's election while at the same time maintaining a human being's "free choice" through making increasingly fine distinctions regarding each side. He felt that an intellectually honest account of salvation required responsibly maintaining *both* God's election and human "free choice."

Augustine had developed a more sophisticated psychological model of personal faith than any of his predecessors, leading him to discover

---

1. Nispel, "*De Servo Arbetrio* and the Patristic Discussion of Freedom, Fate, and Grace," in *Logia*, 15.

weaknesses in the positions passed down to him regarding human freedom. In A.D. 392 he wrote that "It was open and perspicuous to all that anyone who sins by necessity doesn't sin at all, and thus God has given mankind free will so that his reward and punishment for righteousness or sins would be just."[2] But five years later he had already modified this to say that human nature could accomplish nothing good on its own. His solution to the problem of God's election vs. human freedom was to redefine the very term "*voluntas*", which we translate as our human agency involving a moral self. Augustine stated that two things were true regarding "free choice". First, our free will was sufficient to do evil, but not good, because fallen man is free from virtue and a slave to vice. (In "Bondage of the Will" Luther takes this position to mean that man is beast that is ridden. He agrees with Augustine that man obeys one of two rulers, but Luther goes further than Augustine by insisting that it does not lie in man's choice which ruler he serves.) Second, Augustine decided that God "determines our wills when we will what is good, and also that such willing is nonetheless free choice, for which we are responsible."[3]

Enter Pelagius, a contemporary theologian, who taught that free will was a gift of God to man. In order to preserve the concept of "grace" Pelagius redefined it as "the gift of creation", the "gift of free will," or "the gift of the law", which shows man how to live with his free will. Voila! Grace suddenly changes the critical agency affecting salvation from God to man. This redefinition of grace makes salvation into a human righteousness project rendering help from God or the cross of Christ either ancillary or unnecessary. This did not prove difficult to refute, using only basic biblical witness. Moreover, as Luther later pointed out, two marvelous ironies develop, demonstrating that this theology is almost comically false. First, the Law, which is spoken by God to *kill,* is used by Pelagius as a vehicle to achieve *life*! But this refutes Paul's whole argument in Galatians, where he clearly states that there was never, ever a law given that could give life. (Galatians 2:16, 3:21, 5:1-4) Second, instead of the Gospel *resurrecting* and creating a whole new person, it is used to be a crutch for the *dying* person! And so, as Luther said in the Heidelberg disputation, without the cross man uses the best things in the worst way.

Augustine's struggle with Pelagius made him aware of further difficulties relating righteousness by faith to man's free will. "He came to believe that the Bible demanded him to confess that faith itself, the very *beginning* of salvation, is the gift of God. Thus, the solution to the question of why

---

2. *Nicene and Post Nicene Fathers*, 4:117-119.

3 O'Daly, *Predestination and Freedom in Augustine's Ethics*, 86-87.

some are saved and not others is no longer found in human choice, but rather in God, who has mercy on some, but not on others." "Free will" was becoming perilously close to vanishing into a non-entity!

Still, there stood the very problematic scripture that "God wills all men to be saved and to come to the knowledge of the truth." So how was one to deal with that assertion in the face of the overwhelming evidence that men were everywhere perishing like flies? Augustine tried distinctions again. "All men" could mean "All the elect" or "men of every kind". Again, he chooses to leave all the choice up to God, distinguishing between the two calls of God: one by preaching, and one which is "effective", based upon the foreknowledge and predestination of God. Luther pointedly differs from Augustine here, in that Luther's critical distinction between "the God preached" and "the God not preached" makes the certainty of election rest upon the event of proclamation (God preached) as that which reveals *the only will of God that can ever be known to humans.* For Luther, "the God preached" depended, in turn, upon God's sending the proclaimer—thus reverting all the agency back to God alone. The difficulty of Augustine's resulting theological position can be roughly summed up this way: Augustine, by so strongly asserting that predestination was actively caused by God, had endangered the rule of faith accepted by the fathers, by threatening the essential universality of the Christian message of salvation ("it is God's will that all men should be saved . . . ").

Ultimately, the controversies of the Pelagian debate led to the Synod of Orange, which vindicated Augustine's essential argument. While toning down his views on predestination to punishment, it continued the emphasis upon God's election. Jaroslav Pelikan has termed the result "the Augustinian synthesis", where a semi-Pelagian doctrine came to be accepted. That is, some agency was maintained for man's "free will" in the economy of salvation. The principle was that "we ought to believe both the grace of God and the free will of man, neither without the other."[4]

One or Both?

We arrive at the great divide of the Reformation, which in my view, is that of a vast theological current split into two streams divided by a middle island, formed in 1526. One stream represents the Catholic/Arminian position of maintaining the tension between free will and grace, while the other stream represents the Calvinist tradition, which deals with the tension of the Augustinian synthesis through double predestination where God not only

4. Pelikan, *Growth of Medieval Theology*, 81.

foreknows the elect, but also foreknows the already damned. Luther will not countenance the dogma of predestination to damnation. Both the Catholic/Arminian stream and the Calvinist stream reject or ignore the position taken by Luther—a position that extends and modifies Augustine's developments. Ironically, the Catholic and the Arminian traditions, so vehemently opposed to each other on such basics as grace, sacrament, and the location of authority for faith, find themselves in virtual agreement in using "the Augustinian synthesis" of the Synod of Orange to inform their theological positions regarding the relation of "free will" and "grace"!

In what follows, I shall argue Gerhard Forde's assertion that only four theological positions remain possible regarding the issue of the relation between God's election and man's "free will": [5]

- The *Augustinian Synthesis* (preserving some activity of "free will")
- The assertion of *Double Predestination* (Calvin)
- The assertion of *Universal Salvation*, or
- Luther's position: that *in the event of proclamation itself*, God does the electing, present tense, here and now

Each of the first three positions destroy preaching. The first destroys preaching, by making the act of proclamation into an appeal to the human will, rather than actually giving the gift of salvation via the Word. The second renders preaching moot, since everything has happened already regarding one's salvation, or, at best the sermon in this case becomes mere information about such things. The third, again renders preaching moot, since salvation will happen eventually anyway.

Luther refused to treat such a mortal danger to faith as the semi-Pelagian doctrine either by synthesis or by theological distinction. The danger of the semi-Pelagian doctrine can be summed up in this way. Treated as a theological abstraction, the relationship between "free will" and "grace", understood as an irresolvable paradox, threatens the very continued existence of human faith, by rendering the God we must absolutely trust, into someone who is ultimately capricious. This threat cannot be dealt with by subtle distinction. Nor can one deal with this threat by hiding such problems from the average Christian (that is to say, by keeping such debates confined safe within the confines of a more informed magisterium—which was Erasmus' proposal). Luther recognized the threat here as the very same threat which had almost cost him his faith. It was no abstraction for him. The relation

---

5. Forde, from my notes from his lectures.

between free will and grace needed to be met head on, forthrightly, clearly, definitively, once for all.

He did so in the 1526 treatise "Bondage of the Will", a work he considered almost his greatest theological triumph. The warrant for such an accolade from him could only rest upon what had accorded him, at last, his own peace of conscience. In other words, it established categorically that God's authority and action served as the sole and absolute criterion for certainty of faith. Luther, like Augustine before him, takes seriously the psychology of faith. *But Luther builds the whole psychological structure upon a brand new foundation.* The foundation consists in this: that women and men are related to God, as well as being fundamentally defined, *by their ear*. When Martin Luther says "*coram deo*", he means "we are addressed." For him, that is the irreducible core to all viable biblical anthropology—definitely not: "I think, therefore I am." For Luther it became "I hear, therefore I am." Moment by moment, man is constituted by what he hears from God. We are absolutely dependent upon God's continued address and his graciously pursuing question, "Adam, where are you?" If we are ever to be free, it will not be through some imaginary claim that we are autonomous, but rather through becoming rightly related to God through His Word.

Descartes creates an imaginary false autonomy upon which to build certainty, arrived at through asserting what was "indubitable." Yet this imaginary (and solipsistic) claim to human autonomy is insisted upon in unison by every recognized Enlightenment philosopher. Hume, Kant, and Hegel leap to mind. Hamann and Kierkegaard are the lone (and disregarded) dissenting voices, contemporary to these established Enlightenment philosophers. Both of these lone protesters root their cases variously upon Luther's position. Kierkegaard can hardly restrain his vituperative scorn for his *bête noir* (black beast*)*, Hegel, who claimed an imaginary uninvolved ability for humans, to observe and judge both history and all reality, from an "objective" position. However, there is no such uninvolved, autonomous position, says Kierkegaard, and what is more, real truth is subjective, not objective!

Luther refuses to leave free will and grace in tension. He refuses the solution of double predestination as well, for the reason that both of these attempted solutions are poisonous to faith. He refuses "reason" as an adequate foundation for faith because it, too, is fatally compromised by the Fall. In fact, any and all attempts by human agency, whatsoever, are forfeit for the same reason. That leaves God alone, His Word alone, and Grace alone as the only foundations for Christian certainty.

CHAPTER FOUR

The Objective of Christian Preaching: Certainty of Faith

THIS CHAPTER SEEKS TO make the case that Luther's over-riding and controlling concern was a pastoral one: *to establish certainty of faith*, first for himself and then for his hearers. He writes in the interpretation of Hebrew 4:16 in 1518 that we should come before God with the *confidence* of presuming the divine promise.[1] He wrote

> "I have been baptized. I have been absolved. In this faith I die. No matter what trials and cares confront me from now on I will certainly not be shaken; for He who said: 'He who believes and is baptized will be saved' (Mark 16:16 and 'whatever you loose on earth shall be loosed in heaven' (Matt. 16:19) and 'this is My body, this is My blood, which is shed for you for the forgiveness of sins' (Matt. 26:26, 28)—He cannot deceive or lie. This is certainly true."[2] And again, "the following is the reason why our theology is certain; because it tears us away from ourselves and places us outside ourselves. It does this in order that we would not lean on our strengths, our conscience, our mind, our person, our works, but rather lean on that which is outside of us. What is outside of us is, namely, the promise and truth of God that cannot lie."[3]

To demonstrate that this concern for certainty of faith was the overarching objective that not only drove every one of his sermons, but also centrally informed the whole understanding of his office, hardly any other work of Luther's serves better than "The Bondage of the Will."

1. WA 57/III:171.4-8.
2. LW 8:193-94.
3. WA 40/I:589.25-28.

Historical Setting

As was noted in the last chapter, theologians had carried on a centuries-long dispute over the extent, if any, of human free will in its relation to God's grace, especially in regard to salvation. The results were varied, and, considering its importance, surprisingly thin. The Synod of Orange had articulated an uneasy middle position, which failed to end the controversy. Luther appealed to Laurentius Valla, a Renaissance philosopher, who did not exclude the freedom of the will completely but who severely limited it. He also, more appropriately, appealed to Wycliff. But most importantly, he chose as his title for the whole treatise from the single occasion in Augustine's writings where Augustine used the term "servo arbetrium" (captivation of the will), in order to clearly show that his position was, with the Church Father Augustine, against any variation of the Pelagian doctrine.

Luther took more time writing this treatise than any other. It occupied him from June to almost December of 1525, when it went into print. During this time he was establishing a home with his new bride, forced into dealing with the Peasant's revolt, responding to Muntzer's super-spiritual heresy within his own faculty, and beginning the long controversy over the real presence of Christ in the Lord's Supper with the Swiss.

To set the stage for this historically monumental treatise, it is helpful to note the vast disparity that obtained between the two disputants in this very public and international debate. On the one side stood the rightfully eminent humanist scholar, Erasmus, a full generation older than Luther, at the height of his career, renowned on the whole continent not least for his part in the rediscovery and usage of the Greek manuscripts to create a better foundation for translating the New Testament. As a respected scholar, Erasmus had no peer in all of Europe. His authority was unchallenged. He was celebrated in all universities. On the other side stood Dr. Martin Luther, now only 42 years old, only eight years into what was still a quite small reformation movement, teaching at an upstart university far from any of the renowned centers of learning, such as Louvain, Cologne, and Paris. The vital contest between the two (and for all subsequent theology) is fired by Erasmus' 1524 treatise "*De Libero Arbitrio Diatribe Sive Collatio* (Of Free Will: Discourses or Comparisons), in which he lampoons Luther's view that the will is not free. With his reputation as a polished and refined scholar at stake, Erasmus strives to lay down both sides of the free will argument impartially, while still making his own case in the most devastating academic fashion possible.

Both disputants in this matter demonstrate that they are very conversant with the scope and arguments of the theological controversy to this point in history. In coming to his definition of free will, Erasmus is very careful not to treat it as a philosophical problem but to base his position upon scriptural citations. Here is the carefully stated definition for his whole argument: "By free choice in this place we mean a power of the human will by which a man can apply himself to the things which lead to eternal salvation, or turn away from them."[4] He argued that to take Luther's extreme position of denying such a freedom completely would lead to godlessness. He cited the scholastic distinction between unconditioned necessity and conditioned necessity[5] to argue that God effects some things only through secondary causes. Above all, he opposed the idea that God would harden the heart.[6] In summary, Erasmus held that while God was the primary cause of salvation, humans had to have some secondary responsibility. Otherwise, for him the New Testament doctrine of rewards would make no sense.

A second contrast between the two disputants resides in their fundamental approach to their underlying subject—the Word of God. By his very use of the term "*diatribe*" Erasmus was staking his whole position upon a deliberative rhetoric which avoids any definitive decision, but rather is oriented to prudence and temperance. The "Diatribe" did not encourage any definite action. This was its merit to the followers of Erasmus and its fault in the eyes of the Luther. In his treatise, Erasmus had taken the cold, dispassionate, objective approach, which is appropriate in all academic endeavors. The argument of his treatise was to the effect that some things in God's Word were obscure, and others were about subjects too dangerous for church-goers to handle. Thus, to keep peace and security intact, he opined that it would be better to leave to theologians alone, such subjects as divine election. At the very least, it would be better for the sake of church peace not to express any definite opinion about such things. Erasmus' entire treatise did not even conceive of treating God's Word in any other way than dealing with the Word at the level of signification.

In utter contrast, Luther's approach—highly personal, hotly involved, passionate, pastoral—derived from his conviction that the very matter in question, God's Word, demanded a different approach than what academia prescribed. Luther's beginning point was that the Word of God primarily needed to be understood at the level of *effect*. The Word *did something* to both the proclaimer and to the hearer. What it did, demanded proclamation. It demanded confession. It, alone, created clarity in the midst of confusion. Indeed, the whole effect of God's Word is to engender a new kind

---

4. *Luther and Erasmus: Free Will and Salvation*, 47.
5. *Luther and Erasmus: Free Will and Salvation*, 68.
6. *Luther and Erasmus: Free Will and Salvation*, 65.

of speech called *confession*—speech fundamentally characterized by certainty. This part of the argument is centered upon the term which Luther drives home as the only kind of speech appropriate to faith—assertions. The loudest crescendo of this treatise, and its final line, is about the necessity of making assertions. All of this was precluded by Erasmus' method, yet demanded by Luther's method.

So that you do not miss that "The Bondage of the Will" formulates what Luther considered *fundamental to his entire life's work, as well as outlining the major presuppositions of his thought*, he later wrote, "Only this book was really a book of mine."[7]

A Pastoral Project Whose Object is Certainty

I propose that this treatise, "Bondage of the Will", is a certainty project (that is: the fight for the very ground of faith) in the sense that it seeks to create the criteria to establish, and grammar to express the certainly true. All discussion regarding certainty involves agency—God's, Man's, or the devil's. So it is significant that the title of Luther's treatise is rendered more properly as "The Captivation of the Will", in that "captivation" vitally brings to the fore whose agency it is who captivates. As already mentioned, the defining characteristic of this treatise derives from its commitment to be pastoral rather than primarily academic. In turn, this pastoral approach is demanded by God's Word itself, which is not sent primarily to be informational, but to be a personal encounter both confrontational and transformational. Therefore, Luther feels driven by personal conviction to relay what the Word has done to him and what he expects it to do for everyone. It follows that the whole treatise must be a pastoral project working to establish the conscience of the hearer secure under the address of a gracious God.

For this reason, it must additionally be a hermeneutical project (a project dealing with scriptural interpretation), which, for the sake of certainty, requires that two additional goals be achieved. Each of the two goals discovers and founds the certainty of a Christian in God's work alone. In order to place the entire issue of one's salvation totally in God's hands it is first necessary to establish the criterion that the Scripture (understood as God action through His speaking, here and now) must be the sole criterion and authority in this action. It, alone, has the power to secure or establish the conscience safe from condemnation. Second, it is vitally necessary to secure a consistent interpretation of that Word.

---

7. WA Br 8:99.

Luther's thought characteristically flows from a dominant central core. He is like a pit bull, who having secured the vital spot, will hang on to that one spot despite every attempt to dislodge him. And the vital core for Luther was the conscience, for the simple reason that he understood that at our most fundamental vital human core, we are *creatures who are addressed*. For the purposes of the argument here, it is necessary to lay aside all the more modern accretions to the definition of "conscience", and simply work with Luther's concept that, though conscience can be a broken and confused forum, nevertheless conscience is the forum God uses to speak to humans. None of us can escape God's original word after the Fall, "Adam, where are you?"

Through Luther's own most bitter anguish, and through his own most astonished relief, he continued to discover that the very same power which had terrified his conscience, also had the power to graciously establish his conscience safely in God's care. The power he most feared was God's election. Yet the power that delivered him from this fear was God's self-same election. His whole pastoral project arose from his own experience of constantly living within the dynamic tension between these two opposed effects of God's Word. The electing power which terrified him and revealed his helplessness (*"What if God does not choose me? Then I can do nothing about it! I am brought to a complete end. I die."*)—this necessary terror he termed Law. Yet the very same power, which did not relent one iota upon this conclusion, but which pushed the situation further, revealed that in the cross, God had elected him in love through Jesus Christ. This electing power he called the Gospel. His experience of living under both words, within this inescapable irresolvable tension, he defined pastorally by formulating the continuing question for every Christian: "How can I know for sure that I have a gracious God?" The affirmative answer to that question is rendered triumphantly at the end of each of his expositions of the three articles of the Creed (the summary God's action, alone) by the phrase, "This is most certainly true!"

Most assuredly this conclusion does not arise in finding a way to *resolve* the tension described above, for the simple reason that one always remains a sinner! Amazingly, this certainty arises out of what is apparently its dynamic opposite—out of living in the unresolved tension itself! The day by day experience of dying, which to Luther meant dealing each day anew with of the terrors of temptation (Anfechtungen) and personal sin, together with being rendered again and again helpless, and being delivered ever again by God's grace—this is the hot forge from which Christian faith and certainty arise anew each day! Whoever is willing to come and die, they alone, will live; they alone will know certainty; they alone will know that the peace of God which passes all understanding resides only in the midst of the conflict between life and death.

Luther's treatise, so unfortunately shaped by its point by point refutation of Erasmus' positions, and not by his own organizing principles, comes into remarkable focus and unified clarity if one "follows the money", which in this case is Luther's pastoral concern for proper Christian certainty of faith. Thus, the work can be helpfully considered pictorially as a light with seven rays, or as a flower with seven petals. Each of the seven themes addresses some issue regarding the core concern: that God's Word is always sent to secure and create in the hearer an unshakably certain faith.

The seven themes are:

- The necessity of assertions
- The assertion of the clarity of Scripture
- The assertion of the captivation of the Will for the sake of establishing a secured Conscience
- The assertion that salvation must belong to God alone
- The necessity of distinguishing between the two effects of God's Word: Law and Gospel
- The necessity of distinguishing between the God Preached, and the God Hidden
- The art of becoming a theologian of the Cross

1. The Necessity of Assertions

Luther begins with a devastatingly short section on the necessity of assertions. The whole section is illuminated by its summary sentence: "The Holy Spirit is no Skeptic, and it is not doubts or mere opinions that he has written on our hearts, but assertions more sure and certain than life itself and all experience."[8] Six reproaches to Erasmus' treatise follow. First, "A man must delight in assertions or he will be no Christian. And by assertion I mean a constant adhering, affirming, confessing, and unvanquished persevering."[9] Second, Luther quotes Scripture: "How often, I ask you, does the apostle Paul demand that *plerophoria* (full assurance), that most sure and unyielding assertion of conscience?" He then cites Romans 10:10; but Colossians 2:2, I

---

8. LW 33:24.
9. LW 33:20.

Thessalonians 1:5, Hebrew 6:11, and 10:22 can be cited as well.[10] Third, he writes, "The Spirit Himself, goes to such lengths in asserting, that he takes the initiative and accuses the world of sin." (John 16:8)[11] Fourth, what Christian would despise assertions? "That would be nothing but a denial of all religion and piety, or an assertion that neither religion nor piety, nor any dogma is of the slightest importance."[12] Fifth, "Anathema (damned) be the Christian who is not certain and does not "grasp" (apprehend with certainty) what is prescribed for him!"[13] Sixth, "If it does not matter to you what anyone believes anywhere, so long as the peace of the world is undisturbed", then Christian dogmas are no better than philosophical and human opinions. "By such tactics you only succeed in showing that you foster in your heart a Lucian, or some other pig from Epicurus' sty, who, having no belief in God himself, secretly ridicules all who have a belief and confess it."[14]

One can stand amazed at the unyielding confidence with which Luther takes on not only the whole established academic community, but also a whole continent. Both the assured confidence of his expression and his barely contained outrage serve implicitly and quietly to demonstrate that the case which he seeks to verbalize, flows from and is demonstrated by the *person* who speaks here. Only the Word itself could create such a phenomenon, a person with such unshakeable confidence! The summary of this first point is that the certainty which is created by God's Word in a Christian is revealed most saliently by the new way in which Christians speak—confidently, boldly, surely, by *asserting*.

But if a Christian is asked how it is that he or she has become so sure of these matters of faith, not one will be able to tell you anything of the process itself. It becomes quickly evident that the Holy Spirit is the one who has mysteriously written upon our hearts in such a way that it engenders a confidence that no empirically based knowledge can even touch, as Luther's summary so aptly asserts. To repeat: the whole point of the discussion requires that it be removed from academia and to be treated pastorally. Just as night follows day, a Christian gladly speaks and must "confess" these things *appropriately*, that is: confidently, assertively, and boldly. In fact Christians just can't keep it to themselves! This is the language and grammar of faith. Its very sound makes it unique.

---

10. LW 33:20.
11. LW 33:21.
12. LW 33:21.
13. LW 33:24.
14. LW 33:24.

2. The Assertion of the Clarity of Scripture

Luther's second major assertion, the clarity of scripture is also astonishingly brief. "That in God there are many things hidden, of which we are ignorant, no one doubts . . . but that in Scripture there are some things abstruse, and everything is not plain—this is an idea put about by the ungodly Sophists . . . but they have never produced, nor can they produce, a single article to prove this mad notion of theirs."[15] "Texts" in Scripture are obscure not because of the majesty of their subject matter, but because of our ignorance of their vocabulary and grammar. But these texts in no way hinder a knowledge of all the subject matter of scripture . . . Take Christ out of Scriptures, and what will you find left in them?"[16] The problem is not that Scriptures are unclear, but that our own minds are senseless and darkened. "Let miserable men, therefore, stop imputing with blasphemous perversity the darkness and obscurity of their own hearts to the wholly clear Scriptures of God."[17] Luther ends up by discussing the two clarities of scripture—external and internal—what we today refer to as objective and subjective.[18] Objective clarity has to do with the clarity of Christian witness, while subjective clarity has to do with the inner clarity of the heart of the hearer or reader of the biblical witness. Externally or objectively nothing in scripture is ambiguous or obscure. Internally, however, qualification needs to be made. "If you speak of the internal clarity," writes Luther, "no man perceives one iota of what is in the Scriptures unless he has the Spirit of God . . . So, everything there is in the scriptures, has been brought out by the Word into the most definite light, and published to all the world."[19] In other words, the Word interprets the Word.

Notice two things here. First, the requirement of the Holy Spirit's revelation, absolutely removes control of Scripture from man's hands. Second, the very formulation of the last quoted sentence indicates that the clarity of scripture does not wait upon the research of a chosen magisterium of scholars but is secured by the Word, Himself.

An example of how this plays out in practice is on historical display, when American Lutherans, in attempting to "out-fundamental" the fundamentalists in a 1930 Iowa convention debate, adopted the word "inerrancy" as a proper vehicle for their church constitution to convey that

---

15. LW 33:25.
16. LW 33:25-26.
17. LW 33:27.
18. Althaus, *The Theology of Martin Luther*, 78.
19. LW 33:28.

which constituted the authority of the Word of God. (The first appearance of "inerrancy" as a descriptor of God's Word among American Lutherans may have occurred in the Minneapolis Theses of 1925.) But allowing this concept, so foreign to God's Word, fails to grasp Luther's central point here. To assert "inerrancy" as a means to establish the authority of God's Word is to make at least four errors.

- First, it claims for Scripture, what Scripture does not claim for itself.
- Second, it seeks the authority of Scripture in the wrong place. The authority of Scripture does not inhere in its "inerrancy", but simply in the fact that *God speaks it*. The Word alone convinces each hearer of its truth, and does not depend upon some human contrivance, activity, or ability to do the job (and which might render the Word more comfortable or tame it down for our tastes).
- Third, claiming inerrancy for the Word of God is docetic (an old heresy which asserted that Jesus only "appeared" to be merely and completely human) in that it makes the written Word so heavenly that it *cannot be permitted* to participate in our normal fractured and imperfect human discourse, but must be absolutely perfect, something completely heavenly.
- Fourth, it seeks to reduce the Word of God to a "thing" which seems to need our control and protection, rather than realizing that God's Word arrives as an "event", properly belonging to God alone, whose action is fundamentally beyond our control.

3. The Captivation of the Will is required to Secure the Conscience

This brings us to the third main point of Luther's argument—the knowledge, so vital for a Christian, of what power "free-will" has. The issue here for Luther is that any cooperation by humans at all in our own salvation, results in an uncertain calculus regarding how much is done by God versus how much is still required by man. The only solution, for the sake of certainty and conscience is to say, "God alone." For Luther, this comprises and sums up the whole issue underlying the debate. His chosen title for this entire treatise demonstrates the same fact.

Luther writes,

> "But when you tell Christians . . . not to be inquisitive about what they can and cannot do in the matter of obtaining eternal

salvation, this is beyond question the truly unforgivable sin. For as long as they are ignorant of what and how much they can do, they will not know what they should do; and being ignorant of what they should do, they cannot repent if they do wrong; and impenitence is the unforgivable sin. This is what your moderate Skeptical Theology leads us to. . . . This is the cardinal issue between us, the point on which everything in this controversy turns. For what we are doing is to inquire what free choice can do, what it has done to it, and what its relation is to the grace of God. If we do not know these things, we shall know nothing at all of things Christian, and shall be worse than any heathen. Let anyone who does not feel this confess that he is not Christian, while anyone who disparages or scorns it should know that he is the greatest enemy of Christians."[20] "It behooves us to be very certain about the distinction between God's power and our own, God's work and our own, if we want to live a godly life."[21]

One is able to express the alternatives almost mathematically. The assertion of free will inevitably results in an uncertain calculus. Mixing God's work and our own in the matter of salvation requires a calculus not one of Luther's teachers could resolve for him, so that he could find peace of conscience. The official doctrine passed down in the church was that, subsequent to the Fall there still remained in man a spark which was able to respond to God's grace. Instantly the calculus is required. "How much do I have to do?" And critically important, "What will be sufficient for salvation?" The pious answer: "A Christian can never know." This thought world created and drove whole medieval systems and constructs to flee from the "corrupting" world to become "good" or at least "better". The terror is expressed in the innumerable depictions in European cathedrals of Christ as threatening judge on the throne. The attempt to satisfy an angry God by seeking personal piety through fleeing the world was the entire motivation driving Luther to become a monk.

The only other alternative drives one to completely renounce all efforts required by such a calculus and to assert that humans can do absolutely nothing toward their own salvation. God finds us as sinners, calls us by His mercy, and redeems us by sheer grace. When God alone does everything, it first creates sheer terror (again, "what if God does not choose me? There is nothing that I can do about that!" "I am brought to an utter end." "I die."). But it *also* unshakably creates certain faith anchored in the only sure

---

20. LW 33:34-35.
21. LW 33:35.

foundation—God alone, including God's call and election alone. The two alternatives can be expressed:

Asserting **Free** Will → **Bound** Conscience

but

acknowledging **Bound** Will → **Free** Conscience (that is: secure)

4. Salvation Must Belong to God Alone

The next point concerns whether or not God knows things contingently (depending upon human response) or whether he knows things necessarily and immutably. "But how will you be certain and sure unless you know that (God) knows and wills and will do what he promises, certainly, infallibly, immutably, and necessarily? . . . therefore, Christian faith is entirely extinguished, the promises of God and the whole gospel are completely destroyed, if we teach and believe that it is not for us to know the necessary foreknowledge of God and the necessity of the things that are to come to pass. *For this is the one supreme consolation of Christians in all adversities, to know that God does not lie, but does all things immutably, and that his will can neither be resisted nor changed nor hindered.*"[22] (my italics) Here you see that Luther's whole pastoral project regarding both the certainty of faith and the good news of the Gospel is rooted in one foundation—God's election

For Luther, this foundation upon which all Christian faith is built is non-negotiable. "Let me tell you, therefore—that what I am after in this dispute is to me something serious, necessary, and indeed eternal, something of such a kind and such importance that it ought to be asserted and defended to the death, even if the whole world had not only to be thrown into strife and confusion, but actually to return to total chaos and be reduced to nothingness."[23] Luther reproaches Erasmus for advising, "That as a favor to pontiffs and princes or for the sake of peace, we ought if occasion arises, to give way and set aside the most sure Word of God. But if we do that, we set aside God, faith, salvation, and everything Christian." [24]

---

22. LW 33:42-43.
23. LW 33:50.
24. LW 33:51.

5. The necessity of Distinguishing between Law and Gospel

Luther reproaches Erasmus most indignantly over completely and totally missing "theology 101", thus creating the human darkness which results from being unaware of the fundamental distinction between the *effects* of God's commands (Law) and the *effects* of God's promise (Gospel). Luther's primary exhibit of how disastrous this is to Christian faith is located in Erasmus' and Luther's conflicting assertions regarding the proper understanding of Ezekiel 18:23. This is where God says, "I desire not the death of a sinner, but rather that he may turn and live." Erasmus infers from his own view of free will that this verse is proclaiming the fact that the reason sinners die is that they choose to do so.(!) In this manner, Luther expostulates, Erasmus transforms what is the sweetest gospel of Scripture, "I desire not the death of a sinner" into the severest command: "If you want to avoid death, stop sinning!"

First, that is not what the very clear Word says. Second, by Erasmus' imposing his own false presuppositions upon God's Word, he completely *reverses* God's intended effect of these words upon the hearer! What God intended as promise and comfort is rendered into terror and threat. Luther writes, "What does almost more than half of Holy Scripture contain but sheer promises of grace in which mercy, life, peace and salvation are offered by God to men? And what else do words of promise have to say but this: "I desire not the death of a sinner"? Is it not the same thing to say, "I am merciful" as to say, "I am not angry, I do not want to punish, I do not want you to die, I want to pardon, I want to spare"?[25] "Hence nothing could have been more inappropriately quoted in support of free choice than this passage of Ezekiel, which actually stands in the strongest opposition to free choice . . . So you can see that not only all the words of the law stand against free choice, but also all the words of promise utterly refute it; which means that Scripture in its entirety stands opposed to it."[26] But most importantly, by failing to distinguish properly between Law and Gospel *one loses the Gospel entirely.*

---

25. LW 33:136-137.
26. LW 33:138.

6. The Necessity of Distinguishing between the God Preached and the God Hidden

We now arrive at the most bitterly contested and fought over three pages of this entire work—pages 138-140. Luther himself offers and brings up "another question" not dealt with by Ezekiel in this passage. Ezekiel has been dealing with the will of God that is preached, revealed, offered, and worshiped, and not about God as he is not preached, not revealed, not offered, not worshiped. "To the extent that God hides himself and wills to be unknown to us, it is no business of ours."[27] Luther claims he is authorized to make this distinction between the "God Preached" and the "God Hidden" by the Apostle Paul in 2 Thessalonians 2:4 where we read that the Anti-Christ will exalt himself above every God that is preached and worshiped. "This plainly shows that someone can be exalted above God as he is preached and worshiped, that is above the word through which God is known to us . . . God must therefore be left to himself in his own majesty, for in this regard we have nothing to do with him, nor has he willed that we should have anything to do with him. But we have something to do with him insofar as he is clothed and set forth in his Word, through which he offers himself to us and which is the beauty and glory with which the psalmist celebrates him as being clothed."[28] And again, "In this regard we say, the good God does not deplore the death of his people which he works in them but he deplores the death which he finds in his people and desires to remove from them. For it is this that God as he is preached is concerned with, namely, that sin and death should be taken away and we should be saved . . . but God hidden in his majesty neither deplores nor takes away death, but works life, death, and all in all. For there he has not bound himself by his Word, but has kept himself free over all things."[29] Luther does not flinch from the accusation here that *God does absolutely everything*. But the God who does absolutely everything is the "God not preached", and therefore not available to us to either explain or understand. The "God preached", Jesus, and Him crucified, and raised for sinners, we stick with that. Seeking to push beyond that revelation leads only to crushing terror and despair.

In the classic four theological choices we have already listed regarding God's basic relation to us—Free Choice, Double Predestination, Universalism, and Proclamation itself, of God's deed in Jesus' death on the cross and his resurrection—while the first three destroy actually preaching, at least the

---

27. LW 33:139.
28. LW 33:139.
29. LW 33:139.

first makes what should be proclamation into something which says, "It's up to you!" But this would then make preaching into some sort of sales job where the preacher seeks to convince the hearer enough or dress up Jesus enough to make him attractive enough for the hearer to make a choice for God. It might be a sales pitch, but it would not be preaching. The paradigm absolutely precluded by Luther is that of preachers being God's prosecuting attorneys, seeking to bring in a verdict for God. Rather, the fundamental presupposition of Luther's preaching model is the absolute inability of the hearer to respond. Just as Ezekiel preached to the dry bones to create the ears, bodies, and breath, which they no longer had, so preaching creates in the hearer the faith to receive the amazing effect produced by God's promise. The Ezekiel event demonstrates visually Jesus own words: "Apart from me you can do *nothing*." (John 15:5) A Christian's confidence is first created, and then secured, by the effect of the promise of the Gospel—*which creates the very faith that establishes the accused conscience safe within the announced mercy and grace of God.*

Paul's triumphant climax of four questions in Romans 8:31ff all call for a single repeated phrase, the shouted Christian response: "No one!" If God is for us, who is against us? "No one!" Who shall bring any charge against God's elect? "No one!" Who is to condemn? "No one!" Who shall separate us from the love of Christ? "No one!" Paul's highly personalized summary of the argument of the entire previous eight chapters' presentation of the Gospel has nothing whatsoever to do with free choice, double predestination, or universalism. Instead it reports the results of an encounter created by proclamation. It announces the result to persons who hear what has been objectively and historically completed by Jesus Christ. It is for you, in this present moment, something that is not yet to do. It is a declaration completely about God's agency and not ours, about what God did for we humans, in our history, in our place, just as He did in the original Exodus. Such proclamation ends with neither an assignment, nor a "to do" list, nor a suggested proper application, nor an "offer". It simply announces the unbelievably good gift. That is what true proclamation sounds like. And such proclamation, alone, creates resounding joyful faith.

Under the heading which addresses the question of whether the truth of God's necessitating will should be suppressed, we get Luther's astonishing insights from the Heidelberg Disputation, not one of which he has relinquished, and which have sharpened in the intervening eight years.

> "In order that there may be room for faith, it is necessary that everything which is believed should be hidden. It cannot, however, be more deeply hidden than under an object, perception,

or experience which is contrary to it. Thus when God makes alive he does it by killing, when he justifies he does it by making men guilty, when he exalts to heaven he does it by bringing down to hell . . . thus God hides his eternal goodness and mercy under eternal wrath, his righteousness under iniquity. *This is the highest degree of faith, to believe him merciful when he saves so few and damns so many, and to believe him righteous when by his own will he makes us necessarily damnable, so that he seems, according to Erasmus, to delight in the torments of the wretched and to be worthy of hatred rather than of love. If, then, I could by any means comprehend how this God can be merciful and just who displays so much wrath and iniquity, there would be no need of faith.*[30] (my italics)

Finally, "Salvation is beyond our own powers and devices, and depends on the work of God alone . . . For if it is not we, but only God, who works salvation in us, then before he works we can do nothing of saving significance, whether we wish to or not."[31] We are like a beast that is ridden. Of our will Luther says, "If Satan rides it, it wills and goes where Satan wills, nor can it choose to run to either of the two riders or to seek him out. But the riders themselves contend for the possession and control of it."[32]

The definition of "free choice" as "a power that can turn itself freely in either direction, without being under anyone's influence or control" is precisely what Luther objects to.[33] This, he says, is a power that describes God alone, which could even serve as a *name* for God, since he alone can do and accomplish whatever he wills in heaven or on earth. It certainly is not a human attribute to be able to accomplish whatever we will.

7. The Art of becoming a Theologian of the Cross

In Romans 5:1-5 Paul promises that the Christian can be certain of two things—peace and suffering. It is not possible in this land of temptation, in this place where the "already" is also "not yet", to escape the irresolvable tension of the competing and opposing effects of the condemning power of Sin and the absolving and reassuring power of Grace. To willingly bear the suffering of this tension as we wait patiently for the revealing

---

30. LW 33:62-63.
31. LW 33:64.
32. LW 33:65.
33. LW 33:69.

of Christ's final kingdom is to become "a theologian of the cross." Luther describes it this way:

> There is in the saints and the godly a battle between the Spirit and the flesh, so fierce that they cannot do what they would. From this I argued thus: If human nature is so evil that in those born anew of the Spirit it not only does not endeavor after the good but actually strives and fights against it, how should it endeavor after the good in those who are not yet born anew but are still "in the old man" and in bondage to Satan? . . . For my own part, I frankly confess that even if it were possible, I should not wish to have free choice given to me, or to have anything left in my own hands by which I might strive toward salvation. For on the one hand, I should be unable to stand firm and keep hold of it amid so many adversities and perils and so many assaults of demons . . . on the other hand, even if there were no perils or adversities or demons I should nevertheless have to labor under perpetual uncertainty and to fight as one beating the air, since even if I lived and worked to eternity, my conscience would never be assured and certain, how much it ought to do to satisfy God. For whatever work might be accomplished there would always remain an anxious doubt whether it pleased God or whether he required something more . . . as I myself learned to my bitter cost through so many years. But now, since God has taken my salvation out of my hands into his, making it depend on his choice and not mine, and has promised to save me, not by my own work or exertion but by his grace and mercy, I am assured and certain both that he is faithful and will not lie to me, and also that he is too great and powerful for any demons or any adversities to be able to break him or to snatch me from him.[34]

Luther's Five Point Summary of the Argument

1. If we believe that God foreknows and predestines all things, that he can neither be mistaken in his foreknowledge nor hindered in his predestination, and that nothing takes place but as he wills it, then on the testimony of reason itself, there cannot be any free choice in man or angel or any creature.

2. If Satan is the ruler of this world, who is forever plotting and fighting against the Kingdom of Christ with all his powers, so that he will not

---

34. LW 33:288-289.

let men go who are his captives unless he is forced to do so by the divine power of the Spirit, then again it is evident that there can be no such thing as free choice.

3. If we believe that original sin has so ruined us that even in those who are led by the Spirit it causes a great deal of trouble by struggling against the good, it is clear that in a man devoid of the Sprit there is nothing left that can turn toward the good, but only toward evil.

4. If the Jews who pursued righteousness to the utmost of their power, rather ran headlong into unrighteousness, while the Gentiles, who pursued ungodliness, attained righteousness freely and unexpectedly, then it is also manifest from this very fact and experience that man without grace can will nothing but evil.

5. If we believe that Christ has redeemed men by his blood, we are bound to confess that the whole man was lost; otherwise, we should make Christ either superfluous or the redeemer of only the lowest part of man, which would be blasphemy and sacrilege.[35]

Erasmus ends his "Diatribe" by saying "I have discoursed, let others pass judgment." The very last words of Luther's whole treatise contrast pointedly: "I, for my part in this book *have not discoursed, but have asserted and do assert,* and I am unwilling to submit the matter to anyone's judgment, but advise everyone to yield assent. But may the Lord, whose cause this is, enlighten you and make you a vessel for honor and glory." (his italics) [36]

The Council of Trent, following soon after Luther's death, had numerous objections to Luther's assertions regarding the captivation of the will, among which are these:

> CANON V. If any one saith, that, since Adam's sin, the free will of man is lost and extinguished; or, that it is a thing with only a name, yea a name without a reality, a figment, in fine, introduced into the Church by Satan; let him be anathema.
>
> CANON IX. If any one saith, that by faith alone the impious is justified; in such wise as to mean, that nothing else is required to co-operate in order to the obtaining the grace of Justification, and that it is not in any way necessary, that he be prepared and disposed by the movement of his own will; let him be anathema.

---

35. LW 33:293.
36. LW 33:295.

CHAPTER FIVE

The Reformation Discovery

WHAT WAS IT THAT transformed Luther's very person? What created his unbelievably firm conviction that all theology must concern itself centrally with the pastoral problem of God's justification of the sinner? More narrowly, what was the *content* of the "Reformation Discovery"? When did it occur?

In the century since Holl sought to provide rigorous research to seek answers to the last two questions, arriving at an "early date" for Luther's discovery of roughly 1514, many others including Vogelsang, Bizer and Bayer have offered modified conclusions regarding the date, some arguing for a "late date" somewhere around 1518. Regarding the "content of the reformation discovery" there has been similar wide divergence of opinion. However, one can state three things upon which there has emerged consensus on all sides:

1. According to Luther's testimony from 1532,[1] the Reformation Discovery is *a specific event*.

2. Also, according to similar testimony in 1538[2] and 1542[3], it has to do with *Luther's new understanding of the concept of God's righteousness as defined by Paul in Romans 1:17.*

3. Finally, this discovery is created entirely by the new, what we would now call existential way that Luther began to read scripture. "Existential", a maddeningly elusive word, has been given such latitude in definition as to render it almost useless for precise argument. For purposes of this argument, however, I will use it to mean that the Word of God works primarily at the level of *effect*, creating two the basic events in a person's *experience* during the encounter with that Word—being

---

1. LW 54:193.
2. LW 54:308.
3. LW 54:442.

killed and being resurrected. The experience of being thus brought to an utter end, and then of being completely remade new by the Word, requires the interpreter to give a report that experience, to bear witness to what has happened, in a way that far surpasses a mere description of the Word's operation at the level of symbol or signification. Gerhard Ebeling puts it succinctly in his early work "*Martin Luther: an Introduction to his Thought*": "The less one approaches the scripture from a previously established position, looking for specific answers to specific questions, or in order merely to enrich one's knowledge, and the more radically one accepts the challenge to one's own existential life of an *encounter* with the scripture, concentrating upon a single fundamental question aimed at human existence itself and touching one's very conscience, the more one looks ultimately for only one thing in the scripture, *the word which brings certainty in life and in death*."[4] (my italics) This is his description of Luther's experience.

What Luther Received from Others

The central contention in this chapter is that the basic Reformation discovery most fundamentally resulted from Luther's uncomfortable discovery that *he* was "being read by scripture" and that proper hermeneutics required acknowledging and reporting upon this existential event. Expositing scripture and proclamation, for Luther as he heard it in its clear literal sense, entailed a requirement to attempt to create *an honest report from the battlefield*, that is, a personal report of what he was experiencing during the process of devotedly seeking to convey what scripture was speaking to him. This, in turn, forced him to create a whole new interpretive system which he eventually called the theology of the cross. This, he received from nobody.

It has been widely taught that the Reformation discovery consisted of the new insight that the righteousness of God was not something demanded of the sinner but graciously imputed by a justifying decree of God through the death and resurrection of Jesus. (cf. items 1 and 2 above) In other words, the Reformation discovery centered around the redefinition of God's righteousness not as a requirement but as a gift. But that is only part of the story. Luther's new hermeneutic, shaped wholly, and not in part, upon the growing conviction that he was "being read by scripture"—*that* is the more fundamental Reformation discovery. *That* made the exposition of scripture into a report from the battlefield where two events characterized every encounter: the death of all hopes of personal

---

4. Ebeling, *Martin Luther: An Introduction to his Thought*, 97

righteousness for the sinner under the word of Law, and the resurrection to life *ex nihilo* (new creation out of nothing) by the declaration of promise, the word of the Gospel. All exposition now becomes "bearing witness" to the living encounter created by God's Word.

Luther's Reformation discovery absolutely precludes three more modern ways of exposition or proclamation:

- *theorization* which makes faith into insight or knowledge;
- *moralization* which makes faith the enactment of the deed; and
- *psychologization* which makes faith into a reflection upon the experience of human life.

"Luther's great hermeneutical discovery, strictly speaking, *is* his Reformation discovery. *Namely, that the linguistic sign itself is the thing; it does not represent a thing that is absent but it presents a thing that is present.*"[5] (his italics) "It is rather a *promissio* in the form of a speech act that creates a relationship—between the person in whose name it is spoken and the person to whom it is spoken, who believes or does not believe the promise. If we consider the unconditional word of absolution as the basic word, model, and matrix of an evangelical sermon, then there are four decisive features . . .

1. The sermon is not a discourse in the third person, about something, but an address in the second person, where an "I" addresses a "you".
2. The verb is formulated in the present tense or in the present perfect.
3. The performative verb used in the present or present perfect is semantically and pragmatically that of "promise"—a valid promise with immediate effect; it creates community.
4. The "I" of the preacher who speaks, legitimates herself or himself, implicitly or explicitly, as authorized to make this promise—like the prophet with the message formula, 'Thus says the LORD'. The preacher is an authorized representative who stands in the place of his Lord and is authorized and empowered to speak on his behalf."[6]

This more foundational description of the Reformation discovery can be described first as a verb, and only then, more abstractly, as a noun.

- As a verb, the Reformation discovery is an existential event, resting upon the discovery that the living voice of the Word of God (read or preached) is an ongoing event, where God's commanding voice, in a

---

5. Bayer, in *Justification is for Preaching*, 202.
6. Bayer, *Justification is for Preaching*, 202.

highly personal encounter, creates a confrontation between the Holy God and a sinful creature. This verb-oriented, existential and highly personal encounter forces the total revision all previous definitions of the four theological categories listed below.

- Subsequently as a noun, "justification", involves a word-constellation describing the entire Christian experience not as the "exodus from vice to virtue," but as the "exodus from virtue to Grace."[7] What this "exodus" describes (now as a noun, justification) *abstracts* the living, verbal character and content of the Reformation discovery.

Before proceeding further, the received interpretive system with which Luther began needs brief description, in order to give some sense of the almost apocalyptic upset that ensued in biblical interpretation. Luther had been trained in was called the *Quadriga*. This interpretive method from his scholastic training had come originally from the Greeks. It was called the Quadriga because it maintained that there were four levels of meaning to a given text:

- the *literal/ historical*, which pointed to the past, concerning actual events;
- the *allegorical*, which pointed upwards toward the heavenly, what you should believe;
- the *tropological* or *moral*, which pointed downwards toward the human, how you should behave; and
- the *anagogical* which pointed toward the heavenly future, what you should hope for.

The main emphasis in this method was to arrive at the spiritual sense rather than the "mere" literal sense of scripture. Greeks were interested in the more spiritual interpretive sense than in the literal sense, in that they were understandably reluctant to treat all their myths literally. However, in scriptural interpretation, Luther was becoming more and more convinced that the only meaning of significance was the literal. Although one can still see vestigial remains of the "spiritual meaning of the text" in the Church Postil of 1520, it has now become a postscript to the model sermons. In 1540 Luther said at table, "When I was young . . . I dealt with allegories, tropologies and analogies and did nothing but clever tricks with them. If somebody had them today they'd be looked upon as rare relics. I know they're nothing but rubbish. Now I've let them go, and this is my last and best art,

---

7. Forde, *Exodus from Virtue to Grace*, 32.

to translate the Scriptures in their plain sense. The literal sense does it—in it there's life, comfort, power, instruction, and skill. The other is tomfoolery, however brilliant the impression it makes."[8]

From Johann von Staupitz, Luther's confessor while he was at the Augustinian monastery, Luther learned the importance of meditating upon the crucified Christ as the heart of any devotional exercise. From this center of his devotional life arose Luther's conviction that everything is interpreted by the revelation of Jesus Christ critically at the cross. Luther was open to figurative meanings in scripture, but Luther saw the figurative as having a truth in itself which bore witness to another profounder truth. For Luther the figurative operates very much like the seven "signs" in the Gospel of John, each revealing a deeper truth.

This discipline of focusing upon Christ, and him crucified, served to convince Luther that the prevailing interpretive methods did not sufficiently relate everything in scripture to Christ, nor, more importantly to the cross. This conviction, over time, built a distinct distrust in the rather mechanical approach of the Quadriga's hermeneutic. The whole system gradually collapsed before Luther's singular concentration on what the literal meaning, in each case, newly revealed about Christ. Luther struggled to find and then bear witness to the nut and kernel of scriptural witness, because he understood that to be the non-negotiable task laid upon him by the church which had conferred upon him the office of Doctor of Theology. He suffered greatly under the immense struggle to be thus accountable.

Incidentally, another Greek import into western interpretive theory, which survives to this day, is also one that Luther implicitly destroyed by his discovery—the concept of "timeless truths." Greek historiography does not share the unique perspective of the Christian faith that history has a goal which will derive all its meaning in the final revelation of the coming of Jesus Christ and his kingdom. Instead, for the Greeks, time went round and round. It only made sense then, to distil from the continued revolutions of history, "timeless truths" so that one could order one's life a little better. Subscribing to this Greek notion, and presenting God's Word in the form of the "moral of the story" or the "timeless truth", as if the Gospel is not a living, present, I-you word, destroys preaching! Using the "Aesop's Fable format", interpreting everything as something that merely goes round and round, something that can be canned, or stored, or filed in a folder for future use—this fundamental misunderstanding of the actual dynamics of Christian proclamation completely betrays and undoes the office of biblical preaching.

---

8. LW 54:406.

But back to what Luther received from others. "From Augustine Luther learned that the letter is dead until made alive by the Spirit. From Augustine he also learned to draw the distinction between letter and spirit."[9] Luther utterly transformed and enlarged this binary interpretive method until it became his own unique interpretive method, what he came to call Law and Gospel. Instead of seeing the letter as dead, Luther experienced the Law (with Paul) as an active power which killed the sinner. But the Law is only one of the two ways in which the voice of God engages human sinners. The Gospel is also the voice of God engaging human sinners, but this time delivering them from sin, death, and the power of the devil. The essence of scriptural interpretation became how to rightly prepare the two words of the one Voice for proper proclamation. This required that the Law be preached first, to kill the hearer's false beliefs and hopes, in order to preach the Gospel could resurrect the hearer through the promise, who is Jesus Christ. Luther insists that this always has to be the order of things. "God cannot be God unless He first becomes a devil. All that God speaks and does the devil has to speak and do first. And our flesh agrees. Therefore it is actually the Spirit who enlightens and teaches us in the Word to believe differently. By the same token the lies of this world cannot become lies without first having become truth. The godless do not go to hell without first having gone to heaven. They do not become the devil's children until they have first been the children of God."[10]

> "These strange words begin to yield some sense when one thinks as a theologian of the cross and "tells it like it is." Unconditional grace must first be an absolute threat to us as theologians of glory. There is no "cure" for the theology of glory. No mere "change" of mind or opinion is possible. Grace therefore can only appear as nothing but wrath. The executor of the wrath of God, however, is the devil. God therefore first becomes a devil. All that God says and does the devil must say and do first. One must first go to hell before one can be raised. There is no other way here. God must be accorded the absolute right to do this. The sinner must suffer this if there is to be life."[11]

Occam was another important influence upon Luther's evolving approach to scriptural interpretation. Occam (1288-1348) was an English Franciscan friar and a scholastic philosopher who distinguished between the truths arrived at by objective reason, and the truths of theology which

---

9. Harrisville, *Pandora's Box Opened*, 17.
10. LW 14:31.
11. Forde, *On Being a Theologian of the Cross*, 90.

appealed to revelation. His distinction between these two levels of knowledge was so rigorous that he was charged with advocating a "double truth." Occam asserted that it is impossible for reason to recognize what is beyond sense, driving him more and more to the particular. But of incredible import for our argument is that Occam had great skepticism regarding any knowledge arrived at through the "universal concepts" of Aristotle, and posited instead that the basis for knowledge is the human experience of the particular. "Occam's influence on Luther was threefold—in his emphasis on the authority of scriptures, in his conviction that human reason cannot attain to sure knowledge of the realities of faith, and in his emphasis on the absolute power of God. The obstacle set by Occam to Luther's understanding was his accent on the capabilities of the human will, an emphasis that plunged Luther into a profound distress of conscience and compelled him to follow the way of self-perfection to the verge of despair."[12]

"Experience" is the key word in this interpretive system, and Luther was agreeing. The entire last chapter of this book will be devoted to that single subject. Luther was discovering more and more that instead of reading scripture as an object over which he was the master, he was finding himself the object of the decrees of God spoken therein. Not only that, but he was also discovering that he was the one being shaped and created by those words, as they were spoken to him in his study. In his first Psalm lectures is this famous quote: "And note that the strength of Scripture is this: that it is not changed into him who studies it, but that it transforms its lover into itself and its strengths . . . Because you will not change me into what you are (as heretics do) . . . .but you will be changed into what I am."[13] I think it is proper to characterize how Luther was teaching his students here as an "existential" reading of scripture, or, more simply stated, "bearing witness." Again, in the Romans commentary he repeats this point: "He justifies, overcomes, in His Word when He makes us to be like His Word, that is, righteous, true, wise, etc. And He thus changes us into His Word, but not His Word into us."[14]

This idea was independently developed by Luther. Here he went far beyond his favorite church father, Augustine, who had taught that "love changes the lover into the beloved." And this, as much as any narrowly defined "content" to the Reformation discovery, seems to be precisely what decisively aided Luther in overcoming his *Anfechtungen*—his terrors over death, predestination and God's judgment. Lohse observes, "It must be

12. Harrisville, *Pandora's Box Opened*, 17.
13. LW 10:332-3.
14. LW 25:211.

stated that (in his Romans commentary) Luther set what Paul had to say about righteousness and justification at the center, and from that center interpreted all of Paul's theology. In doing so *he made the person under spiritual attack his point of reference.*"[15] (my italics)

"The person under attack" is evident in the highly personal way Luther described what he meant by his *Anfechtungen* in his 1518 "Explanations of the Disputation Concerning the Value of Indulgences":

> I myself 'knew a man' (2 Corinthians 12:2) who claimed that he had often suffered these punishments, in fact over a very brief period of time. Yet they were so great and so much like hell that no tongue could adequately express them no pen could describe them and one who had not himself experienced them could not believe them and so great were they that, if they had been sustained or had lasted for half an hour, even for one tenth of an hour he would have perished completely and all of his bones would have been reduced to ashes. At such a time God seems terribly angry, and with him the whole creation. At such a time there is no flight, not comfort, within or without, but all things accuse.
>
> At such a time as that the Psalmist mourns, 'I am cut off from thy sight' (Ps 31:22), or at least he does not dare to say, 'O Lord . . . do not chasten me in thy wrath.' (Ps 6:1) In this moment strange to say the soul cannot believe that it can ever be redeemed other than that the punishment is not yet completely felt. Yet the soul is eternal and is not able to think of itself as being temporal. All that remains is the stark-naked desire for help and a terrible groaning, but it does not know where to turn for help. In this instance the person is stretched out with Christ so that all his bones may be counted, and every corner of the soul is filled with the greatest bitterness, dread, trembling, and sorrow in such a manner that all these last forever. To use an example: If a ball crosses a straight line, any point of the line which is touched bears the whole weight of the ball, yet it does not embrace the whole ball. Just so the soul, at the point where it is touched by a passing eternal flood, feels and imbibes nothing except eternal punishment. Yet the punishment does not remain, for it passes over again. There if that punishment of hell, that is that unbearable and inconsolable trembling, takes hold of the living, the punishment of the soul in purgatory seems to be so much greater. Moreover, that punishment for them is constant. And in this instance the inner fire is much more terrible

---

15. Lohse, *Martin Luther's Theology*, 94.

than the outer fire. If there is anyone who does not believe that, we do not beg him to do so, but we have merely proved that these preachers of indulgences speak with too much audacity about many things of which they know nothing or else doubt. For one ought to believe those who are experienced in these matters rather than those who are inexperienced.[16]

What is written here describes the experience of the immediacy of death and terror resulting from personal helplessness before the power of predestination, where the issue is not despair or sorrow, but *the experience of God's wrath*. Already in his first lectures on the Psalms Luther writes, "No one arrives at a knowledge of the Godhead if he is not first brought low and has descended to a knowledge of himself. For there he also arrives at a knowledge of God."[17] Later, in his conflicts with the Roman church, another source of *Anfechtung* and torment would be the question hurled at him by his opponents, "Do you claim to be the only one who has the true Word of God and no one else has it?"[18] Luther describes similar testings at table later in life, "The devil has often troubled me by saying 'who commanded you to teach against the monasteries?' Or again, "'Before there was glorious peace, but now you have disturbed it, and who ordered you to do so?'"[19] and, " I have other temptations from the devil. He often throws this up to me: 'How many people must you have led astray!'"[20] In any case, his *Anfechtungen* were not something that passed from his experience when he grew as a Christian, nor were they solved by the "Reformation Discovery." But they did serve as the ongoing crucible *through which* he came to faith and certainty. "Whether God wishes to take me hence now or tomorrow, I want to leave this bequest, that I desire to acknowledge Christ as my Lord. This I have not only from the Scriptures but also from experience, for the name of Christ often helped me when nobody else could. So I've had words and deeds in my favor, scriptures and experience, and God gave me both in abundance. It was hard for me during the temptation, yet it has been good for me."[21]

Other notable contributors to Luther's development into possibly the finest expositor of scripture that the world has ever known—were Faber Stapulensis (1455-1536) at the university of Paris, Ruechlin for his work in

16. LW 31:129-130.
17. WA 55 II 1, 2, 137, 8-11.
18. LW 54:18.
19. LW 54:96.
20. LW 54:95.
21. LW 54:94.

preparing a definitive text for the Hebrew scriptures, and Erasmus of Rotterdam who had gathered the most comprehensive collection of New Testament witnesses to create a definitive Greek New Testament.

What followed the Discovery: the complete Redefinition of Five Theological Fundamentals

One can discern how Luther gradually departed from the received late scholastic theology which he had been taught at Erfurt, by tracing out, first, in the Psalm lectures (1513-15), and then in his subsequent lectures on Romans (1515-16), Galatians (1516-17), and Hebrews (1517-18), the development of the following concepts:

1. his articulation in a dynamic, unprecedented way of this new concept of the **Word of God as personal encounter**, refusing any treatment of scripture other than as personal address;

2. his deepening and radicalizing of the concept of **Sin;**

3. his treatment of **God's righteousness** understood as completely obliterating all claims to human righteousness, through a judgment always heard in the present tense, a judgment which entails hearing both the Law as well as the Word of Promise as God's decree;

4. his redefinition of **Grace**, no longer as an abstract attribute but now understood as the present tense, performative declaration of God's promise to the sinner,

5. his articulation of **Faith** is understood now no longer as merely believing that some theological concept is true, but as humanity's holding firmly to said declaration *(promisio)*, and nothing else at all. Faith now becomes, more and more, a highly personal confidence in God's present tense declaration of the word of promise;

All of the above jointly aid Luther in addressing decisively the anguish of his *Anfechtungen*, the dealing with the testing and inner conflict that he calls "temptation."

I will argue that each of these concepts emerged newly shaped with their peculiar definition through the fearful yet lively encounter with God's Word. The revised concepts of scripture itself, of sin, of God's righteousness, of grace, and of faith—all utterly defied received scholastic theology at critical points, at first creating a horrible disconnect in his thinking, and finally changing Luther's very mode of thinking itself. The horrible disconnect with received scholastic theology he expressed in what was to become his continuing and characteristic exasperated expostulation during lectures to his students: "*O stulti, O Sawtheologen!*" (O fools, O pig theologians!)

One of the first fruits to emerge from this highly intense personal testing of everything by the address of the Word of God, was his growing conviction that there must be a brand new foundation as to what could be accorded authority over faith and life. It had to be the experienced Word alone, and not tradition. These diverse elements then slowly coalesced into an identifiable core formed by a driving concern—that all scriptural exposition (especially preaching) must serve the sole purpose of creating certainty of faith in its hearer. Lohse asserts that in describing Luther's theology as a whole, his Reformation breakthrough, and thus the doctrine of justification, that this pastoral aim must assume a central place. His question is, " . . . are we not dealing with the theme of salvation as the aim and goal that must always be at the center in the discussion of every other theological theme? . . . Or more basically put: What weight does doctrine have alongside preaching? It is certain that for Luther *the question of the assurance of salvation and thus of preaching stood at the center.*"[22] If Luther's concern regarding assurance of salvation actually governs his whole theological approach, then that concern must be exhibited throughout his writings in a readily accessible way and in a way that continues to embrace his whole endeavor. And it clearly is so exhibited throughout his career, evident for instance in all the sermons of the Postil of 1520, Bondage of the Will, both Galatians commentaries, and in his exposition on the Gospel of John, to name a few.

More than any other theologian, Martin Luther is driven by a single, central controlling core pursuit. If that pursuit was and continued to be for him the assurance of salvation via the decree of a gracious God, then that core issue demanded Luther's highly personal, intimate reading of the Word—first recognizing God's Word as an address, and then submitting to its judgment which kills and makes alive.

If Luther's "Reformation Discovery" indeed entails his being shown how assurance comes to a Christian through submitting to the power of God's accusing word of Law and then being resurrected by the accompanying word of promise and grace, then that discovery also fulfills what he had early set out as his goal in a letter to his friend, Eisenach priest Johannes Braun, in a letter written March 17, 1509, stating that he sought "for a theology that gets at the meat of the nut, at the kernel of the corn, or the marrow of the bones."[23] Whereas philosophy always seeks to arrive at a knowledge of God apart from sin and judgment, only on the basis of creation, Luther

---

22. Lohse, *Martin Luther's Theology*. p. 7.
23. Br 1 Nr 5, 40-46.

was becoming convinced that *there is no saving knowledge of God* apart from the knowledge of sin, from being brought low, in fact from being brought to complete nothing, under the experience of God's absolute judgment. True knowledge of God is existential knowledge that comes through dying, and being made alive again.

In the introduction to his later exposition of Psalm 51 (written in 1533) we read, "The proper subject of theology is man guilty of sin and condemned, and God the Justifier and Savior of man the sinner. *Whatever is asked or discussed in theology outside this subject, is error and poison.* All scripture points to this, that God commends His kindness to us and in His Son restores to righteousness and life the nature that has fallen into sin and condemnation."[24] Again, "Knowledge of God and man is divine wisdom, and in the real sense theological. It is such knowledge of God and man as is related to the justifying God and to sinful man, so that in the real sense the subject of theology is *guilty and lost man and the justifying and redeeming God. What is inquired into apart from this question and subject is error and vanity in theology.*"[25]

Here, the older Luther has articulated that the "discovery" had coalesced for him into a sharpened point—that all preaching, all hermeneutics, indeed all scriptural exposition have this one controlling feature. The Augsburg Confession of 1530 likewise stipulates what constitutes the core of the "Reformation Discovery", where Luther describes Article IV on Justification as the single criterion upon which the church stands or falls: "It is also taught among us that we cannot obtain forgiveness of sin and righteousness before God by our own merits, works, or satisfactions, but that we receive forgiveness of sin and become righteous before God by grace, for Christ's sake, through faith, when we believe that Christ suffered for us and that for his sake our sin is forgiven and righteousness and eternal life are given to us. For God will regard and reckon this faith as righteousness, as Paul says in Romans 3:21-26 and 4:5."[26] (translated from the German language version, regarded as the more accurate)

Unfortunately, the living nature of God's address has been lost in this latter quotation, through its attempt to render in more systematic, compact, abstract form, that which creates the justified sinner. Nevertheless, the core content in both these later citations is clear. This content describes two continuing events, involving these actions: first, that God judges Man who acknowledges himself Sinner under God's judgment; and second, that God

---

24. LW 12:311.

25. WA 40 II 327 11-328,3.

26. Tappert, *Book of Concord*, 30.

justifies the same Sinner, who is justified again by the same God's judgment, but now a judgment which has become a declaration of grace through the new testament of the blood shed at the cross. Luther, together with later Lutherans, began to use shorthand for this, calling these two related events as the Law/Gospel hermeneutic, that is, the sole interpretive method for reading all of scripture aright.

This discovery of Luther coalesced into an inescapable violent either/or combat with all competing hermeneutical systems. *Either Luther, or his enemies, must be in hell because one of them is wrong.*[27] Already, at age 33, Luther makes this assertion to the Lateran Council in Rome: "*Everything rests on the preaching of the Word and with it stands or falls the decision of the legitimate reformation of the Church as well as the foundation of a pious life. So let your thesis stand firm: that the Church will not be born and cannot stand according to the ways of men, because it has its being in and through the Word of God. As it is written: "He has called us through the Word of Truth." (James 1:18)*[28] (my italics)

1. The discovery that the Word of God is personal encounter

To repeat, the key to this whole Reformation process, and the central reason that it took the shape that it did, is rooted in Luther's existential reading of scripture. As he wrestled with questions regarding a warrant or foundation from which he could obtain certainty of faith—a warrant which neither received scholastic theology nor to which church leaders could provide answers—he brought those questions to bear in a highly intense struggle with the very scripture he was commissioned by his office to teach and interpret clearly and honestly. In the process, he discovered that the scriptures were changing him! Astonishingly, in the process of being submitted to the terror of God's judgment, without excuse, he also discovered that that very same judgment *delivered his longed for mercy, without any qualification*. In other words, Christian certainty did not arrive through the removal of all terrors and darkness, but rather it arrived precisely through undergoing them. A Christian never lives without stress, never lives by sight or completely by experience, but always lives in temptation, always lives by faith, always lives by hearing the present voice of the Word ever anew. (Isaiah 50:4)

The term, "theology of the cross", while serving rightly as shorthand for a whole interpretive method, obscures the critical feature of Luther's

27. WA 23:33, 17.
28. WA 1:12, 11ff.

discovery, that a *theologian* of the cross, gives primary place to submitting to the Word operating at the level of *effect*, over trying to understand that same word at the level of *signification*. Having said this, the "theology of the cross", as an interpretive method, is violently polemical to all competing hermeneutical methods for the simple reason that it begins with these non-negotiable presuppositions:

- that Christ is the "magister" while the interpreter, himself, is not;
- that all scripture is about Christ; and further,
- that the key to understanding any of it, is that it is about Christ, *and him crucified*.

Luther often cited I Corinthians 1:18-25 to anchor this assertion. "For the word of the cross is folly to those who are perishing, but to us who are being saved it is the power of God." 2 Corinthians 3:14 is also instructive in this regard: "But their minds were hardened; for to this day, then they read the old covenant, that same veil remains unlifted, because only through Christ is it taken away." With Paul, the "theology of the cross" carries a corresponding conviction that without the cross, all scripture remains in darkness. But this cross kills the hearer/reader in order to create the sight of faith. "Therefore having this ministry by the mercy of God we do not lose heart . . . .And even if the gospel is veiled, it is veiled only to those who are perishing. In their case the god of this world has blinded the minds of the unbelievers, to keep them from seeing the light of the gospel of the glory of Christ." (2 Corinthians. 4:3-4)

Luther's interpretive method or hermeneutic derived from his understanding that the gospel is defined as "that which gives or carries Christ." Writing that, "just as his deeds, so Christ's commandments and his exposition of the law are not yet the gospel," he asserted that the gospel becomes clear only *when a voice is heard* to announce that, "Christ is your own—with his life, teaching, works, dying, and rising." So, Luther writes, since much more is involved with the *word* than with the *deeds* of Christ, if one should ever lack the deeds or the word of Christ, it would be better to do without the deeds and the history than without the word and the preaching. "The deeds," Luther adds, "are of no help to me, but his words—they give life as he himself says." For this reason he states, those books are most highly to be praised which deal most with the words of Christ. In fact, if there were no marvelous deeds of Christ, and we knew nothing of them, we would still have enough in the word without which we cannot have the life. Luther thus assigned inferior status to the Synoptic Gospels. The epistles, he wrote, especially those to the Romans, Galatians, Ephesians, together with

First Peter were the books that show Christ, and teach everything needed, though one should never see or hear of any other book. These were the real core and marrow among all the writings of the New Testament. These were the best evangelists, and deserved first place, since they set forth how Faith in Christ alone makes righteous, and thus were more a gospel than Matthew, Mark and Luke, who did little more than describe the history of the deeds of miracles of Christ. Luther reflected an astonishing freedom toward historical questions, and the conscious separation of them from matters of faith. As it happened, both the Orthodox and the Pietists have totally suppressed Luther's critical stance, whether respecting the *res* (the thing itself, or the content thereof) or the history.[29]

Because I am going to take the modern historical-critical method to task in a whole later chapter, it must be clear that I do not deny that critical biblical method has its place. After all, Jesus himself required critical reading of scripture from the professional Jewish theologian, the scribe, when he asked him, "How do you read?" (Luke 10:26), thus indicating that there were alternative ways to understand scripture, and, more importantly, one must be aware of the interpretive criteria one was using to ferret out the truth. The scribe described his criteria to Jesus' satisfaction, stating that the summary of God's revelation was contained in two sentences—the two tables of the law. Jesus himself used critical biblical method to arrive at the most astonishing results. For example when he was being mocked by the Sadducees for believing in the resurrection of the dead, Jesus quoted the Word, "I am the God of Abraham, Isaac and Jacob", (Mark 12:26) using the *present tense* of that sentence as sole and sufficient warrant to prove resurrection. After all, God did not say, "I was the God of Abraham . . . ." Now, there is biblical interpretation at its core, taking the literal word, extremely literally!

The prevailing modern interpretive method, unknown to Luther, because it is an Enlightenment creation, is ironically, the current reigning, almost uncontested interpretive method taught in most seminaries—the historical critical method and its variants. For those who claim to be Lutherans this is ironic for at least three reasons:

- Ironic, because it roots in Enlightenment *philosophy* and not in theology (that is, not in the Word of God.)
- Ironic, because it is a hermeneutic of *doubt* or *suspicion,* which, by its very structure and by its own admission *cannot* deliver certainty of faith!! (This result alone is directly contrary to Luther's whole preaching effort.)

---

29. von Lowenich, *Luther als Ausleger der Synoptiker*, 1954.

- Ironic, because the historical critical method begins with the basic assumption that man is the master over the text (which is commonly referred to as "material") rather than God Himself, together with His Word, being the operative agents to change the reader into what is proclaimed.

Before continuing, it is necessary to understand what we mean when we say that the historical critical method is a hermeneutic (interpretive method) of doubt or suspicion. This method was developed, and worked admirably, in sifting through the documents of the Middle Ages to determine whether they were valid expressions of the truth or forgeries. The process began with assuming that any document under examination was a forgery or a fraud. Then corroborating evidence was sought, and if there was a balance of witnesses in favor of said document, then it was declared *probably* true. I say probably, because for this interpretive method nothing is certain, and nothing can be certain! The highest degree of certainty is some percentage figure.

Although that is a very simplistic summary, consider now the same interpretive process being applied to God's Word. We begin by assuming that the "material" in front of us is a fraud, created by "redactors" and other copiers to serve their own purposes and not necessarily the truth. Thus, some Epistles of Paul are probably not his, but written under a pseudonym or acolyte, etc. etc. Soon, non-negotiable features of the faith become suspect. Basics of faith are directly questioned. "Was Jesus really God?" and, "Is the resurrection merely wishful thinking created by disappointed apostles?" (Sadly, it has become necessary for N.T. Wright to write a magisterial 800 page volume "The Resurrection of the Son of God" just to refute all the current counter claims of the historical fact of the Resurrection, by some of the most reputable current theologians.)

Practically, let's see how this plays out in proclamation. Fairly recently, in a church not far from a famous seminary the pastor commenced his sermon by saying essentially, "Since this story occurs in all three synoptic gospels, it very probably happened." Many professors from the neighboring seminary attend this large, architecturally and musically gifted church. No controversy at all attended this outrageous remark. This kind of "proclamation" regularly goes unchallenged. But how does this sort of thing build faith? More to the point, how does it not *destroy* the faith of the hearer, who has his or her foundational authority for faith thus directly undermined and eroded?

To take another example of how the "hermeneutic of doubt and suspicion" affects the church, consider any funeral sermon. Funeral sermons distill the Christian faith. The unspoken question in the room is, "Did aunt

Martha make it?" or, to ask more narrowly the same thing, "Preacher, what is your warrant for making the claim that she did make it?" Preachers who don't take this challenge head on need to find another occupation. So, our historical critical proclaimer sallies forth armed with high probability statistics, to fight the foe, whose entire stratagem is to sow doubt. This proclaimer, well prepared by academia, might say, "The resurrection very well may have happened historically, and is probably not an imaginary fiction. And, if that is so, there is a good chance that it may somehow reach or impact our aunt Martha! Amen." Practitioners of the historical critical method should do a month of funeral sermons, before going back to their lecterns.

Of course, all this "probability" is precisely the nexus of Luther's terrors. This same probability was precisely what was rooted out by Luther's being willing to become a theologian of the cross, to be brought low, in fact to be brought to an utter end by the word he was hearing. But by insisting on such a rigorous literal reading of scripture, at the level of effect, he found that through that very same death arose certainty about God's purpose for him, as well. That certainty arose precisely from utter helplessness—*such helplessness driving to the conviction that God must do everything*. With God alone doing everything, for the first time certainty became not only a possibility, but an established event. Now Luther had his controlling pastoral task defined—to create the same certainty in his hearers.

The introduction to the 1535 commentary on Galatians (by the much more seasoned Luther) is amazing in articulating this singleness of purpose for prospective and current pastors.

> The righteousness of faith, which God imputes to us through Christ without works . . . is a merely passive righteousness . . . For here we work nothing, render nothing to God; we only receive and permit someone else to work in us, namely God. Therefore it is appropriate to call the righteousness of faith or Christian righteousness 'passive.' This is a righteousness hidden in a mystery, which the world does not understand. In fact, Christians themselves do not adequately understand it or grasp it in the midst of their temptations. Therefore it must always be taught and continually exercised. And anyone who does not grasp or take hold of it in afflictions and terrors of conscience cannot stand. For there is no comfort of conscience so solid and certain as is this passive righteousness."(p.4-5) "It is impossible for the human mind to conceive any comfort of itself, or to look only at grace amid its consciousness and terror of sin . . . therefore the afflicted conscience has no remedy against despair and eternal death except to take hold of the promise of grace

offered in Christ" (p. 5) "This is our theology, by which we teach a precise distinction between these two kinds of righteousness, the active and the passive, so that morality and faith, works and grace, secular society and religion may not be confused."(p.7) "I am indeed a sinner according to the present life and its righteousness, as a son of Adam where the Law accuses me, death reigns and devours me. But above this life I have another righteousness, another life, which is Christ . . . Thus as long as we live here, both remain. The flesh is accused exercised, saddened, and crushed by the active righteousness of the Law. But the spirit rules, rejoices and is saved by passive righteousness . . . Paul is concerned to instruct, comfort, and sustain us diligently in a perfect knowledge of this most excellent and Christian righteousness. For if the doctrine of justification is lost, the whole of Christian doctrine is lost."(p. 9) "For by this doctrine alone and through it alone is the church built, and in this it consists . . . .*Therefore I admonish you, especially those of you who are to become instructors of consciences, as well as each of you individually, that you exercise yourselves by study, by reading, by meditation, and by prayer, so that in temptation you will be able to instruct them from the Law to Grace, from active righteousness to passive righteousness, in short, from Moses to Christ. In affliction and in the conflict of conscience it is the devil's habit to frighten us with the Law and to set against us the consciousness of sin, our wicked past, the wrath and judgment of God, hell and eternal death, so that thus he may drive us into despair, subject us to himself, and pluck us from Christ. (p.10)*[30]

Further on in the same commentary Luther asserts that practicing this distinction between the Law and the Gospel is "an art" at which he is still not very good, but a practice necessary to console the conscience as well as a practice which constitutes the summary of all Christian doctrine.[31] "You who are to be consolers of consciences that are afflicted, should teach this doctrine diligently."[32] Faith *is* the practice of this dialectic.[33]

All this demonstrates why the "theology of the cross" tolerates no rival interpretive system, whatsoever. The bloodless, "objective", and "empirical" historical critical method knows nothing of such hot passionate engagement with opposing spiritual powers, and disdains all claims thus made for truth or validity as hopelessly "subjective" (and therefore suspect or worthless). In

30. LW 26:4-10.
31. LW 26:115-117.
32. LW 26:138.
33. LW 26:141, 161-3.

contrast, a theologian of the cross has arrived at the truth bloodied, terrified, humbled and killed—but newly certain of God's grace.

Each hermeneutic begins its task so differently that even the basic starting point—"knowledge of God"—is defined, respectively, in two totally irreconcilable ways. The philosophic one (the historical critical method) begins with the conviction that creation, inquired into by proper scientific and objective method, will yield (factually) what we need to know about God; while the other begins with the terrifying discovery that we, the sinner, know *nothing* about a holy God, driving to the non-negotiable conclusion that we *can* have no saving knowledge, nor any certain confidence about Him apart from having Him reveal our sin to us and then experiencing His gracious decision to deal with that sin by a word of promise whose warrant is that the cross of Christ has already borne your richly deserved condemnation.

2. How The Doctrine of Sin Changed

Regarding Luther's immense contribution to the doctrine of sin, and to see how radically he departed from his received scholastic training on this subject, it is instructive to begin at the developed conclusion exhibited richly in the 1533 lecture on Psalm 51.

> 'I know my transgressions,' does not mean, as the pope taught, to call to mind what one has done and what one has failed to do; but it means *to feel* and *to experience* the intolerable burden of the wrath of God . . . A theologian discusses man as a sinner. In theology, this is the essence of man. The theologian is concerned that man become aware of this nature of his, corrupted by sins. When this happens, despair follows, casting him into hell. In the face of the righteous God, what shall a man do who knows that his whole nature has been crushed by sin and that there is nothing left on which he can rely, but that his righteousness has been reduced to exactly nothing? When the mind has felt this much, the other part of this knowledge should follow. *This is not a matter of speculation either, but completely of practice and feeling.* A man hears and learns what grace and justification are, what God's plan is for the man who has fallen into hell, namely that He has decided to restore man through Christ. Here the dejected mind cheers up, and on the basis of this teaching of grace it joyfully declares: '*Though I am a sinner in myself, I am not a sinner in Christ, who has been made Righteousness for us.* (I Cor. 1:30). I am righteous and justified through Christ, the

Righteous and Justifier, who is called the Justifier because He belongs to sinners and was sent for sinners.' This is the twofold theological knowledge which David teaches in this psalm, so that the content of the psalm is the theological knowledge of man and also the theological knowledge of God.[34] (my italics)

Besides demonstrating how Luther hears God's Word at the level of effect more than at the level of signification, these words demonstrate that Sin also gets treated at the level of effect, that is to say, as the *event* of being personally accused. Sin no longer is *a* problem. Sin becomes *the* problem. Long after the "Reformation discovery", Luther is settled on this point. For him, what it means to be a human being is to be a *hearer*, someone who is seized, claimed and subject to judgment. If that is so, then one's whole being depends upon and hangs upon the word of absolution, the decree of mercy and of promise that reaches us and touches our inmost self (what he called the conscience).

Early inner conflicts (it would not be too strong to call them terrors or torments) included a near death experience while caught in a storm out in the open, the death of a close friend, and the continuing unanswered question regarding the question of his personal salvation or damnation pressed upon him by the biblical emphasis on God's election—these torments not only drove Luther to the monastery but forged the most salient feature that came to characterize the new thing his theology brought to the church—that the goal that theology must be, *in every situation,* the question of salvation. In turn, this focus drove, very early on, to some radical departures from the received scholastic doctrine regarding sin. Luther so radicalized the doctrine of sin that the whole medieval system of penance, designed to be a stop-gap measure between a Christian's baptism—understood as the original "infusion of grace"—until one's death, together with purgatory, and masses for the dead, were all about to be overturned. Again, from Luther in 1533:

> They have applied this psalm (51) to the penance of works, to actual sin, which they define as 'anything said, done, or thought against the Law of God.' This definition is far too narrow to portray the greatness or power of sin. We must look at sin more deeply and show more clearly the root of wickedness or sin, not simply remain with the 'elicited act,' as they call them. From this error, their failure to understand sin properly, there comes of course, the other error, their failure to understand the nature of grace properly either. This accounts for their ineptitude in

---

34. LW 12:310-311.

comforting timid consciences and consoling hearts against death and divine judgment. How can anyone give consolation if he does not understand what grace is? Hence they fell into the foolishness of persuading men troubled with sorrows of conscience to put on cowls, accept monastic rules, and the like, by which they believed they would please God. This clearly shows that they did not properly understand either sin or grace and that they were simply teaching a theology of reason without the Word of God. They taught the same way about repentance: people were to collect all the transgressions of the past year, sorrow over them, and expiate them by satisfaction. I ask you, does not a judge hang a thief if he confesses his theft and is sorry for it? Yet these people think God is satisfied if they pretend to be sorry by dressing differently, walking differently and eating differently. The reading of this psalm will be especially useful in teaching us to understand these points of our doctrine properly and in providing us with a learned and serious refutation of our opponents, who argue so wrongly about such serious issues. I have experienced for myself how useless their profane arguments were when my conscience was in need.[35]

The received scholastic theology which Luther had been taught, was expressed in Bonaventura's formula, "If a man does all within his power (*facit quod in se est*), God gives him grace." We know, from countless Reformation stories how well this worked in practice for Luther! In his commentary on Romans, Luther angrily came against the scholastic doctrine that sin was the "absence of original righteousness" and that original sin was merely the absence of a quality of the will. He was discovering while he taught the scriptures, that in the Word, Sin was not merely the absence of righteousness, but rather was the total lack of righteousness in all faculties of body and mind and spirit, inner and outer, besides the set inclination to evil at all times. In Luther's exposition of Psalm 51 in his first lectures, we find the following definition of sin, which goes far beyond Lombard's "Sentences":

> *First.* All men are in sin before God and commit sin, that is, they are sinners in fact. *Second.* To this God himself bore witness through the prophets and established the same at last by the suffering of Christ, for it is on account of the sin of men that He made Him suffer and die. *Third.* God is not justified in himself, but in his words and in us. *Fourth.* We become sinners then when we acknowledge ourselves to be such, for such we are before God . . . Hence these things conflict with each other:

35. LW 12:304.

Denying that one has sin, or not confessing it—and justifying God. Justifying oneself before God—and glorifying God. Therefore God is not justified by anyone except the one who accuses and condemns and judges himself."[36]

This is new: that the essence of Sin is the constant attempt to create one's own righteousness before God, and until that attempt is slain, there is no hope for God's righteousness to save the sinner. In the Romans commentary Luther advances the further characterization of Sin as the condition of being "curvatus in se", (curved in on oneself) always seeking to have everything serve the self. "The reason is that our nature has been so deeply curved in upon itself because of the viciousness of original sin that it not only turns the finest gifts of God in upon itself and enjoys them (as is evident in the case of legalists and hypocrites), indeed, it even uses God Himself to achieve these aims, but it also seems to be ignorant of this very fact, that in acting so iniquitously, so perversely, and in such a depraved way, it is even seeking God for its own sake."[37] Scholastic talk about grace "improving the human condition" (*forma*) was as ridiculous as placing a patch on a mortal wound. Equally ridiculous was scholastic use of the Greek ethical teaching of "habitus", which described the remedy for sin as more rigorous practice of virtue. If "habitus" could change the predicament of human sin, why would there be the necessity of divine atonement? "It must be added that for Luther apart from a true knowledge of sin's nature there is knowledge neither of grace nor of the righteousness of God."[38] Iwand adds this of Luther's theology : "To recognize God in Jesus Christ means to recognize oneself as a sinner and one who needs Jesus Christ. Thus, two things come together that would otherwise be mutually exclusive, namely, the recognition of God and the recognition of sin. Recognition of Sin *is* recognition of God . . . All knowledge of sin that is not gained from the revelation of God—but that is gained by one's own knowledge or experience—will contain in itself it own error and, accordingly, will disguise the true nature of sin."[39]

When Luther described Paul's goal in Romans as "making sin great", he was demonstrating that he no longer would have anything to do with sin defined with the volitional abstractions and distinctions about human ability that he had been taught. Sin for Luther was an *event* caused by the confrontation with an almighty holy God, not an abstraction. "I am accused." Since Adam's original sin, that is humanity's most fundamental definition,

---

36. LW 10:235-236.
37. LW 25:291.
38. Lohse, *Martin Luther's Theology*, 72.
39. Iwand, *Righteousness of Faith According to Luther*, 26-27.

as fundamental and as axiomatic as "I think" was for Rene Descartes. And this accusation has a specific venue—the conscience. This accusation places man inescapably before a holy God, *coram deo*, the relational location where the continuing determinative judgment takes place.

This knowledge of sin, moreover, is not some sort of speculation or an idea which the mind thinks up for itself. It is a true feeling, a true experience, and a very serious struggle of the heart, as (David) testifies when he says (v.3), "'I know (that is, I feel or experience) my transgressions.' This is what the Hebrew word really means. It does not mean, as the pope taught, to call to mind what one has done and what one has failed to do; but it means to feel and to experience the intolerable burden of the wrath of God. The knowledge of sin is itself the feeling of sin, and the sinful man is the one who is oppressed by his conscience and tossed to and fro, not knowing where to turn. Therefore we are not dealing here with the philosophical knowledge of man, which defines man as a rational animal and so forth. Such things are for science to discuss, not for theology.[40]

It is worth noting here that Descartes' whole effort, as well as the whole Enlightenment enterprise which followed him, could be accurately described as an attempt to discover a new basis for human certainty (in the recent loss of the foundational truism that the earth was the center of the universe). This search for a foundation which provides certainty, Luther and Descartes have in common. However, Descartes decided that certainty lay in what philosophy calls "indubitability"—that is, in that which cannot be doubted. In utter contrast, Luther discovered certainty through undergoing the opposing, terrifying event of being completely stripped of all certainty. He found absolute faith through undergoing absolute terror. Certainty, for him was not indubitability, but was grounded precisely and necessarily in human helplessness. Certainty could only obtain where God does everything and man can do nothing.

It is a theological commonplace these days to hear reputable theologians, such as Luther Seminary's recent homiletics professor, dismiss Luther's question, "How can I find a gracious God?" as no longer the question of modern man.[41] If that is so, I would challenge them to demonstrate just how graduating into the wonderful current world of "post modernism"[42] somehow erased or removed the intractably sinful nature that each of us inherited from our original parents. We must have already found our way back to the

---

40. LW 12:310.

41. Baccalaureate address at Luther Seminary, 2014.

42. "Post-modernism", a reaction to "modernism", denies the belief that absolute Truth and objective reality underlie all empirical scientific endeavor.

Garden! Repeatedly, however, each and every daily newspaper together with any kind of informed sane reasonable telling of has current facts, bears common, unbending, daily witness that this is not so. And so, in this passing age, and in all the time antecedent to the resurrection from the dead, the covert hope of our ticking little Pharisee hearts, that we will someday somehow graduate from the need for forgiveness, remains unfulfilled. We need to find a gracious God, or we are lost. Thank goodness He has found us and called us to be His very own! I am told that the ancient Chinese word-symbol for forgiveness contains the picture of the sacrifice table. Sinners always have been, and remain, the only people whom God addresses. Sinners are the only ones whom God loves. You qualify. We all do.

3. God's Righteousness

God's righteousness is no abstraction for Luther. In the same way that God's Word is a living Word, and Sin is a living accusation, so also God's righteousness is an event—a once-for-all-time event completed at the cross, which event is delivered personally to you through the hearing of a brand new verdict declared on your behalf. But this declaration or promise that justifies the sinner, heard as a voice, *coram deo*, always competes with the voice of the accusing conscience. The necessity of faith is clearly seen at this critical juncture in that the voice which accuses the conscience has the empirical evidence of self-knowledge that the accusation is richly merited, while the opposing decree that you, the sinner, possess an alien righteousness, cannot be apprehended by any of our five senses. It must simply be believed.

If there is a narrowly defined "content" to Luther's redefinition of the concept of the Righteousness of God, it involves the contrast between the righteousness which humans must achieve in order to be saved, to the righteousness which is not achieved, but given and imputed to believers as a completed, heavenly, and wholly alien righteousness that doesn't even reside in them but rather resides in Christ. The very word "impute" implies necessarily that the righteousness given in this way cannot reside in the sinner, otherwise imputation would not be necessary. "Impute" implies, as well, that the receiver remains a sinner, or again the imputation would not be necessary. The newly defined content of God's Righteousness can be found literally on the very first page of the Romans commentary, where Luther describes the whole Christian enterprise as a new Exodus. As we have said, the Christian life of faith is no longer an "*exodus from vice to virtue*" but an "*exodus from virtue to grace*." This simple formulation absolutely precludes any possible notions of penance, indulgences and the entire system and practice of masses then in place. It is the nuclear explosion that required an entire new theology now known as the Reformation.

The phrase, "the exodus from vice to virtue" wonderfully describes the whole scholastic theology so succinctly articulated by Bonaventura. The following is a list some of its problems in practice:

- It is an analog system, always emphasizing "progress" on a continuum, always partial, never complete;

- The direction of this proposed human exodus is "up, up, up" (which is the direction always suggested by the evil spirit) forcing attention on the person and the performance, rather than on Christ, who comes down;

- It drives inevitably to self-justifying which always competes with and eventually must drive out God's justifying deed in Christ;

- Worst, it can never provide an answer as to when one has achieved enough to satisfy the Law's demands for adequate righteousness. There is never a *terminus ad quem*. (a description of the final goal) The proper terror engendered by the Law arises from the fact that its demands are never ending, a fact which this theology seems to blissfully ignore.

In contrast, the "exodus from virtue to grace" is a mortal attack at every point on the preceding system.

- Grace is not analog, but rather is 100%. Grace is analogous to the state of pregnancy. One cannot be 85% pregnant. The Grace of Jesus Christ is total or nothing. Thus, the coming of grace must be preceded by God's total assault on any and all human claims to righteousness, (God's intended use of the voice of the Law) as well as on any of our efforts to totally "fulfill all righteousness." (Matthew 3:15, Jesus' first words in this Gospel to describe what *He* came to accomplish).

- The direction of this exodus is "down, down, down"—the direction of the Holy Spirit. God only justifies sinners. And sinners they remain! But now the justified who have God's Righteousness are *simul*—at the same time 100% righteous by imputation of an alien complete righteousness, and still 100% sinner, by reason of indwelling original sin and because we have not yet been raised. (This *simul* formulation is non-negotiable, central and unique to Luther.)

- God only justifies sinners. Thus, we don't have to be good enough. Thus, we no longer have to self-justify.

- Best of all, the answer as to when adequate righteousness has been achieved for you, the sinner, is, "Already!" The Last Judgment has been passed *already* in one's baptism, which connects us to the Last Judgment of the cross where Jesus proclaims the same when he cries out, "It is Finished!" God's Righteousness is already complete. It is not something yet to be done or to be achieved.

This exodus from virtue to grace Luther characterizes as passing from actively seeking one's own righteousness to receiving a "passive righteousness"—having the righteousness of Christ imputed or declared as your own. (cf. especially in that above quoted introduction to the 1535 Galatians commentary). In view of all of this, it easy to see why, in his Romans commentary, Luther characterizes the essence of Sin as any human attempt to achieve one's own righteousness, that is, to justify oneself. There is no means of salvation other than Jesus Christ. Either we are faced with eternal death or we take hold of this passive, declared righteousness by faith. Interestingly, many scholars find that, even with all the emerging insights relating to righteousness in the Romans commentary, Luther has still not arrived at his driving pastoral goal there, of articulating the grounds for proper Christian assurance.

4. Luther's redefinition of Grace

Grace is now defined no longer as some infused quantity which allows the penitent to improve his life, but rather as the operative voice to which faith attends, that convinces us that all that ever was required has already been done. Grace is the living, present tense, decree of absolution, "Your sins are fully forgiven for Jesus' sake." The only question remaining is, "What are you going to do now with that you don't have to do anything? How will you use such freedom?"

I discovered how such grace operates, at an "existential" level, when an old professor who had escaped the Soviet invasion of Latvia, and had emigrated to Minnesota, was assigned the task of getting us first year seminary students interested in reading the church fathers in the original Greek. (a very daunting task) He began the whole enterprise, astonishing all of us, by announcing in the first class that, no matter what, we would all get an A for the course. He wanted us to be motivated in our studies by grace, and not by fear. Hopefully that would allow proper curiosity and interest. He was as good as his word. How I treated this grace was shameful. When the semester came to an end and the threat of grades pressed in from all the other courses, I slacked off on Professor Smits' course. It has bothered me all the rest of my life, that I repaid such a gift of grace in this way. Grace calls forth and exposes our true character. One can trash Grace! I have learned this to my great sorrow, and not just from that course. The value of what Dr. Smits taught me there has probably exceeded in value almost anything else I learned from the entirety of three years preparatory to ordination.

One can trash Grace, but does that means that Grace is weak or ineffective? Look at the results! Isn't it marvelous how Grace still prevails and accomplishes its convincing through the persistence of God's active love? (which is what Grace is)

Already in the first Psalms lectures Luther is giving special emphasis to the effect of Christ's saving work as a voice that liberates the conscience. "Therefore Christ's coming *is* our goodness, for He has taken away, first from our conscience, the punishments which are our evils, and then He will also remove them from the body, and so our goodness will be perfect."[43] Nevertheless, it must be acknowledged that grace gets far less emphasis than Sin, God's righteousness, faith, or justification in Luther's early theological development.

5. Luther's concept of Faith

It is necessary here to alert all readers, right here, that *Luther's concept of faith had nothing whatsoever to do with how the word's current prevailing definition*. That is to say, "faith" for him, was never volitional nor an act of the will. The entire treatise "The Bondage of the Will" (1525) is bent on nothing else than completely and categorically obliterating that notion. Nevertheless, both in Europe and in the United States, in reading Luther's works, we insist on giving faith the definition that was not only foreign to his thinking but inimical to his whole theological effort. In the United States, with our history of awakening movements, we are so used to hearing faith defined volitionally as "accepting Jesus as your personal savior" that one wonders why no one ever notices that nothing like that phrase ever occurs in the whole of the New Testament. If fact, the word "accepting" might occur twice in the whole New Testament, and in those places the Greek can also be rendered just as well "receiving." Salvation, in this understanding, becomes something that is "offered" by God, and all we have to do is reach out and accept it.

In contrast to this Arminian or even Pelagian theology, which both teach that somehow the human will remains intact after the Fall, denying

---

43. LW 10:458.

its slavery to an alien power, Luther insists upon the bondage of the will for the central, singular pastoral purpose which arose from his own struggles over how to find a gracious God. Insisting upon freedom of the will places one instantly right back into "the exodus from vice to virtue", with all its attendant, cursed inability to arrive at any assurance before God. However, insisting that faith does not lie within any human ability, but is rather a miraculous gift of God, created "ex nihilo" (out of nothing) by the hearing of the Word—this understanding actually defines the central event of the "exodus from virtue to Grace" as well as placing us safely within that saving exodus. *The very definition of salvation as well as any hope of proper Christian confidence, hangs in the balance in how "Faith" is defined.*

Luther is not the sole voice in this matter. Even the most famous Baptist preacher defers to the authority of scripture when it opposes the "free will" dogma of the Arminians. In his exposition of Ephesians 1:19-20 C.H. Spurgeon writes,

> "In the resurrection of Christ, as in our salvation, there was put forth nothing short of *a divine power*. What shall we say of those who think that conversion is wrought by the free will of man, and is due to his own betterness of disposition? When we shall see the dead rise from the grave by their own power, then may we expect to see ungodly sinner of their own free will turning to Christ. It is not the word preached nor the word read in itself; all quickening power proceeds from the Holy Ghost . . . . No sin, no corruption, no devils in hell nor sinners upon earth, can stay the hand of God's grace when it intends to convert a man. If God omnipotently says, 'Thou shalt,' man shall not say, 'I will not . . . The same power which raised the Head works life in the members. What a blessing to be quickened together with Christ! "[44]

Scripture reveals a reality completely unreckoned with by any Enlightenment scholar—that there is an operative agent who can obscure our knowing. All knowing, regarding salvation, comes not from us but from the agent opposed to the evil one, that is, the Holy Spirit. Unless the Spirit comes to us, all is lost. In the controversy with the theological faculty at Jerusalem in John chapter 8:43 and 46-47 Jesus asks, "Why do you not understand what I say?" (The cause of their misunderstanding does not lie in Jesus' lack of clarity nor does it lie in their low IQ.) "It is because you cannot bear to hear my word. You are of your father the devil and your desire is to do your father's desires . . . If I tell you the truth, why do you not believe me? Whoever is of God hears the words of God. *The reason why you do*

---

44. Spurgeon, *Morning and Evening* (for the evening, Sept 8).

not hear them is that you are not of God." Here, Jesus is making no "offer". Here, Jesus is preaching God's Word. Here, as God's Word is preached, God is doing the electing. Here, man is decidedly not doing the electing. The reason that they do not "accept Jesus" has nothing to do with human will, and everything to do with the one to whom they already belong as helpless slaves. In other words, the act of preaching has this unbelievable power: it divides hearers, already, into sheep and goats. While it delivers the sheep, preaching also exposes the previously hidden. Preaching creates the ongoing prosecution of the kingdom of God. Preaching is the very creation of a *kairos* moment of time. (*Kairos* is a seminal biblical Greek word denoting what scripture teaches throughout—that all "times" are not the same. Some moments are God-filled, and thus irreplaceable and incalculably valuable. They cannot be predicted nor created by man, but are defined by *God's decision to come. Kairos* moments are the very definition of judgment, either for salvation or for condemnation.)

Please note! The subject of God's election becomes dangerous to faith the moment that it is made into an abstraction, as Luther was extremely well aware. The question, "What if God has not elected me?" if understood only as an abstraction or an idea, leaves human beings with absolutely no recourse or answer, and is thus both damning and damnable. But God's election is *not* an abstraction. It is not an idea. It is an *event*. Every time the Word is rightly preached God's kingdom comes! Every time there is scriptural preaching, the preacher "brings it" in that he or she is announcing God's gracious choice in favor of the sinner. Dr. Gerhard Forde memorably said, "The solution for the absolute God is the absolution!" Luther said the same thing in making his distinction between the God preached and the God not preached.[45] The God preached is Jesus who died on the cross for sinners. The God not preached comprises all our speculation about a God who necessarily does everything. But if God does everything, including all the calamities in nature and history, then he is a terrifying God. So God has insisted that He shall be known in Jesus, and nowhere else. There are things which we are not given to know. In the event of proclamation, God is causing salvation to happen, when and where He chooses, by revealing himself clothed in the promise, "I am the Lord your God", clothed in the person of Jesus Christ, and mediated by the cross. The results of such preaching are hidden, even to faith, but we know that preaching always works, because God's Word never returns to him void, without accomplishing the purpose for which He sent it. (Isaiah 55:11)

---

45. LW 33:138f.

So, scripturally at least, faith cannot be described as a human act of volition or will. It is a creation of God, "ex nihilo" (out of nothing), whenever and wherever this word is rightly preached. And, by extension, any preaching directed toward an appeal to the will, not only completely misunderstands the office of biblical preaching, but has reduced such preaching to a "sales job" which seeks to supplant the work of the Holy Spirit, who always comes in the proclaimed Word. Insisting on an appeal to human will, or relying rather upon human rhetorical skills of persuasion, is a failure to believe the power of the Word to do what it says! Yet, this misunderstanding is what is explicitly taught in homiletics almost all of the largest seminaries in the United States.

Whenever people do respond with faith in the New Testament witness, it is always because they heard the Word, and it is always the power of the Holy Spirit who has promised to use that Word as His medium, which creates the miracle of faith "ex nihilo." And this, not only at the moment of conversion, but every living moment after. Luther is adamant about the necessity of the return to the scriptural definition of faith, which he found especially in Romans. It contrasted mightily to the rather confused picture of faith he had gotten from received scholastic theology.

In the Psalm lectures Luther writes, "Faith means to believe in Jesus' humanity, given us in this life as our life and salvation. For he himself, through faith in his incarnation, is our life, our righteousness and our resurrection."[46] Luther was going beyond the definition of faith as "holding something to be true" and "what is emerging is the substance of an idea that cannot as yet be found in the marginal notes, that is, the category of *hiddenness*: in the hiddenness of the incarnate Christ, God is present; in the hiddenness of the cross our salvation is effected, and to his hiddenness of the divine saving activity corresponds the hiddenness or non-demonstrability of faith."[47] Aristotle is already a "chatterbox" as Luther insists more and more upon scriptural usage and definition.

Luther gradually abandons the scholastic distinction between "formed faith" (that is, faith that does the works of love) and "unformed faith"[48] because it just cannot be made to fit with what scripture depicts to be the case. In contrast Luther writes, "(Scholastics) say that we must believe in Christ and that faith is the foundation of salvation, but they say that this faith does not justify unless it is 'formed by love ... What they have taught about justifying faith 'formed by love' is an empty dream. For the faith that takes hold

---

46. WA 9, 92, 38–93,7.
47. Lohse, *Martin Luther's Theology*, 47.
48. Aquinas, Thomas, *Summa Theologica*, II—II, Qu. 4, Art.3.

of Christ, the Son of God, and is adorned by Him is the faith that justifies, not a faith that includes love. For if faith is to be sure and firm, it must take hold of nothing but Christ alone; and in the agony and terror of conscience it has nothing else to lean on than this pearl of great value."[49]

So also *habitus*, the Aristotelian position that taught that morality is shaped by repeated practice, is abandoned as a philosophical category and not scriptural. While in the later Romans commentary, faith acknowledges that the judgment of God is right in order to share the Righteousness of Christ, in the Psalms lectures we find the first movement in that direction: "And faith in Him is then acknowledgment and beauty, which He puts on spiritually. For through faith we confess Him and honor and adorn Him."[50] Here it is clear that justifying one's self and justifying God are mutually exclusive acts. Only those who humble themselves honor God, while those who would exalt themselves deny God honor. But only faith gives God the honor, and so faith is the only decisive thing in one's relation to God. In the Galatians lectures of 1531 Luther wrote, "Faith . . . is the creator of the Deity, not in the substance of God, but in us."[51] In Luke 7:29 we read the strange and unique phrase that "the people justified God." For Luther, in regards to faith at least, that just about says it all. The miracle of justifying God brings to an absolute end of self-justifying, anywhere at all. To justify God requires the end of all self-justification, for the two absolutely exclude each other. And the simple reason for this is that God and human-kind are related not by analogy but by contradiction.

Luther weaves all these component parts together in describing how the truth of the Gospel is identified and confirmed in the testing and inner conflict which he called "temptation." But that will take us to another whole chapter.

---

49. LW 26:88-89.
50. LW 11:317.
51. LW 26:227.

CHAPTER SIX

Preaching as the Prosecution of God's Election

A CHRISTIAN'S CHIEF AND ONLY comfort is this: **God cannot lie**. We fearfully ask God, "Do you promise?" And God says, "Yes, I do." The Bible's attestation of promise is expressed most fundamentally in God's predestination. Luther, when seized by the crisis of his most fearsome *anfechtung* that he may not be among the elect, preached to himself, "I am baptized!" That was the same as his claiming, "God cannot lie!" God predestines immutably, he predestines in time, he predestines in Jesus Christ, and he predestines in the living present. So it is critical to understand this: God's eternal resolve and immutable necessity stand behind each proclamation.

Grace, like love, has to be its own apology. That is, grace self-authenticates. As the saying goes, "Wine is like love, you know when you have found the right one." But God's promising word of grace is also dangerous. Like love, it may not happen. Its "For you!" may not be heard. Then we are lost. And so, the purpose of proclamation is to *make it happen*. The purpose of proclamation is to greet each hearer with the joyful news, that God's promise, together with the predestining nature of the whole of the salvation story, was designed always, and ever will be, "For you!" If there were no immutable promise, how could God say to Jacob and Jeremiah and others at their call, I knew you before you were born? How else could we hear the word that the Lamb of God was slain before the foundation of the world? All this was done, so that you may hear again and again, "For you!

"Behold, I have given you authority to tread upon serpents and scorpions and over all the power of the enemy; and nothing shall hurt you. Nevertheless do not rejoice in this, that the spirits are subject to you; *but rejoice that your names are written in heaven*." (Luke 10 19-20) In other words, arguably the most problematic doctrine for theologians of all time—God's election—is, according to Jesus, the most fundamental cause for Christian rejoicing!

The Biblical Concept of Election

The Greek word-constellation consisting of *eklegomai* (to elect or choose), *ekloge* (election), *eklektos* (the elect), *kaleo* (to call), *klysis* (your call), and *proorizo* (predestined) are basic for the most fundamental biblical understanding of all human relationship to God.

Eklegomai (to elect)

Beginning with the verbal form, the Hebrew scriptures use the verb "to elect" to refer to God's activity one hundred and five times. Curiously, the verb is used very rarely in the reverse sense of humans choosing God or gods, one significant case being Joshua 24:10ff. In that case, the command, "Choose this day whom you will serve" is being asked for, as a confession of a reality which has already been previously established by God's election. In another case, Judges 10:14 mocks the disaster of human election when it becomes a confession of idolatry. "Go cry unto the gods which you have chosen: let them deliver you in time of your tribulation!"

From Deuteronomy on, the concept of God's electing is established in the sense of the designation of Israel as "the people of God."[1] However, negatively, electing one nation means rejecting other nations. Other nations did not experience what Israel experienced. Worse, the extreme gulf between the one true God of the Israelite nation and the false gods worshipped by their neighboring nations required an all-out conflict between them regarding the faith. The narrative in Joshua and Judges seems fanatical at times. And it is incomprehensible without an underlying knowledge that this contest on a historical level is only a reflection of the mortal spiritual contest for people being waged between God and his continuing adversary. With the coming of the new covenant, the temporary rejection of other nations is ended when God sends His Son to extend the election to be His very own people, to all the nations of the world. The Deuteronomic conception of "the people of God" gets a new definition in the books of Paul, most notably in Galatians and Romans as the people newly called to belong to Jesus Christ.

God is called upon to elect in certain situations where an unknown needs to be revealed. For instance, in the case of Achen's sin (Joshua 7:14ff), it was necessary for God to reveal to His people precisely where the pathology in the community lay, by casting lots in order to discern the will or choice of God. In I Samuel 10:17, casting lots revealed from which tribe and family, and finally, which individual should be king. In each case, "There is

---

1. Schrenk, "Eklegomai," 163.

no question of any act of will on the part of the assembly. Its role is purely passive. God elects in its place and from within it."[2]

In our modern day, the concept of God's electing is notorious for eliciting more grievous anxiety than perhaps any other concept in the Bible. That is ironic in the extreme, since the will of God, His unbreakable resolve which underlies even the most minimal conception of God's covenant faithfulness throughout the entire Old Testament, His tenaciously held gracious determination concerning His people which defined the very content of God's Great Name—*is meant to exclude all doubt!* Hosea 11:1-9 comes to mind. "When Israel was a child, I loved him, and out of Egypt I called my son . . . It was I who taught Ephraim to walk, I took them up in my arms but they did not know that I healed them . . . How can I give you up, O Ephraim! How can I hand your over O Israel! . . . I will not execute my fierce anger, I will not again destroy Ephraim; for I am God and not man, the Holy One in your midst, and I will not come to destroy." It is *God* who suffers by reason of his tenacious, gracious resolve. The people are meant revel in His election, and they did.

However, we New Testament Christians have completely reversed God's intended purpose for His tenacious, gracious election, which was always meant to serve both as the primary source of our comfort in temptation as well as our refuge and security when under the attack from various doubts. For example, when God in the gospel reveals his gracious will of expanding his election in the coming of his Son, Jesus Christ, to include us who belong to "all nations," we perceive God's election as an attack upon our cherished autonomy. Instead of Good News, we hear God's election as the worst of all possible news. Unbelievably, we seek to completely undo it by replacing it with our own election!

But I am getting ahead of my argument.

Turning to the New Testament, in Mark 13:20, the elect, whom God chose (both words from the very same root) designate God's selection from a larger number to be the community of the last time. In the Gospel of John the word is used to treat the problem of how Judas can belong to the twelve and still be a traitor. Jesus succinctly states the case in John 6:70, by asking, "Did I not choose you the twelve, and one of you is a devil?" One could rightly ask, "Is not Jesus very office of electing challenged by the existence of such a traitor?" The answer is that the Father's counsel and guiding power is over all these things, and it is He who will bring to fulfillment the prediction of Psalm 41:9, in the person of Judas. These things "must be" in order that the scripture may be fulfilled. Jesus, in this gospel is always the one

---

2. Schrenk, "Eklegomai," 157.

who elects with solemn "I" statements. With the coming of Jesus, election ceases to be a secret counsel of God. It is now enacted by the spoken word of Jesus, and the Father always confirms this word. We do not choose. We are chosen. (John 15:16) The ones God has elected are revealed in this single characteristic, which cannot be counterfeited: chosen ones believe Him and His Word. They love His Word. They live His Word. In short, they show by this whose "begotten" child they are. (John 1:13) God's electing them "out of the world" results in the world hating them. Finally, God's electing is for the vocation of all who are so chosen to bear fruit, fruit that will last.

In the book of Acts God's electing holds a relatively minor place. The story of Cornelius shows how God's election is meant for all nations and all people. And, as in the Old Testament, casting lots is done to reveal God's choice of the person to replace Judas, where, again, the community remains completely passive.

In Paul's writings, God's electing serves to emphasize three things. The first is the eternal basis of our justification. The second is that God's election brings with it the eschatological promise of our "sonship" or "being-made-like-Christ" (Romans 8:23, Ephesians 1:5, and Galatians 4:5) Often the identical technical term found in these three places is wrongly translated as "adoption-as-sons". But translating this term as "adoption" instead of "sonship" goes against the entire Old Testament witness where one is "born into" an office such as being the "people of God" or being born into the office of being a priest of the tribe of Levi to God's people. Nowhere will you find anyone "adopted" into any important vocation in the Old Testament. Additionally, "adoption" goes against the entire witness of John 1:13 and 3:3-5 where one is "begotten of God." Why would one be "adopted" if one is already a natural born child?!

In the third case, God's electing, gives the Holy Spirit who enables a responsible walking in love and ends self-seeking. The Spirit also prevents the perversion of election, namely, the idea that the community of God is more important than the whole world.[3]

Significantly, "Nowhere in the New Testament is election explicitly contrasted with reprobation."[4] It is unfortunate that damnation has been linked in any way to God's electing. Both Romans 9:13 and 18 are based upon their reference to Malachi 1:1-5 where the comparison between Jacob and Esau is referred to the temporary supersession and hardening of Israel, while, in contrast, the Gentile church is flourishing.

---

3. Schrenk, "Eklegomai," 175.
4. Schrenk, "Eklegomai," 175.

Ekloge (election)

In I Thessalonians and in Romans "election" describes not the salvation, but the position and historical task of the patriarchs. In Romans 11:28 it is used to refer to all Israel. Everywhere else in Paul's writings, when referring to the Christian community, election is manifested by the powerful operation of the Holy Spirit. Here, God's election is not primarily a dogmatic thesis so much as an event confessed in shared Christian experience. Sometimes Paul uses "election" to denote the selection of a part of Israel to distinguish this part from the whole of Israel. When, in 2 Peter 1:10, the apostle calls for us to "be zealous to confirm your call and election, for if you do this you will never fall," we see once again, that "election" is not to be understood as some kind of static dogmatic abstraction. The responsible use of your ordination for God's service, will, in the progress of such service, confirm the fact to you that you "will never fall."

Ecklectos (the elect or the chosen)

Matthew 22:14, "Many are called but few are chosen" stands as a biblical problem. "The word 'chosen' has exactly the opposite meaning in Matthew that it has in Paul, where it is mainly used to *assure* of salvation. In Matthew's context 'chosen' is a goal-word, not (as in Paul) a source-word; it is a word of admonition more than a word of comfort; it is ethical, not predestinarian. For Paul, the bond between election and calling was fast, giving assurance; for Matthew, the bond is open, urging sobriety . . . Whereas Paul instructs Christians to live in a way that is 'worthy' of those who are "chosen", Matthew enjoins them to live in a way that would ensure at the end that they are among the chosen (at all)."[5] In I Peter God's election is the theme of the whole book where, in spite of dispersion to outlying areas, and in spite of being Gentiles, they are united by being "chosen and destined by God the Father and sanctified by the Spirit for obedience to Jesus Christ."(I Peter 1:2) Everything is worked out with this controlling concept, showing most clearly here the careful choice by the early Christian community for its self-reference as "the elect."

---

5. Bruner, *Matthew: a Commentary*, vol. 2:778.

Kaleo (to call)

Found in almost all the New Testament writings, this verb is particularly common in Luke-Acts, fairly common in Matthew, and less so in Mark. John seems to have his own vocabulary to convey the synonymous concept. In Paul, Peter, and Hebrews, it is also fairly frequent. The bible uses the verb denoting God's call in at least three ways. First, God is the one who calls all things into existence. Second, God is the one who calls his people, before the foundation of the world, to belong to Jesus. Third, at the last Day, God will call you from the grave of death into eternal life. Jesus, Himself is presented as "called" and fulfills all the functions demanded by the term. God "calls" Christians into fellowship with his Son. Christians are "called" in the absolute sense. Throughout Paul's writings God "calls" people in Christ through His own means and for his own purpose. God is the sole agent in all calling.

Klysis (your call)

In Paul's writings, this is a technical and highly precise term upon which one can build one's faith. It is the "source" of proper Christian confidence. When Paul says, "consider your call brethren," in I Corinthians 1:26, he refers them instantly to the fact that God elected them with absolutely no correlation to their piety or goodness. Rather, they are in the family of God by sheer grace. Additionally, on the level of ethics, he also uses their "call" to point out to them that the Spirit's power, which provides all the gifts needed for their new walk in this grace, is also found fully in Jesus Christ and not in themselves. The passage from I Timothy 1:9-10 is the most complete usage of the term in Paul's writings. "God saved us and called us with a holy calling, not in virtue of our works but in virtue of his own purpose and the grace which he gave in Christ Jesus ages ago, and now has manifested through the appearing of our Savior, Christ Jesus, who abolished death and brought life and immortality to life to light through the gospel." Finally, when Paul addresses his Galatian congregation he reminds them that it is God who calls all things into being. His call brings from death to life. God's call is therefore not mere invitation but the effective Word which brings about what it states. In their case, God's call has not only been refused, but his work emptied and erased, and his Word contradicted. God's call is an *event*, and that is the decisive criterion in his argument. Christ could be mistaken for an idol and the Gospel for an ideology, but Paul asks the Galatian to consider what has befallen them on the basis of what they have *experienced*. This criterion for the truth of the Gospel precludes all efforts to make it merely a matter of opinion.[6] God's call to His people has the power to defeat death.

Proorizo (to Predestine or Foreordain)

This extremely powerful verb is used only six times in the New Testament, most notably at the climax of Paul's salvation description in Romans 8:29-30 and in Ephesians 1:5 where Paul is describing the fundamental basis for our Christian confidence. The mystery of God's hidden wisdom is revealed in Acts 4:28 where Pilate, Herod and the crowd do "whatever thy hand predestined them to do." Thus all history, and every person in it, serve the purposes foreordained by the God who rules all history, directing it to history's goal—the feet of Jesus Christ. We, who are called, foreknown, predestined, justified and glorified get to taste the future in advance.

This cursory survey should make obvious that God's primary concern throughout scriptural witness is to let us in on the mystery of what His foreordained will actually is. The purpose of this revelation, made known only to His people, is not to terrify us, but to serve for us as an unassailable buttress for faith and proper Christian confidence. God's Word of promise is what secures our confidence. That Word of promise finds its foundation in the absolute nature of God's fore-ordination.

Preaching as Election: *God's Attack* as well as *God's Foundation for Faith*

Biblical preaching does three things:

- it proclaims, prosecutes, executes, performs, conducts and extends God's election;
- it begins by asserting the captivation of the human will; and
- it takes its shape from the cross, because in it we are brought *through death* to life. (it kills by revealing to sinners their sin, and it resurrects by announcing the absolution in Christ)

Christians are never so nervous and divided as when it comes to election, hearing that our wills are captivated, or seeing the serious implications of the cross of Jesus for their own lives. According to abundant scriptural witness it is evident that it is not an incidental truth, but

---

6. Ebeling, *Truth of the Gospel*, 126-127.

a fundamental truth, that God is an electing God. This God speaks a living Word to accomplish his choice. Since this is so, it is necessary that someone come to speak to us, in the present, here and now, someone who can actually do the electing in the name of God. (Romans 10:14-15) It is necessary that there be a *preacher*, a speaker of the Word of God. Without an actual speaker, election becomes only an abstract idea that threatens to destroy us. The only solution to the threat and destruction of election, considered as an abstraction, is for someone to come and actually do the electing.[7] Electing, in God's way, can only be rightly done present tense, here and now, I-you discourse—or not at all.

Early in his career as an expositor of scripture, Luther experienced his single greatest theological terror (*Anfechtung*) over this constant scriptural theme of the election of God. The terror for him—the very same terror for *every* Christian who takes the biblical teaching of election seriously—is the question, "what if I am not among the elected?" If I am not, then there is nothing that I can do about it. Election, taken thus as an abstract concept, presents to us only a God we don't know about, a *hidden* God. We can do a lot of guessing about Him, but without fail, apart from God's revelation of Himself and His will at the cross of Jesus Christ, He turns out to be a capricious God who cannot be trusted, a God who gives me absolutely no warrant to believe that judgment will be in my favor. He remains and always will be, without the Gospel and without the cross, a God of wrath who punishes some people and not others. The doctrine of election drives to the distinction Luther insists upon, unique to him—the vital difference between the "God preached" and the "God not preached."[8] He concludes from this that there is a will of God that is not preached. "But this God must be left to himself in his own majesty, for in this regard we have nothing to do with him, nor has he willed we should have anything to do with him. But we have something to do with him insofar as he is clothed and set forth in his Word."[9]

But if God's Word is a living Word, tied to the specific revelation at the cross which definitely and once for all shows God's will concerning sinners, then election is no abstraction, but the moment by moment hearing of a gracious decree pronounced over one's head. Ephesians 1 is emphatic. One's election cannot be understood Christianly apart from God' electing deed for sinners at the cross. As the apostle Paul wrote,

---

7. The argument in the preceding two paragraphs is from an essay by Gerhard Forde in "*Called and Ordained: Lutheran perspectives on the Office of Ministry.*
8. LW 33:138-147.
9. LW 33:139.

"Blessed be the God and Father of our Lord Jesus Christ, who has blessed us in Christ with every spiritual blessing in the heavenly places, even as he *chose* us in him before the foundation of the world, that we should be holy and blameless before him. He *destined* us in love to be his sons through Jesus Christ, according to the purpose of his will, to the praise of his glorious grace which he freely bestowed on us in the Beloved. In him we have redemption through his blood, the forgiveness of our trespasses, according to the riches of his grace." (Ephesians 1:3-7)

Frederick Dale Bruner notes in his Matthew commentary that three miracles happened at the baptism of Jesus: the heavens were ripped open, *skizomenos,* (nowhere noted to be ever be closed again), the Spirit descended, and the Father proclaimed, "This is my beloved Son with whom I am well pleased." In our own baptism we receive the very same three gifts—an open heaven over us, the Holy Spirit within us, and the Father's decree of righteousness, "You are my beloved child, with whom I am well pleased." This covenant act of God, this ongoing living proclamation, is the sole defense against the terror of predestination understood as an abstraction.

Luther would proclaim to himself in the midst of the temptation to terror regarding God's election, "I am baptized!" He placed God's covenant promise *prior to every other word of scripture. He heard it as a living word. He used it to set the limits of the Law's accusation.* He learned from taking God's Word seriously, that if certainty of faith were to survive or even exist, that it must all depend upon God's grace, upon God's mercy, and upon God's doing. *Salvation is no guessing game.* It is an on-going mortal struggle between life and death, where life prevails only in the present tense hearing of the Good News. Certainty of salvation was revealed to him, and was experienced by him in a process of being brought through death to life. In bearing witness to this phenomenon, salvation, for him, came existentially in this sequence: only by suffering the death of every human pretense to his ability to save himself, did he come to the resurrection to life through faith. This process described the entire way in which he came to know God. This process became the entire way in which he interpreted scripture. That is to say, it became his entire hermeneutic. This process informed absolutely every syllable he proclaimed and taught as God's Word. The teaching concerning "Justification" or the forgiveness of sins (shorthand for the entire process) was, he passionately stated, the doctrine upon which *the entire Church stood or fell.* (Article IV of the Augsburg Confession) He expressed the miraculous nature of this process in writing the following meaning to the third article of the Creed on the Holy Spirit: "I believe that I cannot, by my own understanding or effort, believe in Jesus Christ or come to Him, but the Holy Spirit has called me by the Gospel . . . ." The wrack of existential pain caused by God's total assault on his own abilities, and the amazing certainty that resulted from it he described in those creedal reflections. Each one ends with this confession: "This is most certainly true!" The "theology of the cross" is simply an attempt to describe the very personal, the very event-oriented nature of this attack by God's living Word, and the amazing resurrection to proper confidence which follows.

This problem of dealing with a God who elects and determines absolutely everything, is what drove Luther to become what he called in his Heidelberg Disputations of 1518, a *theologian of the cross*. Please note that "theology" and "being made a theologian" are not even close to being congruent concepts! A *theology* of the cross is an *abstraction*, while the ongoing trauma of becoming a "theologian of the cross" is an *experience* of the trauma and restoration that occur in relationship under God's spoken word. It inheres most centrally in this: that if a person has to know for the sake of one's salvation and certainty, what one is capable of with regard to his salvation, then that person evidently knows neither what he is capable of, nor what God is, *until he knows for certain that he can do nothing towards his salvation*. But, undergoing that terror of helplessness, that very inability, opens up the prospect of the certainty of salvation for the very first time, because it is based upon the act of God alone. Luther later said of this discovery that he never realized how closely together sheer terror and absolute certainty of faith reside. Luther simply bore witness to the fact, confirmed from his own experience, that no one, *absolutely no one*, apart from the killing intervention of God's Law, will admit that they are helpless sinners. Apart from God's spoken accusation, we will always justify ourselves and refuse to die. There is no exception to this axiomatic rule in the entire scriptural witness (or in the entire human race). That is why Luther said that God must be our devil before he can be our savior. That is also why he said that we will always relate to God on the basis of our sin, and not on the basis of our righteousness. Because God's election mortally wounds the old man, and yet is the very heart of all comfort to the new man, it requires a death and a resurrection to be executed by the electing Word. This death and resurrection entails an absolute end to any claims of agency by the old man and a complete surrender to the power of the agency of Another.

Since we never get on well with an electing God, and no one willingly braves the terror of God's surgery, we devise detours around the problem, which will obviate and remove the sting of God's total assault upon our old nature. For example, the scholastic teaching which sought to accomplish this, was the assertion that there remains a divine spark within each of us, after the Fall, which, by using God's "grace", becomes capable of both response and reform. Salvation thus became a calculus (an uncertain calculus, however, absent any *terminus ad quem*) concerning the relationship of God's activity and our response. It depended upon some free will on the part of man. The danger of God's electing was thus removed. The attack was deflected. After all, the idea that God elects becomes just the last straw. *Why preach, if all has been decided from eternity?* In this Scholastic view, rather than the being the fundamental reason for proclamation, election, understood as an abstraction, becomes the rock upon which all preaching is shipwrecked.

But preaching does not come off better by constructing and conveying better and more accommodating ideas about how God relates to man, but by speaking precisely the living Word of God. God does not call off the election because it makes us uncomfortable, or because we experience it as an assault upon our cherished prerogatives, but God simply goes ahead and elects concretely wherever the Word is rightly preached.

Where this definition of preaching is not understood, a marvelous irony develops. The minister can only serve by attempting to **undo** God's election. Since (it is held) that God does not in fact elect, the only remaining definition for preaching lies in making it into an appeal to whatever degree of "free will" is deemed to have survived in the hearers. *If God does not elect we must do so for ourselves.* Ministry becomes a sales job rather than proclaiming. Preaching, understood in this fashion, requires preachers to be God's "prosecuting attorneys", who understand preaching to be an enterprise defined by seeking to bring in a favorable verdict for God. In this understanding, no sermon is really complete without an altar call. Or perhaps preaching becomes a therapy hour whose goal is to make us feel better about ourselves or perhaps more successful, by removing any and all controversial or confrontative passages that might stand in the way of this objective. Thus preaching comes to depend completely upon the art of human persuasion, classically taught as the field of rhetoric, rather than relying on the power of the Gospel itself to do the deed which God sent it to do—to kill in order to make alive.

When ministry is not the concrete carrying out of divine election it becomes a matter of appealing to human wills. This results in two main possibilities: 1) the Catholic/Anglican mode where preaching is no longer central, but is replaced by the re-presenting the ritual of sacrifice, which subtly changes the agency in the sacrament from God to man as well as changing the direction of the sacrifice from "down" to "up"; or 2) the Calvinist mode where preaching gets reduced to the more cognitive task of informing the elect about such matters and the consequences thereof, or making proclamation into a rhetorical challenge where the objective is to sway the will of the hearer.

The commission that impels preaching in this fallen world is the death and resurrection of Jesus Christ. We are called to publicize this! Paul says, "God was in Christ, reconciling the world to Himself!!" The cross of Jesus becomes news about *how* God has done his election, and *for whom* he has made his choice. Evangelical preachers proclaim the astonishing news that God's chooses sinner! His love is for sinners! Therefore, you qualify!! Forde has characteristically pithy statements on page 121 of his essay already cited: "Since Jesus commanded, 'Go, baptize, preach, teach, absolve!' . . . we live in a world that cannot believe its good fortune . . . Go do the electing authorized by the death and resurrection of Jesus Christ!"[10]

The electing God, hidden by the world behind all its methods of denial, makes people unable and unwilling to believe the mystery. The fact that the world will not hear of an electing God is because it cannot of "its own reason or strength believe." That is to say, that all are afflicted with a captivated will. All are blind and need to have their eyes opened. (John 9)

Preaching the Law ruthlessly exposes our denial of God. It reveals the foolishness of our saying that we already see. Our sin is so hideous and hidden that it needs to be revealed to us. And the sin involves blindness: our refusal to see that we are helpless, our denial of death, our denial that there is any god but us. The Law exposes all this and brings old beings to an utter end, *so that* we might hear the good news of the new life in the resurrected Jesus. The point of the distinction between Law and Gospel is to make public God's deed, making it hearable in a world that will not hear it. The drive behind ministry is to *say* it, to have the courage to *do* the electing deed, to *bear witness* to it, to *make it public*, "to make all people see."[11]

Preaching is an act of God the present, the link between Christ's resurrection and the resurrection of all the dead . . . the question of Christ's resurrection cannot, however, be treated as a matter of purely scientific truth. Paul says not only that preaching is vain if Christ is dead, but adds: 'and you are still in your sins' (I Corinthians 15:17) According to the same basic conception of preaching that we have often outlined, the word of the preacher is an attack on the prison in which man is held."[12]

No wonder Jesus felt that the urgency of proclamation was paramount over all other ministry concerns. And if that was the case for Him, it is also the case for us. God sends preachers who, after they themselves have gone through the event of the encounter with the Word of truth, can bear witness to the events which that Word produced in that event—death

---

10. Forde, *Called and Ordained*, 121.
11. Forde, *Called and Ordained*, 118-124.
12. Wingren, *Living Word*, 123-4.

and life, Law and Gospel. Above all, these witnesses announce the forgiveness of sins: the now-completed, the specific, the cross-revealed shape of the mystery of God's merciful will for sinners. It was hidden until these last days, but He has now commissioned preachers to proclaim this revealed will to you, to me, to us all.

The electing Word goes something like this. "You are the man! You are the sinner! Yet God loves sinners. (After all, there seems to be no one else for Him to love.) He loved sinners so much that He sent His only Son to be lifted up upon the cross, bearing your sin, and the sin of the whole world. This mystery of this salvation was foreordained before the foundation of the world, but now has been brought here to you. Because Jesus has died and has been raised again, I have the warrant to proclaim to you, here and now, that in spite of your grievous failures, your sins are fully forgiven for Jesus' sake."

Here, Gerhard Forde's aphorism, "The only solution for the absolute God is the absolution" extends its meaning to summarize what biblical proclamation must always sound like.

CHAPTER SEVEN

Preaching the "Non-Asterisk Absolution"

MARTIN LUTHER DEFINED HIS understanding of the Gospel very succinctly and helpfully in this short phrase: "whatever gives Christ." "Christ himself says in John 15:27, 'You shall bear witness to me.' All the genuine sacred books agree in this, that all of them preach and give (*treiben*) Christ. And that is the true test by which to judge all books, when we see whether or not they give Christ."[1] The verb in this formula is critical. Luther never tired of contrasting the defining characteristic of the Law, which is to demand, with the defining characteristic of the Gospel, which is purely and unqualifiedly to give. Giving Christ to sinners, who have no way to rid themselves of sin and its guilt, is the sole function of preaching. When a sinner hears that he or she is absolved for Jesus' sake, then the ambassador of Christ has delivered the goods that God sent his officer deliver. What preachers give with one hand, they should not take back with the other!

In one of the most famous portraits of Luther, "The book of the Bible is not tightly clutched and closed; it is no fundamentalist weapon, so to speak. Rather the book lies open. It is opened by him who is alone able to open it: the crucified One who lives. Luther's index finger rests on a specific passage in the open book of the Bible. On which passage? Romans 3:25 may be recalled: the one who FORGIVES SIN. Of all the verses in his Bible, Luther distinguishes only this one phrase with capital letters. In a marginal gloss, he calls this clause 'the main part' and the 'central place of this epistle and of the entire Bible.'"[2]

Dr. Gerhard Forde, the advisor for my doctoral studies, would sit attentively during each worship, carefully listening for the Gospel, hoping that the preacher that day would "deliver the goods." Too often he would leave quietly disappointed. Even though the sermon might be a

1. LW 35:396.
2. Bayer, *Luther's Relevance for Today's Rupture of Times*, 40.

theologically correct exposition in every other way, it failed to deliver the goods if somewhere in the development of what the text authorized the preacher to say that day, there was not a simple, clear, declarative sentence asserting something that somehow conveyed the "last word", the final word of all: "Your sins are forgiven for Jesus' sake." Luther was very clear that this was the defining feature of all Reformation preaching, the single theme of all proclamation. In Article XII of the Apology to the Augsburg Confession he writes, "This is the very voice of the Gospel, that by faith we obtain the forgiveness of sins"[3] and again, "The power of the keys administers the Gospel through absolution, which is the true voice of the Gospel. In speaking of faith, therefore, we also include absolution since 'faith comes from what is heard,' as Paul says (Rom. 10:17). Hearing the Gospel and hearing absolution strengthens and consoles the conscience. Because God truly quickens through the Word, the keys truly forgive sin before him according to the statement (Luke 10:16), 'He who hears you, hears me.' Therefore we must believe the voice of the one absolving no less than we would believe a voice coming from heaven . . . So faith is conceived and confirmed through absolution, through the hearing of the Gospel."[4]

Given that clear mandate, it is amazing how much Lutherans, who should be leading the way among Christian denominations, have more characteristically managed to place all sorts of qualifying asterisks around any such declaration, or worse, delete any formal liturgical announcement of absolution entirely. Commonly, the declaration is so carefully qualified, that any assurance that a Christian might justly be expected to derive from God's messengers becomes tenuous at best. The pious motivation of these preachers seems to be that one does not want the wrong ears to hear the unqualified declaration, "Your sins are forgiven for Jesus sake." Should the unrepentant hear that, they would surely be comforted into continuing unabated in their sinful ways. So the qualifying asterisks begin.

Lutheran worship services characteristically begin with an opening confession of sins and absolution. That way, if the preacher that day totally fails to understand his or her function, the congregation can at least hear the Gospel in the absolution. Fortunately, this worship feature also gives a tool to empirically track the raging theological contest among Lutherans seeking the proper way to deliver the Gospel over the last century in North America.

I grew up in the Scandinavian Midwestern expression of Lutheranism under three hymnals: The *Concordia* hymnal published by Augsburg in 1932, the *Service Book and Hymnal* shared by eight Lutheran denominations and

---

3. Tappert, *Book of Concord*, 182.
4. Tappert, *Book of Concord*, 187.

published in 1958, and the *Lutheran Book of Worship* designed for the three major denomination of Lutherans in North America, published in 1978. The authorized absolutions from each will now be considered in detail.

Absolution: the First Iteration

1. "Almighty God, our heavenly Father, hath had mercy on us, and hath given his only Son to die for us, and for his sake forgiveth us all our sins. To them that believe on his name he giveth power to be come the sons of God, and hath promised them His Holy Spirit. He that believeth and is baptized shall be saved. Grant this O Lord unto us all."

(This absolution is shared almost verbatim by the majority of other Lutheran hymnals including the 1917 *Common Service Book with Hymnal*, the 1938 UELC hymnal, the *Lutheran Hymnary* of 1913 and 1935, and all the Missouri Synod hymnals from 1931, 1982 and 2006. The variations will be noted below.)

Everything is fine until the seemingly innocuously pious last sentence. It compromises the whole thing. Why? Consider at least two things that it does to the hearer. First, the English language has verbs in three different "moods"—declarative, subjunctive, and imperative. That last sentence takes the mood of all absolutions, the declarative, which is used to express the factual and the certain, and now switches to the subjunctive, the mood used to convey wishes or hopes rather than certainty. "May the Lord go with you," is an example of a subjunctive expression. "Grant this O Lord unto us all," is certainly hopeful, but not declarative! Second, is the hearer to understand that not "all" would be covered by the preceding declaration? This sows just that little seed of doubt about one's personal standing before God. After all, one should never be absolutely sure about these things! Here Pietism joins hands with Catholic Orthodoxy which, according to the Council of Trent, asserts that Christ earned for us the *chance* to earn salvation; not the gift itself is given, but the opportunity to merit it.[5] Both the subjunctive formulation and the question over whether you belong to the "all", work to subtly but effectively call into question, if not outright yank away, any assurance of pardon, together with its attendant assurance of God's restored relationship. Yet this proper confidence is what centrally defines a Christian, according to Luther! "It is impossible for the human mind to conceive any comfort of itself, or to look only at grace amid its consciousness and terror

---

5. Jedin, *History of the Council of Trent*, 249 ff.

of sin, or consistently to reject all discussion of works. To do this is beyond human power and thought . . . Therefore the afflicted conscience has no remedy against despair and eternal death except to take hold of the promise of grace given in Christ, that is, this righteousness of faith, this passive or Christian righteousness, *which says with confidence*: 'I do not seek active righteousness.'"[6] (my italics)

An interesting divergence from this pretty much settled absolution can be found in the *American Lutheran Hymnal* (Wartburg Press 1930). Here we find new qualifications:

> "**If this be your sincere confession, and if with penitent hearts you earnestly desire the forgiveness of your sins, for the sake of Jesus Christ, God, according to his promise forgiveth you all your sins; and by the authority of God's Word and by the command of our Lord Jesus Christ, I declare unto you that God, through his grace, hath forgiven all your sins in the name of the Father, and of the Son and of the Holy Ghost.**

Before getting to the final declaration we have had to consider the sincerity of our confession, the penitence of our hearts, and the earnestness of our desire for forgiveness! If these are not present, then what follows does not apply to you!

Absolution: The Second Iteration

Moving now to 1958, we get options! (These options were also included in *The Common Service Book and Hymnal* from 1917, the 1925 *Hymnal and Order of Service* from the Augustana Synod, and are now in the new Lutheran hymnal *Reclaim*.) The very necessity of options betrays the certain fact that there was blood on the floor among the theologians whose responsibility it was to design worship and convey the Gospel to Lutherans for the next decades. The fact that two options were *required* obviously implies the total inability to arrive at any theological compromise on the issue. Comparing the two options reveals clearly that the issue was anxiety over just leaving the declarative statement hanging out there for everyone to hear, that Jesus forgives sinners, without some qualification. Here are the 1958 absolutions:

> 2. (Then the minister, standing, and facing the congregation, shall say) "**Almighty God, our heavenly Father, has had mercy upon us, and hath given his only Son to die for us, and for his sake forgiveth us**

---

6. LW 26:5.

all our sins. To them that believe on his Name, he giveth power to become the Sons of God, and bestoweth upon them the Holy Spirit. He that believeth and is baptized shall be saved. Grant this, O Lord, unto us all."

(or he may say)

"The Almighty and merciful God grant you, being penitent, pardon and remission for your sins, time for amendment of life, and the grace and comfort of the Holy Spirit."

The second option is regress, not progress! It makes overt and explicit what was previously more covert and implicit. Now the whole absolution is rendered in the subjunctive, making it into a pious wish, rather than a declaration. Worse, it now depends upon your future behavior! The sole warrant for a Christian's confidence and assurance, the dying and rising of Christ on behalf of sinners and for their sake, is not even mentioned! The Christian is thrown back upon himself, responsible now to be penitent enough and life-amending enough. Any hope for Christian assurance is receding rapidly to a far horizon.

In this 1958 hymnal there was included a "Brief Order for Public Confession" which includes, besides the above absolutions, the most clear declarative statement thus far:

"By the authority of God and of this our office and ministry, I declare unto thee the gracious forgiveness of all thy sins: In the Name of the Father, and of the Son, and of the Holy Ghost."

Two things to note here are that, for the first time, the office of ministry is introduced as a warrant for the declaration. Meanwhile the true warrant, the death and resurrection of Jesus Christ, is left implicit. This hymnal also had a more full "Order for Public Confession," where after the "option one" absolution, (no option two here) came this closing qualification:

"On the other hand, by the same authority, I declare unto the impenitent and the unbelieving, that so long as they continue in their impenitence, God hath not forgiven their sins, and will assuredly visit their iniquities upon them, if they turn not from their evil ways, and come to true repentance and faith in Christ, ere the day of grace be ended."

There it is. With the two statements standing side by side, the theological conflict is out in the open, completely unresolved. Observe carefully the effect that it produces. Notice that nothing in this closing declaration is incorrect. In fact, it is helpfully succinct and quite powerful. Indispensable, it needs to be heard in every congregation. Even more, it is a faithful attempt to clearly state the twin power of the keys to open and to shut. The church cannot separate the two nor can it operate one without the other. All that, however, overlooks the very function being performed here—absolution. That last declaration is sheer law. As such, it is misplaced. *Law always precedes Gospel* in God's method of soul care. But here it comes last, precisely where the "last word", the Gospel, should be. Confusion reigns, and so the Gospel is lost entirely. Where the Gospel is not heard, that loss defines the very absence of salvation, which is evil in the strictest sense. The hearer in this situation is supposed to choose which declaration applies to him or to her, the first or the last, the Gospel or the Law. But a terrified, accused conscience will *never* hear the good news when it is presented as a choice. It will always be convinced that it is undeserving.

Yes, public confession is attended by both believer and unbeliever, by both penitent and impenitent. But in being so careful not to "give dogs what is holy or cast your pearls before swine," (Matt. 7:6) has one desisted from casting pearls entirely? And, since it is impossible to preach the Gospel only to those who will believe it and use it in living a faithful life, is it our place to protect the Gospel from misuse? Luther agonized over this as well, despairing over how his German nation was mistreating the Gospel. Nevertheless, he concluded that hedging the Gospel proclamation around with protections was neither his job nor his mandate. God would take care of business, creating faith when and where he pleased, and creating judgment for those who refused to believe His Son. Meanwhile, amongst all this unbelief, it is the preacher's job to give Christ clearly and definitively and without limiting asterisks.

An Excursus on which is the more fundamental: Repentance or Absolution?

A recent book by a Lutheran Professor, Walter Sundberg, is entitled "Worship as Repentance." In it he makes the much needed and impassioned case that repentance is the heart of worship. His basic thesis is that rather than simply being a celebration of God's love where the themes are inclusivity and unconditional love, worship has always had its roots in the declaration of the forgiveness of sins. While I agree with Sundberg regarding the critical importance of repentance in worship, I believe that he could have helpfully gone one step deeper still and made the case that worship at its even more fundamental, is *absolution*. This is not a small point, since repentance tends to highlight human response, even though it is a gift of God, while absolution clearly remains solely in the aegis of God. The gospel, any "last word", any assurance possible in this age, (however one wants to say it) has to have a single source and warrant—God alone. Thus, Luther's insistence upon the "solas"—Christ alone, the Word alone, the Cross alone, Grace alone, Faith alone—all indicated a single foundation, the rock upon which one is built which is able to defy all storms and the one agency powerful enough to do so, God Himself.

To illustrate his case that repentance is vital, in the preface to his own book Sundberg quotes the scene from Evelyn Waugh's, *Brideshead Revisited*, of a priest giving the service of Last Rites to a life-long profligate sinner. "The medieval rite, *unctio extrema*, done word for word, unchanged, accommodating nobody. From somewhere inside his diminished, dying self, Lord Marchmain finds the will to make the sign of the cross. Weak, flat on his back, *in extremis*, he repents. He is forgiven."[7] (thus quotes Sundberg) Yes, Lord Marchmain repents. But why? How? The Word of *absolution* did it, accomplished it, unchanged, accommodating nobody. Father Mackay had begun, "'Try and remember your sins; tell God you are sorry. I am going to give you absolution. While I am giving it, tell God you are sorry you have offended Him.' He began to speak in Latin. I recognized the words *Ego te absolve in nomine Patris* . . . " (I absolve you in the name of the Father . . .) The wicked old man, now shriven, opens his eyes and makes the sign of the cross."[8] (This part of the very same page is omitted by Sundberg) The point Sundberg seeks to make is that everything must critically revolve around the non-negotiable feature of personal repentance. While this is true, repentance remains the *penultimate* miracle and is not the *ultimate* operative power, which is absolution—the point actually being made by Evelyn Waugh's narrative.

Again, in the introduction, Sundberg recounts how he used the almost forgotten complete order for public confession at chapel one day (printed immediately above). The seminary students were aghast at the effect of the "conditional absolution." (His words. page 2) They should be. While the last four lines of *The Order for Public Confession*, "On the other hand, I declare to the impenitent . . . " perfectly accomplish the proper and terrifying accusation of the Law, it certainly declares no absolution. Lutheran teaching requires that Law and Gospel be completely separated and "done to the hearer" sequentially, *in that order*. If one reverses the order or mixes these two voices of scripture, the whole Gospel is lost. Yet both of those

---

7. Waugh, *Brideshead Revisited*, 358.
8. Waugh, *Brideshead Revisited*, 358.

requirements of Lutheran proclamation—separation and proper order—are violated in the "conditional absolution" just cited, and the students' reaction bears witness to the fact that, when that happens, the Gospel is indeed completely lost.

Since Sundberg's book was written to defend himself against the outcry of fellow Lutherans regarding his position that the conditional absolution can be defended as the "Lutheran position" historically, and since this entire chapter and book are written to passionately argue the opposite case, it may be helpful here to list some brief point by point rebuttals of a few of Sundberg's key arguments.

Sundberg sets up Andreas Osiander as a straw opponent to his position. Since Luther did not agree with Osiander, it is implied that it was Osiander's defense of unconditional absolution which was rebuked. But that is not the case. Osiander was a Lutheran pastor, contemporary to Luther and Melanchthon, who asserted, contrary to the practice of the leaders of his city, that absolution must be unconditional or not at all. However, he also wrongly asserted that only private, and not public confession was the proper prerequisite to the hearing of the absolution. When the city fathers appealed to Luther and Melanchthon, their careful joint reply did not support Osiander's insistence upon private confession alone. Part of Luther's reply is this wonderful sentence: "The preaching of the holy gospel itself is principally and actually an absolution."[9] Since preaching is done in public, Luther argues that absolution may be a public affair as well. That was the issue. However, Sundberg interprets the following quote of Luther's response to the city leaders in an alarming fashion. " . . . for each absolution, whether administered publicly or privately, has to be understood as demanding faith and as being an aid to those that believe in it, just as the gospel itself also proclaims forgiveness to all men in the whole world and exempts no one from this universal context. Nevertheless, the gospel certainly demands our faith and does not aid those who do not believe it; and yet the universal context of the gospel has to remain (valid)."[10] Concerning this, Sundberg writes, "A liturgical absolution, they argue, must conform to two characteristics:1) it demands faith, and 2) it is an aid or comfort to those who believe in it. *To make the demand of faith is to subject absolution to a condition.*"[11](!) But this is to completely misread Luther's entire theological position (laid out clearly in Article XII of the Apology to the Augsburg confession and the Treatise concerning the Keys (both from 1530) by

9. LW 50:75.
10. LW 50:.76.
11. Sundberg, *Worship as Repentance*, 92.

- implying that absolution depends upon faith instead of asserting the reverse, that faith could not exist without absolution, which makes absolution absolutely prior to and constitutive of faith; and
- by asserting that faith somehow validates absolution by becoming the "condition" of absolution; and
- by understanding faith as that which can flow from human agency or, what is the same thing, understanding faith as "decision."

A second straw man set up by Sundberg's argument is the Roman theological doctrine of *opus operatum*.[12] This theological position holds that the sacraments operate almost mechanically without regard to the faith of the receiver/hearer. The implicit accusation in this discussion is that if one holds any position other than one requiring conditional absolution, one is treading on this ground. But that is simply not true. Lutherans deny that sacraments work in that fashion. Lutheran theology, again laid out in both Article XII of the Apology to the Augsburg Confession as well as in the treatise concerning the Keys, defends unconditional absolution while clearly requiring faith as the only possible receptor of the gifts of grace. Yes, absolution "demands faith." But absolution also *creates* the very faith that it demands. Since Sundberg evidently does not agree with that last theological assertion, he is driven to understand faith as a prerequisite, existing prior to the absolution, to validate the absolution. But that makes absolution depend upon faith, whereas in fact, faith depends upon, is built upon, and is created by the absolution.

A third argument involves understanding faith as a personal decision. It is the overwhelming consensus among theologians following the Enlightenment that faith somehow involves human volitional agency. This conviction was one of the most constitutive elements in the Second Great Awakening in the United States in the first decades of the 1800's through the preaching of Finney, and has continued on up to the present in the preaching of Billy Graham and in what is loosely characterized as the evangelical movement. In complete contrast, Lutheran theology still defers to what Martin Luther considered his magnum opus, "The Bondage of the Will," which seeks to destroy, uproot, and obliterate any notion of faith as decision, in order to build our faith upon a proper foundation—God's election. Yet Lutheran professor Sundberg interprets the confession of the Samaritan villagers who have heard the testimony of the woman who met Jesus at the well, "It is no longer because of what you said that we believe, for we have heard for ourselves, and we know that this is truly the Savior of the world."

12. Sundberg, *Worship as Repentance*, 81-83.

(John 4:39-42) in this fashion: "What is this 'we have heard for ourselves' if not the knowledge of those *who have come to the decision of faith?*"[13] Further on he repeats this: "But Luther also defends auricular confession in dramatic, existential terms, calling on Christians to make the *decision of faith* to engage in spiritual warfare."[14](my italics) Decision is not the way classical Lutheran theology speaks of or understands faith.

Fourth, Sundberg locates the origin of faith in the "binding key", the key of the Law! Citing Luther from the treatise on the keys, "(the keys) demand faith in our hearts, and without faith you cannot use them with profit."[15] Sundberg writes, "Faith begins with the binding key. Faith allows us to heed the threat of divine judgment and 'thereby come to fear God.' Faith comes to rest in the loosing key."[16] But this, again, is to misread Luther completely. It also goes against Galatians 3:22, "For if a law had been given which could make alive, then righteousness would indeed be by the law." Nothing alive, including faith, originates in the preaching of the Law. Citing scripture, now, instead of theological authorities, one could turn to Psalm 51, which is *the* scriptural locus which generations of people of faith have turned to who are in crisis and distress over their sin. David cries out from the deepest pit of despair he would ever encounter in his entire existence, "Make me to *hear* joy and gladness, that the bones you have broken may rejoice."(Ps. 51:8) Notice that David does not ask for the preaching of more rigor upon which to anchor renewed personal resolve to henceforth live a changed life. In fact, any more rigor at this point would literally kill. So where does faith originate? Where is it born? It does not "begin with the binding key . . . allowing us to heed the threat of divine judgment and thereby come to fear God." This description of events accords neither with David's life nor his prayer. "Make me to hear joy and gladness" is a cry for a saving action completely external to the self, completely residing in God and his mercy. Ears are the least action-oriented of all human members. They are passive. They are receivers. They are not capable of rigor or resolve. Thus, "Make me to hear" has nothing to do with the "binding key" which only deals with human performance. "Faith comes by hearing", says the Apostle Paul in Romans 10:17. But hearing what? That is the issue here. "What is heard comes by the preaching of *Christ.*" And that is how the verse finishes, and that is what is upheld in Lutheran doctrine. David and Paul agree.

---

13. Sundberg, *Worship as Repentance*, 31.
14. Sundberg, *Worship as Repentance*, 73.
15. LW 40:330.
16. Sundberg, *Worship as Repentance*, 80.

Locating the origin of faith in the binding key, which warns and demands moral rigor, and locating faith in some human volitional response make marvelous theological sense if Christian worship really is all about repentance. But it is not. Christian worship is, more fundamentally yet, about absolution, defined as hearing what Jesus has done for sinners—something which we could not do for ourselves. Worshippers gather to hear the Gospel. This Gospel is not about increased rigor or moralism. Surely it includes the call to repentance! But the repentant one is astonished by hearing about a new righteousness completely beyond the highest imaginations of humankind. Biblically, this righteousness consists in just five words: "Because I go to the Father." (John 16:10) An offense to human reason, and an apparent non-sequitur, these words of Jesus completely redefine saving righteousness as residing in and consisting solely of the actions that constitute Jesus' return, including *Jesus'* death on the cross, *Jesus'* resurrection, and *Jesus'* ascension to rule his kingdom. To make the same point, N.T. Wright, in a fairly recent essay, makes the cogent case that Paul, in the three places where he makes his most critically dense theological thesis statements—Romans 3:21-22, Galatians 2:16 and Philippians 3:9—all refer to the faithfulness *of* Jesus (genitive case in all three), not faith *in* Jesus (this would require dative case, which is clearly *not* how Paul carefully laid out his thesis statement) as the content of our righteousness.[17]

Christian righteousness has nothing to do with the binding key, or newly rigorous ethics, or any human action or performance whatsoever! It consists only in hearing and believing the loosing key, that is, Jesus Christ's work. This, God the Father mercifully counts to us as righteousness. Whoever believes it has it! Such declaration, made publicly, will not be believed by all, maybe not even by most. Nevertheless such public declaration needs to be made—unapologetically, *unconditionally*, clearly, boldly, and gladly, confident that if faith is to be created, this, and only this will create it! Why preach at all if this is not the beginning presupposition of the proclaimer? Any other presupposition makes the preacher a huckster of some sort, a salesman perhaps, seeking to make Jesus attractive enough to close the deal, or perhaps God's "prosecuting attorney" seeking a favorable verdict from the jury (which will certainly depend upon his wonderful rhetoric). For those are what preachers become under Pietist doctrine. If God sent Ezekiel to preach to the dead (Ez. 37), and not to the living, or to the sentient, or those who were somehow "free" to respond, then something else than a sales pitch or the convincing practice of rhetoric is going on in genuine biblically conceived preaching!

17 Wright, *Paul In Fresh Perspective*, 110-112.

And so the argument among pious Lutherans goes on apace, never abating. *But perhaps this is the most essential debate to be had among Christians.* It certainly has been ongoing for almost 2000 years, and Lutherans have merely crystallized it. The whole controversy roots in the relationship between human responsibility and God's sovereignty. We have treated this subject already in the chapter on the "Bondage of the Will", giving a brief summary of the theological positions regarding God's election. N.T. Wright labels his argument regarding the faithfulness of Jesus, cited immediately above as "Election Reshaped Around Jesus." And so the debate over the power of the keys among Lutherans distills into two questions:

- whether our faith can properly be understood as a required human responsibility in the pronounced absolution,
- and thus, whether our repentance (the human response/responsibility) is the qualifying factor which makes the absolution valid.

Kurt Marquart writes, "Keeping in mind that in the Lutheran understanding of justification is quite the same thing as forgiveness of sins,[18] we may begin by noting a certain oddity in the wording the fourth article of the Augsburg Confession: "we receive forgiveness of sin . . . if we believe . . . that sin is forgiven us for His sake." Logically there is here at least the suggestion of a circle: On the one hand forgiveness is the result of faith, and thus comes after faith, and on the other hand it is the object of faith and therefore goes before faith."[19]

In order to escape such confusion it is necessary to review the difference in Luther's theology between what has come to be classified in more modern terms as "objective justification" and "subjective justification". Luther explains it in this way:

> We treat of forgiveness of sins in two ways. First, how it is achieved and won. Second, how it is distributed and given to us. Christ has achieved it on the cross, it is true. But he has not distributed or given it on the cross. He has not won it in the supper or sacrament. There he has distributed and given it through the Word, as also in the gospel, where it is preached. He has won it once for all on the cross. But the distribution takes place continuously, before and after, from the beginning to the end of the world . . . .Even if Christ were given for us and crucified a thousand times, it would all be in vain if the Word of God were

---

18. Tappert. *Book of Concord*, 76.
19. Marquart et. al., *A Lively Legacy*, 117.

absent and were not distributed and given to me with the bidding, "This is for you, take what is yours.[20]

So, according to Luther, "objective justification" has already been won. Not only is it completely done and not to do, it is also completely extensive in the sense that the sins of absolutely everybody, whether believer of not, have *already* been forgiven! Luther cites both Isaiah 53:6 that "The Lord laid on Him the iniquity of us all, and John 1:29 "Behold the Lamb of God who takes away the sin of the world." (Which clearly seem to make his case!) The understanding of justification as "not yet to do" is not shared by Roman dogma, while the extensive formulation that such justification includes absolutely everybody is not shared by Calvinist dogma.[21]

Moving now to "subjective justification" we deal with the distribution system which God has appointed to "deliver the goods." "The distributing Word which Luther urges is of course the Gospel, or to say it most pointedly, the absolution."[22] Luther writes, "We should and must constantly maintain that God will not deal with us except through his external Word and sacrament. Whatever is attributed to the Spirit apart from such Word and sacrament is of the devil."[23] Because the Gospel or the absolution is the performative Word of God, it is never a theory or a report about how sins are forgiven. If God's word is seriously believed as performative, then persisting in focusing instead upon human response becomes pointless, if not stubbornly inane. If the preached Word is the "power of God for salvation to all who believe." (Romans 1:16), then what the Word requires, which is faith, must be conceived, born, and come into existence in the very hearing of that Word. It also follows that a division of the whole world occurs in the event of this preaching. Some believe while others do not. We do not know why, nor will we ever find out in this age before the general resurrection. The same thing happened when God Himself preached while he was here on earth. Not everyone who heard him came to faith. So the issue of faith (both its coming into being and its absence) goes back behind human ability, to God's election.[24] It also ineluctably follows (and this establishes Forde's assertion) that all preaching is the prosecution of God's election. In John 8:43 and 47, during Jesus' heated controversy with the Jerusalem faculty, Jesus does not attribute their unbelief to either human reason or will. It seems pretty clear that God's election is the issue here, and just as clearly, not human ability.

20. LW 40:213.
21. Marquart et al., *A Lively Legacy*, 123.
22. Marquart et al., *A Lively Legacy*, 125.
23. Tappert. *Book of Concord*, 313.
24. LW 33:138ff.

And this is the most critical assertion of the Bondage of the Will. "Of course Luther knows that faith is necessary to receive the Gospel's benefits. But he insists that the Gospel . . . has its own power, validity, and dignity, before, apart from, and independently of faith or unbelief. Faith depends on the Gospel, not the Gospel on faith. Our subjective fluctuations, whether of faith or unbelief, cannot make God's Key doubtful or 'wobbly.'"[25]

The "sovereignty of God" side cites Luther as follows: "Whatever does not direct us to God's Word, but rather to our remorse, is a *conditionalis clavis*, a fickle key. If (Christ) should say, 'if you are remorseful and pious then I will forgive you, but if not, I failed,' that would be a *clavis errans* (a defective key) . . . If my remorse is not enough, his word is; if I am not worthy enough, his keys are. He is faithful and true; my sins shall not make him a liar." The "conditional" side could cite Luther as follows: "What the one speaks and the other hears is God's command and word . . . for their souls' salvation both are bound to believe that word as surely and firmly as all other articles of faith . . . We shall and must in all seriousness and confidence believe what God says. Whoever does not believe, let him leave the keys in peace."[26] This latter quote can be understood as making the case that absolution somehow depends for its effect on our faith only upon two conditions:

- that faith is seen as preceding absolution, and
- that faith is somehow a human response/responsibility.

Yet this flies in the face of the most fundamental formulations regarding faith in the Lutheran confessions. If God is the one who creates faith when and where he chooses, and faith itself is born in the hearing of the Word, how can faith be understood as a "human responsibility"? Yet this is a required understanding both implicit and explicit in Lutheran Pietism—the source of all the subjunctive absolutions listed. In both of these citations from his treatise on the Keys Luther is arguing for a declaration which is absolutely unqualified.

Moving beyond the relation between God's sovereignty and human response/responsibility, it would clarify things to coin a new term human "response-ability". For that is the real issue, whether one defines human "response-ability" by the terms "repentance" or "faith" or both. Here Luther laid down the gauntlet in the meaning of the Third Article of the Creed in the Small Catechism: "I believe that I cannot by my own reason or strength believe in Jesus Christ, my Lord or come to him. But the Holy Spirit has called

---

25. Marquart et al., *A Lively Legacy*, 125.
26. LW 40:214.

me by the Gospel . . ."²⁷ In succinct form this says: "I believe that *I* cannot believe," as well as saying, "I believe that I *cannot* believe." Therefore, since faith is the only possible way to receive absolution, and yet faith cannot be understood as that which validates absolution, it must then logically be both commanded and given by God in the self-same Word of absolution!

This meaning to the Third Article is the one sentence summary of the entire "Bondage of the Will". But it is given only lip service by the Pietist wing of Lutheran theologians, and is completely ignored by Calvinists, Catholic Orthodoxy and the various expressions of Evangelicals in North America. Yet a strong biblical argument can be made for this case by citing the one sentence summary of all of Jesus' preaching given to us in the first gospel: "The special salvation time (*kairos*) has been filled up! The Kingdom is right here! Repent and believe while you under the sphere of the power of the gospel!" (Mark 1:15) In choosing that wording I am following Eduard Schweitzer's assertion, "The kingdom is more like an area or a sphere of authority into which one can enter" in his commentary.²⁸ By taking this reading of the last phrase of verse 15, one has complete warrant for understanding that God both commands and, at the same time, gives what he commands, by means of the word that is spoken. If this is so, then preachers don't have to worry about how to make the Gospel effective. All they need to be concerned about is proclaiming what the Word authorizes them to say. And, if preaching, itself, separates believers from unbelievers, then preachers also need to leave to God alone the judgment that will ensue upon those who do not believe the announced declaration.

Luther, himself, admirably summarizes the somewhat extended preceding argument in this statement from his treatise concerning the Keys.

> "Remember that the keys or the forgiveness of sins are not based on our own repentance or worthiness, as they wrongly teach. Such teachings are entirely Pelagian, Mohammedan, pagan, Jewish, like those of the Anabaptists, fanatic, and anti-Christian. On the contrary, our repentance and work, our disposition and all we are, should be built on the keys. We are to depend on them with as daring confidence as on God's Word itself. You must never doubt what the keys say and give you, at the risk of losing both body and soul. It is as certain as if God himself were saying so, which indeed he does. It is his own Word and command. But if you doubt the same you make God a liar. You pervert his order and base his keys on your own repentance and worthiness. You should, indeed, repent. *But to make repentance*

27. Tappert. *Book of Concord*, 345.
28. Schweitzer, *Good News According to Mark*, 46.

the basis of the forgiveness of your sins and of corroborating the work of the keys, is to abandon faith and deny Christ. By means of the key, he will forgive your sins, not for your own sake but for his own name's sake, out of pure grace."[29] (My italics)

Absolution: the Third Iteration

Moving now to 1978, the entire confession-absolution portion of the worship service is made optional(!), another thing Sundberg properly decries, by setting it apart from the Holy Communion Service. (This hymnal, which began as a publication meant to unite the Missouri synod with the majority of other North American Lutheran denominations, but miscarried in that attempt, is unique in rendering confession-absolution optional. The Missouri edition of this project did not do so.) Now, whole synod assemblies of the ELCA began to be conducted with worship services absent *any* order for confession and forgiveness.

Here are the two choices for absolution:

"Almighty God, in his mercy, has given his Son to die for us, and for his sake, forgives us all our sins. As a called and ordained minister of the church of Christ, and by his authority, I therefore declare to you the entire forgiveness of all your sins, in the name of the Father, and of the Son and of the Holy Spirit."

or

"In the mercy of Almighty God, Jesus Christ was given to die for you, and for his sake God forgives you all your sins. To those who believe in Jesus Christ he gives the power to become the children of God, and bestows on them the Holy Spirit."

Finally, we get two fairly robust, straight-forward declarations, *but now rendered entirely optional*! Again, one can argue over whether the phrase "as a called and ordained minister" should be included in an absolution. Good Lutherans could argue that since call and ordination serve the function of "seeing that the Gospel is rightly preached and the sacraments are properly administered", and, since the absolution centrally expresses the Gospel, therefore, it is only proper, while delivering what the office requires, to refer back to the purpose of one's office. However, the contrary argument could also be made that, since the sole warrant and surety of the declaration of

29. LW 40:364.

absolution lies completely in the work of Christ, it is misleading to introduce the subject of the office of ministry, which could easily be misconstrued and heard as an additional warrant for Christian certainty. These two options are also retained and given in the recent "Reclaim" Lutheran hymnal.

Absolution: Current Iterations and Options

Turning now to later additions to this process, the 1991 Hymnal Supplement gives the gift of absolution completely unqualified for the first time:

> "With joy, I proclaim to you that almighty God, rich in mercy, abundant in love, forgives you all your sin and grants you newness of life in Jesus Christ."

One wishes only for some mention of the warrant for such good tidings to be included—some mention of the cross.

With One Voice, 1995, leaves the brief order for confession and forgiveness optional and has these two absolutions:

> "In the mercy of almighty God, Jesus Christ was given to die for us, and for his sake God forgives us all our sins. As a called and ordained minister of the Christ of Christ, and by His authority, I therefore declare to you the entire forgiveness of all your sins, in the name of the Father, and of the Son, and of the Holy Spirit."

or

> "Almighty God have mercy on you, forgive you all your sins through our Lord Jesus Christ, strengthen you in all goodness, and by the power of the Holy Spirit keep you in eternal life."

The second needs only the addition of "may" as the first word to complete the slide into the subjunctive pious wish, as opposed to a clear declaration.

Finally, in 2006, the ELCA published the *Evangelical Lutheran Worship* (Augsburg-Fortress). This edition for corporate Lutheran worship not only makes the confession-absolution service optional, but now one can optionally choose *instead* of any absolution, a "thanksgiving for baptism"! The two alternate absolutions (in the now optional/optional format) are as follows:

> "In the mercy of almighty God, Jesus Christ was given to die for us, and for his sake God forgives us all our sins. As a called and ordained minister of the church of Christ and by his authority, I

therefore declare to you the entire forgiveness of all your sins, in the name of the Father, and of the Son, and of the Holy Spirit."

or

"God, who is rich in mercy, loved us even when we were dead in our sin, and made us alive together with Christ. By grace you have been saved. In the name of Jesus Christ your sins are forgiven. Almighty God strengthen you with power through the Holy Spirit, that Christ may live in your hearts through faith. Amen.

Both absolutions have clear and distinct declarations that deliver the goods. The concern regarding "called and ordained minister" has already been noted. The subjunctive mood of the concluding sentence of option B does not serve as a qualification to the clear declaration, but rather expresses a hope and prayer for its saving effect. It is sad, however, that whole congregations may never hear either of these clear absolutions in their entire lives at worship.

The whole process of first rendering the whole confession-absolution service as optional, and then replacing absolution entirely with a service of "thanksgiving for baptism" is not accidental, but is driven by a critical need in the "new" Lutheran church to quietly move away from any declaration of absolution at all. At least two issues are creating the impetus to move away from an exclusive focus on the cross that comes with absolution.

The first is the issue of religious pluralism, with its question of whether Christ is inclusive or exclusive. Religious pluralists say things such as this: "Christ is the only way to the Father—for Christians. But there are other ways for those who are sincere in other religions and of other convictions. For Jesus Christ is very inclusive in his spirit." In 2008 the bishop of the Episcopal Diocese of Los Angeles, during an Indian Rite Mass with Hindus, issued a statement of apology to the Hindu religious community for centuries-old acts of religious discrimination by Christians, including attempts to convert them. The bishop also said he was committed to renouncing the proselytizing of Hindus.[30] Much evidence can be assembled that main line churches are tending toward the same pluralistic approach exhibited in this instance, in their relationship with the Muslim community.

The second controversy challenging the exclusive focus on the cross is the issue of the acceptance of gays in the church. This controversy is not basically about sexuality, but has been dictated by how the church has decided to handle the non-negotiable demand by gays that their life-style be validated with equal status as the heterosexual life. When this *a priori*

---

30. Bruner, *Gospel of John*, 828.

assumption cannot even be discussed, then the conclusion is already foregone. If a certain life style needs no forgiveness, then part of being "welcoming" or "inclusive" requires that the church find and articulate another gospel, characterized less by forgiveness and more by inclusivity. "But God has consigned all men to disobedience, that he might have mercy on all." (Romans 11:32, and 3:10, 20, 23) The cross of Jesus for *all* sinners, together with the declared absolution based upon it, are sidelined and heard less and less so that worship may be more welcoming. In both cases, Niebuhr's characterization that liberal Christianity preaches "a God without wrath, who saves a world without sin, by a salvation without the cross," has found yet another iteration.

The 2006 Missouri Synod hymnal does not go this direction. Here, the absolutions are basically the same ones classically used by American Lutherans in the whole previous century. However, in setting three we have this:

> "Upon this your confession, I by virtue of my office a called and ordained servant of the Word announce the grace of God unto you, and in the stead and by the command of my Lord Jesus Christ I forgive you all your sins in the name of the Father and of the Son and of the Holy Spirit."

Does "upon this your confession" make dependent on it, what follows? "My office" and "my Lord Jesus Christ" are disconcerting and discordant intrusions into the work that belongs to Christ alone. "My office" runs the danger of reigniting the initial conflict of the Reformation, which contested the claim that "the Roman doctrine of the power of the priest to forgive sins and give absolution was a result of his ordination, which also gave him the power to administer the sacraments. His ordination was by a bishop who stood in relation to the pope, from whom came the apostolic power through Peter."[31] Nevertheless, with this exception, all the absolutions in this hymnal are clear and unqualified.

Summary

This condensed, somewhat distressing history of absolution in the Lutheran churches in North America over the last century has at least this salutary feature. The unremitting, unrelenting and vociferous nature of the struggle over how to convey the Gospel via the absolution demonstrates that it remains the central concern in Reformation worship and preaching;

31. LW 40:323.

it has gradually improved in its expression; and it has never been rendered ancillary, until only recently, and then by only a fraction of Lutheranism in America. And it *should* be fought over, because it is the whole ball game. No generation of Christians or theologians misses that. My father was a discerning and astute Luther scholar. After several decades of preaching and teaching—for twenty five years on a mission in Madagascar and later in a Montana congregation—he came to the conclusion that, in Reformation preaching or practice, "conditional" and "absolution" were mutually exclusive terms. In his 1530 *Treatise Concerning the Keys* Luther wrote, "An uncertain absolution is none at all, but rather deceit and knavery ... For who can say that his repentance is sufficient before God? Not our own repentance, but Christ himself with his suffering must be our repentance and satisfaction before God."[32] If one places *any* condition around the declaration of forgiveness, the gift of certainty regarding one's standing before God, which is the defining characteristic of absolution, is inevitably lost. "If people realize that their endeavors are uncertain, vain, and fraudulent, they help the devil fill his hell with Christian souls and to lay waste the kingdom of Christ."[33] "The result and fruit of such teaching is the destruction of Christendom and the Christian faith. For when a Christian hears and is convinced that the keys may err and fail, it is not possible for him to ground his hopes and belief on what the key promises.....Indeed, unbelief is sure to follow."[34] Again, "Christ says, 'Truly I say to you, whatever you bind on earth shall be bound in heaven and whatever you loose on earth shall be loosed in heaven.' (Matt 18:18) Notice that assuredly, yes assuredly, it shall be bound and loosed what we bind and loose on earth. There is no suggestion of any wrong key."[35] "We possess these two keys through Christ's command ... The key which binds carries forward the work of the law. It is profitable to the sinner inasmuch as it reveals to him his sins, admonishes him to fear God, causes him to tremble, and moves him to repentance, and not to destruction. The loosing key carries forward the work of the gospel. It invites to grace and mercy. It comforts and promises life and salvation through the forgiveness of sins. In short, the two keys advance and foster the gospel by simply proclaiming these two things: repentance and forgiveness of sins. (Luke 24:47)"[36]

32. LW 40:344.
33. LW 40:346.
34. LW 40:348.
35. LW 40:364.
36. LW 40:372-3.

Thus, "conditional absolution" becomes an oxymoron, less comical than "random order", "only choice", or "open secret", for instance, but an oxymoron nevertheless. It becomes an oxymoron because what absolution is sent to convey—assurance and proper Christian confidence—is utterly compromised and removed by any qualification or warrant other than the cross of Jesus Christ. Only what God has done can serve as the rock upon which one is built. The preacher is sent to "give Christ." The preacher is not sent to "sort of give Christ" by taking away with one hand what is given by God's hand alone. A biblical preacher knows that he or she is sent to proclaim a word of God, expecting its power to perform what it was sent to accomplish. The election which God performs, as various people hear that word preached, is up to God and not up to us. God can create faith when and where He pleases, defend the truth of His Word, extend His kingdom, and deal with the judgment that will come upon those who will not believe, all without any careful asterisks on the part of the proclaimer.

The rationale for this whole chapter is the conviction, emphasized by Luther, that preaching and absolution are not related metaphorically, but are rather materially, fundamentally, and literally precisely the same thing. Preaching *is* absolution, that is, the proclamation of the forgiveness of sins together with the warrants given (the cross and the resurrection of Jesus) for a hearer/believer to hold fast to this Word. Preaching delivers God's Word, operative as Law and Gospel, in that order. Preaching gives Christ. Preaching is directed toward the general public, not just the believing few. Preaching has as its central concern, to create proper confidence in Christ alone and His completed work to deliver sinners. And here is the rub: rightly preaching God's grace for sinners runs precisely the same risk as pronouncing the unconditional absolution, which is that cynical hearers may use such unconditional proclamation as an excuse for their moral laxity. Should the preacher then try to deliver the message only to those who will rightly use it? But that is patently impossible. The only remaining option is to proclaim the Good News publicly and boldly, that is, to pronounce the absolution unconditionally. God alone must do the sorting as to what He wills this Word to accomplish.

So that you do not miss that this ongoing controversy remains a significant part of the Reformation conflict with the official Catholic theology, the Council of Trent included these canons:

> CANON XII. If any one saith, that justifying faith is nothing else but confidence in the divine mercy which remits sins for Christ's sake; or, that this confidence alone is that whereby we are justified; let him be anathema.

CANON XIII. If any one saith, that it is necessary for every one, for the obtaining the remission of sins, that he believe for certain, and without any wavering arising from his own infirmity and disposition, that his sins are forgiven him; let him be anathema.

CANON XIV. If any one saith, that man is truly absolved from his sins and justified, because that he assuredly believed himself absolved and justified; or, that no one is truly justified but he who believes himself justified; and that, by this faith alone, absolution and justification are effected; let him be anathema.

CHAPTER EIGHT

Luther's Preaching Model—Conscience as "Man[1] Addressed"

At issue in this chapter on conscience are the three fundamental, intersecting, interrelated questions which every preacher consciously or unconsciously has assumed and determined in advance, even before opening his or her mouth:

- What ability does my hearer have?
- What is the target of my message—the will or the conscience?
- Who is the agent in this encounter—the preacher/hearer, or the Word itself?

How one answers each question has enormous consequences in the understanding of the preacher's vocation and in how one performs the act of proclamation itself.

New Answers From Luther's Reformation Principles

Biblical preaching according to Luther's Reformation principles is exceedingly rare. This is because, even among Lutherans, the answers given by Luther to these three questions, in each case, are directly opposed to the common current consensus. For example, in answer to the question, "What ability does my hearer have?" a Reformation preacher answers, "My hearer's will is captivated, helpless to respond to any appeal from God. Because this is so, the Word itself must do the deed. Therefore my task is to do to the

---

1. I will sometimes use "Man" in the following argument, which continues to serve, in spite of alternate PC requirements, as a more adequate referent to the human race, than the inelegant and more cumbersome term "human being". Common consent continues to confer both "Man and Woman" to the briefer term.

hearers the two things God's Word requires: to *kill them* by literally cutting off all escape and silencing every excuse and shutting every mouth through the preaching God's rigorous Law; and then to *resurrect them* by giving them through preaching the promise of what Christ has done for them." Such a preacher believes that the *use* of the Word has been given to preachers, but the *execution* of that Word God reserves to himself. Such preachers stoutly believe and expect all the power and results will come from the Word itself. Besides being completely independent of human response, a belief that the Word can create faith when and where God pleases makes any humans response completely dependent upon the Word that was proclaimed. These component parts make the "Theology of the Cross" utterly polemical against any competing view.

The primary competing view to Luther's reformation model of preaching is that preachers must convince hearers to make a proper saving response such as "Accepting Jesus as their personal Savior." But this leaves at least part of the warrant for salvation in human hands. Additionally, it makes preachers into God's salespeople who are looking to close the deal for God, or alternatively, God's prosecuting attorneys who seek to bring in a favorable verdict for God. The irony here is that precisely the reverse should be happening: preachers should be bringing to the people a declarative favorable verdict *from* God "that God was in Christ reconciling the world to himself".

The emphasis in this more popular paradigm puts pressure upon preachers to be entertaining, riveting, persuasive, emotional, rhetorical giants, trusting in their own agency to bring in the sale or the verdict, perhaps making Jesus desirable enough to suit our current fancy. More insidiously, it tempts preachers to avoid the controversial or the offensive, as turn-offs to the sales presentation (the overtly stated concern of the Crystal Cathedral ministry).

The second irony is that these preachers seek to un-do God's election! They seek to have their hearers turn from the only source of proper Christian confidence—the goodness of God's election—by substituting a far less intimidating but completely non-functional alternative, confidence based upon our own election! If we ourselves do the electing then we have every right to congratulate ourselves for a job well done. But this would be in total opposition to Paul's word in Ephesians 2:8-9: "By grace you have been saved through faith; and this is not your own doing; it is a gift of God—not because of works lest any man should boast."

And this is already answering the second question, because preaching that is informed by absolute priority of the Word's authority to create the actual encounter between God and man, is what Luther calls "establishing the conscience." The accusing conscience can only be silenced by a higher authority than itself. This reliable authority is the voice of the very God who created the conscience in the first place. In I John 3:19-20 we find this: "If our hearts condemn us, God is greater than our hearts." In other words, the conscience, which is an interior voice (and, in fallen humanity, a now unreliable voice), can only be over-ridden by another higher voice, the exterior voice called the Word of God. Second, the accusing conscience can only be satisfied when the uncertain calculus is removed regarding how much a person needs to do in relation to how much God does. When God does all, only then is the conscience established secure and certain upon the only foundation that can give proper confidence.

In Luther's model, the third question regarding the critical aegis—the actor in this vital encounter—is neither the persuasiveness of the preacher, nor the acquiescence of the hearer, but the performative Word itself, the Word alone. *This Word is able to create the receiving faith which it demands, when and where God pleases, in its very coming to our ears.* Somehow, this last sentence is found to be unbelievable by a large majority of preachers. They demonstrate that this is so by the basic assumptions they use to control what they term "proclamation".

However, the functioning of this entire thesis is impossible without a careful recovery and return to the definition of conscience understood from scripture and articulated by Martin Luther. A brief review of the definitions of conscience first from philosophy (both medieval and eighteenth century) including modern day definitions that lead to such canards as "let your conscience be your guide", along with the definitions of conscience from scripture, all need to be compared, contrasted, and critiqued by the definition of conscience proposed by Luther.

Conscience According to Philosophy

Who are you? "Ontology" is a word from Greek philosophy formed to deal with such things as *substance, essence, accidents, form, material, acts, potential, qualities,* and *relationships* as they regard personal "being." But they are also the central questions handled by God's Word. Human philosophy and God's Word predictably give diametrically opposed answers to questions regarding "being". When Thomas Aquinas, during the excitement of the rediscovery of the Greek philosophers writings in the 12th century, synthesized Greek philosophy and Holy Scripture, the resulting mighty system of thought, which sought to explain virtually everything, was called Scholasticism. However, the result was not wholly congruent with the Christian faith revealed by scripture, and resulted eventually in the collision of the two competing thought worlds, in an event called the Reformation.

To understand the first thought world one begins with Greek philosophy. Both ancient and modern philosophies have defaulted generally to the treatment of man as an observable construct which the Greek philosophers called "persona", one of several categories of "being". Another basic feature of the philosophical ontology regarding man, both ancient and modern, is that all the assertions are rooted in an optimistic view of man. Scholasticism, for example, specifically maintained that there remained in man a divine spark undamaged by the Fall, through which God's grace could be used by man to address and improve the situation brought upon us by sin.

Only a brief recall of the biblical account, shows how far scholasticism is from the interpretation of the early theologians. According to the theology received by Luther, fallen man retained intact his knowledge of good and evil. The entire domain of the conscience and of the intellect supposedly was maintained, while only the will was fallen. "Man, it was asserted, knew the true good but no longer had the power to perform it. This explanation, of course, can be sustained if one starts from certain philosophical premises; and in fact it is on the basis of philosophical presuppositions that Thomas Aquinas builds his system. One can offer any of the possible explanations, and the most diverse, merely by a change in the metaphysical standpoint; but none of that is biblical."[2]

An instance of this same optimistic stance during the later Enlightenment period is the French philosopher Rousseau, who coined the term "the noble savage" to assert that, completely absent the meddling by European (read "Christian") explorers, all the new-found human populations and cultures were better left alone, thank you.

A third philosophical assumption regarding man's basic definition finds its roots more centrally in the Enlightenment. At the risk of horribly oversimplifying the entire Enlightenment project one could argue that it is centrally characterized by an emphatic new definition of "man", who possesses the imagined ability to be an uninvolved, neutral, empirically objective observer of reality. This central tenet of Hegel's impressive philosophical system drove Soren Kierkegaard to distraction and was the source of page upon page of sustained mockery in Kierkegaard's works. "Hegel's philosophy could not produce an ethics, Kierkegaard argued, because its stance was that of a spectator. It does not really let me exist *in* history. I am an onlooker outside it."[3] (his italics) In emphasizing that the truth could only be known existen-

2. Ellul, *To Will and To Do*, 14.
3. Thielicke, *Modern Faith and Thought*, 386.

tially, by personally participating in it, Kierkegaard was objecting to Hegel's "objective thinking" that refused to take account of existence, or personal participation in it, as the very definition of knowing the truth. "Speculatively establishing the mediation of absolute and finite spirit, Hegel thought that he could know Christ directly, but only by an essential falsification, i.e., by de-individualizing, by his reduction to the mere representative of the *idea* of reconciliation. In contrast, Kierkegaard views (Christ) as the God who came to manifestation in an individual. He thus bursts open the continuity of Hegelian dialectic. He makes Christ an absurdity for objective reason, an absolute exception that we can speak about only in the form of paradox."[4] Hamann (another marginalized philosophical name) concurs with Kierkegaard in dismissing Hegel's claimed ability to judge what constituted truth from an uninvolved point of view, as fanciful or even inane.

Although this assumed ability to be an objective, uninvolved observer of reality also accords with the ancient Greek stance, this ability becomes non-negotiable for the entire Enlightenment concept. The Socratic method of arriving at the truth proceeds from the irreducible starting point that the inquirer and the one who is asked share the same basic ontology. But the incarnation of the Son of God himself renders this maeutic method of knowing, which assumes that the truth is latent in the mind of every human, both untenable and obtuse. Here Luther would have appreciated Kierkegaard's insistence that the truth is known only by existentially participating in it.

Additionally, the Enlightenment, which fancied itself as extending the progress of the Reformation, ironically directly denied the central discovery of the Reformation, an urgent need to have one's thinking molded by biblical revelation which insists that the constitutive relation between God and Man is a relationship marked not by analogy but by contradiction. But for the Enlightenment philosophers this submission of their thinking to scriptural authority was impossible because, in their horror of actual excesses in Church practice during the immediate preceding century, they all reacted by seeking to root out everything they regarded as "superstition" in order to replace it with a more secure "objectivity". So the Enlightenment enterprise became characterized by the removal of God (considered as anything beyond an idea) or the necessity of his revelation, as far as possible from any consideration when dealing with humanity.

In summary, and for purposes of this argument, my assertion is that these three philosophical components of the definition of "man"—man as an observable construct, man who (optimistically) retains a divine spark, and man as the capable objective neutral observer of all reality—jointly constitute

---

4. Thielicke, *Modern Faith and Thought*, 509.

the broad outlines of what the current "man on the street" now assumes to be actual descriptions of his own reality, and commonly believes as foundational truth. It is certainly characteristically assumed to be so and taught in academia. I, myself, believed these things to be assumed truth for a long time. But, jointly, these three assertions regarding the definition of "man" require an entirely revised view of conscience as something operating within the construct of *the absolute priority of man*, that is, a construct without relation to any other power or being. Of course, such a view also renders completely impossible the Reformation model of proclamation.

Luther's whole discussion of conscience rejects this entire anthropocentric starting point, together with its definition. In utter contrast, the irreducible beginning point for Luther in any consideration of a true description of reality, is the Word, and not "man". A human person is a conscience-creature first and foremost, because Luther insists that we are at our most fundamental definition, "one who is addressed". And it is precisely in this assertion and at this precise point that Luther loses most modern theologians. The Word is absolutely prior for Luther. The Word of God precedes us, creates us, and then calls us constantly into question in our conscience. The evidence for this is that whether or not one is a believer, in every culture on the planet the religion of the people somehow deals with this underlying anxiety regarding God's unknown verdict over them, making "religion", in turn, a witness for the priority of conscience in the definition of who we are.

As we have said, the definition of who we are, and all descriptions of our "being" are within the philosophical field called ontology. Luther insists that his theological position is a vital challenge to all received ontological teaching. Biblical theology does not allow one to argue in an abstract mode. In fact, Luther's position is that all unbelief produces a deficient description of reality. For example, Hegel considers his postulate of the disinterested observer's complete exclusion from the description of reality, as problem-free. Luther on the other hand, asserts that a truthful description of our reality must include the fact that we cannot escape from our very selves' "being-with-others." Luther's seminal phrase, *coram deo*, (before the face of God, or, in the presence of God) points to the inescapable situation of judgment which this relationship creates. At a minimum our life *coram deo* is characterized by constant judgment. "The ontological relevance that accrues to the Word results from the situation of judgment, which is fundamental for the being of humanity... The difference between the word of humanity and the Word of God is not bridged by translation, but rather has to do with the dissimilarity of their characterization of reality. The word of humanity—no matter whether it may contain information or promise—can deceive and is unable to guarantee its fulfillment as a promise. In any case, it needs an extra deed, which is not the word as such. On the other hand, the Word of God is a speech-act as such, of creative power and infallible reliability . . . That such gravity falls to the Word of God is a biblical peculiarity, which, trinitarianly based, molds the understanding of creation, reconciliation, and consummation."[5]

Our encounter with this Word creates a contest regarding what is real, which is carried out in the conscience. For example, the struggle over whether one is really justified, (which all reason and common sense war against) is carried on in the conscience. "In the *conscientia*, everything has its place: the contestability of *coram*-relationship, the existential power of Word and faith, as well as the implementation of *distinction* and *unio*. (The one Word of God that comes as Law and Gospel) In conscience, Christ has his true dwelling place. *Ubi Christus*, (wherever there is Christ) there should be a *bona conscientia* (good conscience). 'Faith is nothing other than a good conscience.' Thus we can talk theologically only if the spell of an alleged, self-evident understanding of reality is broken." [6]

Conscience according to Scripture

According to scripture, *not one* of either the medieval or the enlightenment beginning philosophical presuppositions hold. When Luther began to experience a growing disconnect between what he had been taught as received doctrinal truth, and what he was struggling to understand as scriptural truth, the disconnect between the two finally grew to be characterized not merely as an *etymological*, but an *ontological* one; that is, not a battle over proper word definitions, but a battle over telling the truth about what constitutes the very definition of reality. Luther's central contribution to the Reformation was to recall theology (or more narrowly, proclamation) to its proper role and function, which includes revealing to people that their sin has made them so blind that the intuitive, the visible, and the rational were no longer reliable ways to the truth. God's truth has to be revealed, because God and man are related not by *analogy* but by *contradiction*. Here Luther staked the claim for his entire position upon Paul's assertion in I Corinthians 1:18-25, which begins, "The word of the cross is folly to those who are perishing." In the Heidelberg Disputation, theses 19-20 we read: "That person does not deserve to be called a theologian who claims to see into the invisible things of God. But (that person deserves to be called a theologian) who comprehends what is visible of God through suffering and

---

5. Ebeling, *Luther's Understanding of Reality*, 65-66.
6. Ebeling, *Luther's Understanding of Reality*, 71.

the cross." Here, "The question of the knowledge of God is directly related to the claim that we can, by our natural powers, prepare for grace by 'doing what is in us.' 'Doing what is in ourselves by natural ability of trying to hold to the efficacy of such doing before God, presumes a natural knowledge of God's justifying action. It presupposes a certain way of knowing and seeing God."[7] But the cross shuts down any other way of knowing God. What is revealed there is precisely that we don't know God.

The only way forward to any reliable, saving knowledge of God, together with all correct knowledge, whatsoever, of what is real, is by believing God's Word, and nothing else at all. But the truth of this Word must be mediated by, interpreted by, and have its entire meaning unlocked by the cross of Jesus Christ. The cross blocks absolutely every other access to knowing God than through dying to all human effort. We are finished. There is no escape. By faith we become a human being, a truly historical person, because there is nothing to do now but wait, hope, pray, and trust in the promise of him who conquers for us the crucified and risen Jesus. By faith we are simply *in Christ*, waiting to see what will happen to and in us. This is no abstract theological problem! "The only solution is the cross itself and the subsequent proclamation of the word of the cross as a divine deed, the work of the Spirit, in the living present. That is to say, as fallen creature and not creators, we will always be threatened by God, who is hidden by the masks of divine majesty . . . The only refuge is the word of the cross in the here and now. Through the preaching of the cross in the living present, not through theological explanations, we are defended from the terror of the divine majesty . . . The 'solution to the problem of God, that is, is not in the classroom but in church. When theologians do not grasp that, or when they forget it, they no longer deserve the title."[8]

Turning to the witness of the Bible, *before we even get to the definition of man*, prior even to the assumed pathways to knowledge such as reason, sight, or intuition, scripture takes us to our preceding reality—the Word of God. "Thou hast exalted above everything thy Name and thy Word."(Ps. 138:2) The Word was in the beginning, and was in relation to God, and constitutes the very being of God (John 1:1); the Word created all things (Genesis 1:1); *in* this Word, and *for* this Word and *toward* this Word we all exist (Col. 1:16-17); the Word remains in eternity after all that is visible has passed away (I Peter 1:25); the Word is no product of evolution but constitutes the continuing animation behind absolutely every living thing (Matthew 4:4 and John 1:3); the Word is the power behind the resurrection from the dead

---

7. Forde, *On Being a Theologian of the Cross*, 71.
8. Forde, *On Being a Theologian of the Cross*, 74.

(John 10:18); and the Word, most critically, awaits us as verdict—the judgment of God—at the end of the world. This Word, as verdict, has determined whose names "are written in the book of life"—a repeated election descriptor throughout scripture. (Psalm 69:28, 139:16, Daniel 12:1, Philippians 4:3, Revelation 3:5, 13:8, 17:8, 20:12 and 15, 21:27) Conscience bears witness to each person on this planet of the priority of this Word, in that every single race and tribe upon the earth knows within their hearts that the verdict over their lives does not rest with them, but with some "higher power", whatever name the Speaker is given. *Conscience in scripture minimally means "Man Inescapably Under the Address of God's Word."*

"While the Old Testament describes the experience but not the notion of conscience in, for example, the stories of Adam, Cain, David, Job; the New Testament, especially Paul, has the word and the reality."[9] Both New and Old Testaments constantly describe the on-going dynamic effect of human conscience throughout the entire narrative. As an example, compare the first recorded words of God to man in Genesis to the first recorded words of Jesus in John. In Genesis God speaks: "Adam, where are you?" certainly not seeking to elicit Adam's location in the garden, but to elicit the word from Adam, confessing his current situation regarding his relationship with God, the complete rupture of which Adam's conscience is bearing witness. In other words, this deceptively simple narrative describes the basic feature of what Luther came to characterize as living *coram deo*, living as a "being-addressed", or living as a "conscience being". Adam's conscience is bearing witness to him that there is now "no way home" for him, with his current capabilities. He will become the first to experience the ultimate judgment visited upon God's people in the Old Testament—being driven from the promised land. (Luther made vivid the stories of Joseph and Abraham via referring to their experience of conscience in the last multi-volume work of his life, the commentary on Genesis.)

Using a demonstration similar to the Old Testament, that even though the term "conscience" is not in use, its function remains front and center to the narrative, consider Jesus' first spoken word in the gospel of John.

In the Gospel of John when Jesus asks, "What are you looking for?", it a word which in some ways invites, but now extends, the response to the question first heard in Genesis, "Where are you?" Jesus ends the short conversation regarding where to find him by saying, "Come and see." Being with Jesus is the answer to everything that was lost in the garden. It is exactly what every conscience seeks post-Fall. Not only are we are always looking for God, but more centrally for the *affirmative* Word of God, which

9. Tillich, *Morality and Beyond*, 68.

was lost when the connection was lost through our defying God's Word. The once enjoyed affirmative verdict upon ourselves is the always elusive goal of our search. And how is Jesus going to create that affirmative word from God, for which we constantly seek? That will take the whole New Testament to describe. It will involve the cross, where God himself enters into the ruptured place, in order to restore us. On resurrection morning God's original question is repeated—both sharpened and extended, again—by the very first word the now risen Jesus speaks: "Who are you looking for?" And, finally, after 39 books of Old Testament narrative, which, too, is all about conscience, we get the amazing news that "being-completely-cut-off" and "the exile from our proper home" is forever ended, by what was done outside of us, by Another. Return has come via a new word, the long sought affirmative Word. It has arrived through him who bore the rupture of relationship in our place, so that we could be restored into conversation once again. Resurrection is distilled in John's gospel into one word—our own name! We now hear Jesus' voice speak, not now in accusation, but miraculously in the tender love of restoration. Resurrection is the beginning of the healing of the ruptured conscience, and happens in one word—"Mary!" Our own name spoken by the one who loves sinners and re-establishes the conscience secure in a love that casts out all fear. These brief examples of "first words" serves as a cursory demonstration of how, even though the scriptural narrative rarely uses the term "conscience", it is centrally dealing with conscience all the way through.

The New Testament's treatment of the term "conscience" extends what is revealed in the Old. In Romans 2:14-15 Paul describes conscience, not as a special quality of Christians, but as an element of human nature generally. Conscience witnesses to the law, but it is not itself the law and so its judgment can be wrong. Nevertheless even an erring conscience must be obeyed because one can lose salvation even when doing something objectively right, if one does it with an uneasy conscience. (I Corinthians 8:7ff) Peter directs the Christian to his baptism into Jesus Christ as the only hope of a *clear* conscience. (I Peter 3:21) This verse lays out the foundation for the only solution to a Christian's sensitive conscience—pointing to the change of location for saving righteousness, which must reside in Jesus Christ while at the same time finding its completion and perfection in Jesus Christ. Hebrews 9:9 agrees with the direction Peter has taken—the sacrifice of Jesus is the only possible way to "make the conscience of the worshiper perfect." Heresy sears the conscience. One cannot be a heretic with a good conscience. (I Tim. 1:19 and 4:2)

LUTHER'S PREACHING MODEL—CONSCIENCE AS "MAN ADDRESSED"

The term used in the New Testament, *syneidesis*, literally means "knowing together with", or "consciousness," particularly consciousness of sin."[10] "(In Paul's use) the reference is to *gnosis* (knowledge), which embraces in a totality the perception of a distinction between the facts, the acknowledgment and choice of divinely willed obligations and self-evaluation."[11]

> "The attitude to one's *syneidesis* is the attitude to oneself, and the attitude to the neighbor's *syneidesis* is the attitude to the neighbor himself. Paul's decisive statements, that in the community of Jesus Christ man is in encounter with the one true but gracious God, impose a restriction on syneidesis, which is at one and the same time both a liberation and a commitment. The liberation is especially for the weak, about whom Paul as one of the strong speaks to the strong, (Romans 14). Members of the congregation who are weak because they are used to idols have not yet won through to the liberating acknowledgment of the truth that they themselves are known and acknowledged by the one true God beside whom there are not other gods but only created things. They are thus threatened at the very heart of their being when as the weak they try to achieve the insight of the strong. But because Christ died precisely for the weak the strong should know and acknowledge a weak self-awareness better than the weak themselves can do. For the self-awareness which condemns itself there is thus set up a liberating boundary *from without*. (my italics) The weak should take the Gospel promise of their acknowledgment by God more seriously than their own knowledge. That is to say they must let their own *syneidesis* be limited and liberated by this . . . .Paul takes *syneidesis* with a comprehensive breath and variety not found in any of his predecessors. For him it is no longer just the popular bad conscience of the Hellenistic-Jewish *elegchos* ("proof" or "inner conviction"). It has now become the central self-consciousness of knowing and acting man. With few exceptions it had never been anything like this before in literature. Combining the Greek view of man as especially a thinking being, with the Hebrew tradition which stressed the primacy of the Word, Paul raises the whole problem of act, being, and knowledge in anthropology—a step of momentous significance for the centuries which followed."[12]

---

10. Maurer, *Synoida and Syneidesis*, 914.
11. Maurer, *Synoida and Syneidesis*, 915.
12. Maurer, *Synoida and Syneidesis*, 917.

Luther's Contribution and Critique from Scripture

Our received Enlightenment science defines man as "homo sapiens" (the wise one)—this title asserting that the central feature distinguishing man from all other creatures is his wisdom or the size of his brain. What scripture teaches, by contrast, is that we, of all God's creatures, are the only ones created "in God's image." Being created in God's image (and science should have noticed more carefully this other salient distinguishing feature of man) we, alone among God's creatures, have been given the gift of speech—the defining feature of God himself. As such, before anything else is said about the reality of who man is, we are constituted and most fundamentally defined as a "being-under-address". According to scripture, *before anything else can be said about man, it must be acknowledged that he is in relationship, a relationship constituted by a spoken word*. He is neither autonomous, nor neutral, nor objective, nor uninvolved. In fact he, himself, *is* a relationship. Man is inescapably in three relations at once: a) to the God who called him into existence; b) to his neighbors; c) but perhaps most frustrating of all, in a complicated relationship to himself. Each of these relationships is an on-going forum where man finds himself judged, where a verbal verdict in some form is rendered upon who he is.

Luther described the scripturally revealed forum, which constitutes all of our true reality, in two ways. First, he used the phrase *coram deo* to assert that, absolutely the whole existence of a Christian (or, for that matter, every person), whether one believes or not, is lived before the face of God. By this phrase he wished to express how fundamentally everything is transformed when we realize that we live "in God's presence", a reality constituted by "intimately hearing his word" as it comes to us new every day. Second, literally everything in his theology drives toward a single point, the forum "where God meets man", and that is the conscience. That is why, for him, conscience forms the only true target and destination of all preaching and proclamation.

Predictably, conscience, the most basic construct for the whole thought world of Luther's Reformation theology, has been rendered incomprehensible through the ensuing centuries by being systematically misconstrued, psychologized, and hopelessly subjectivized. Yet for Luther, conscience required only a very simple definition (in which Sigmund Freud's "id "ego" and "super ego" have no place). "Conscience" simply indicates the reality that man is centrally constituted, defined and judged by the spoken Word he hears. And conscience is both the *faculty* which hears God's Word and the *forum* which God's Word shapes. Conscience is the inescapable forum in which we live our whole life. So, for Luther, we are not "homo sapiens" (the wise or intelligent one) so much as we are primarily *homo auditer*—(the one who listens or hears). As conscience-creatures we are defined most essentially by waiting upon the coming of God's Word, and by our longing for the positive verdict of that Word—a positive verdict which always eludes our control. The very possibility of creating such a positive verdict always lies beyond and outside of us. But this verdict rests in Another—a reality we constantly seek to deny.

"What Luther says of God is concentrated to an extraordinary degree upon the conscience. 'Conscience', of course, does not mean what it means in the usual but questionable interpretation of the conscience as the essence of the normative contents of the consciousness and of he autonomous faculties of judgment, that is, the presence of the decisive norm and appeal within man himself. Rather, what Luther understands by 'conscience' is the reliance of man upon the word, in the sense that he is always, and not merely in some particular respect but in his very person, claimed, commanded, questioned, and subjected to judgment, so that in one way or another he is always a determined, listening and receiving conscience; either confused or arrogant in an imaginary freedom, which means his bondage to the powers of this world; or assured and comforted in obedient attention to God which is true freedom with regard to the world."[13]

Jaques Ellul, in his book *To Will and to Do*, carefully, critically, and unflinchingly lays out both the presenting problem for every existing conscience, as well as defining how conscience is constituted by God's living speech event. This will require an extended quote.

> In the Bible the good is not prior to God. The good is not God. The good is the will of God. All that God wills is good, not because God is subject to the good, obedient to the good, but simply because God wills it . . . From man's point of view the good is not his decision, nor a simple possibility; for that good has, as a matter of fact, an independent reality. 'He has showed you, O man, what is good' (Mic. 6:8), and man is forbidden to discover it by himself. *Man can only act well when he listens to the word of God.* There is never a divine requirement which is abstract, general, inherent, but only divine requirements which are concrete. Now Adam precisely is unable to have knowledge of this good in the situation in which he finds himself; first, because such knowledge would mean that the will of God is set, immobilized in an objectively perceptible content, continuing without change, and that God, in the last analysis is relegated to

---

13. Ebeling, *Luther: an Introduction to his Thought*, 261.

the past... In other words, if man by himself knew the content of the good, that would mean that God is not free."[14] "At this point, Adam's weakness takes on a terrifying character. God's sovereign power of discernment is indeed in his hands, but Adam's hands are not God's hands... it is he who will declare the just and the unjust, yet he himself is not just." (my italics)[15] "Thus sin is not the failure to obey a morality. It is the very desire to determine that morality independently of God, a desire which is at the same time, concupiscence, the will to power."[16] "In scripture, there is no possible knowledge of the good apart from a living and personal relationship with Jesus Christ. In reality, however, man has even less knowledge of the true evil than he has of the good. Man learns what is evil; that is, discovers himself as a sinner, at the time of the revelation of the good as the will of God... He learns it at that time only....He cannot be convinced of sin by confrontation with a good, a morality, a more or less abstract principle, but only when he is confronted by God."[17] "The point is that from the moment one possesses that discernment—the knowledge of good and evil—one also possesses the power to justify oneself. It is because man has become the master for declaring good and evil that at the same time and by the same action he claims to give himself his own justification. Man's thirst for justification rests on his capacity to settle the good for himself. But just as this thirst for justification is nothing other than the desire to flee the judgment of God, so also the settling of the good by man is nothing other than his refusal to be in communion with God.....he can justify himself by invoking the good, by invoking the law... This is also why only the man who acknowledges that he is incapable of that knowledge can find grace with God.[18]

Besides recapitulating Luther's argument from Romans that justifying self and justifying God are mutually exclusive events and actions, this rigorously logical meditation upon the scriptural narrative is centered around "the knowledge of the good" and the impossibility of our knowing it apart from the living word of God coming to us in each new situation. Any effort to discern God's will by using approximation (to the Ten Commandments, say) is an effort of casuistry to place God's will in the past

14. Ellul, *To Will and To Do*, 6-7.
15. Ellul, *To Will and To Do*, 12.
16. Ellul, *To Will and To Do*, 13.
17. Ellul, *To Will and To Do*, 16-17.
18. Ellul, *To Will and To Do*, 19.

so that we can be in control of the discernment. In fact, any effort, whatsoever, to discern "the good" apart from receiving it from God in a living relationship and in a living conversation is the original sin. Instead, a Christian conscience acknowledges and experiences our helplessness and that we are sinners prior to anything else, meaning that the truth is simply not in us. That is why Luther says that we are related to God on the basis of our sin. That is why our justification and our righteousness must be a "passive righteousness", a righteousness which is counted to us, external and alien to us, complete, and not to do.

Jaques Ellul, the Calvinist, and Paul Tillich, the Lutheran, find congruence in their struggle against human morality, which always takes the form of casuistry, and in their struggle to articulate an alternative. Paul Tillich calls his alternative the "transmoral conscience."

The Historical Development of the Term

Moving now from scripture to historical development, Scholasticism employed the term *synteresis* to describe "a perfection of our reason that leads us toward the recognition of the good. It has immediate and infallible evidence, being a spark of the divine light in us . . . .The basic principles given by *synteresis* are: 1) The good must be done; the evil must be avoided. 2) Every being must live according to nature. 3) Every being strives toward happiness . . . Man has an infallible knowledge of the moral principles, the natural law, through *synteresis*; but he has a conscience that is able to fall into error in every concrete decision. In order to prevent dangerous errors, the authorities of the church give advice to the Christian . . . The Jesuits removed *synteresis*, and with it any direct contact between God and man, replacing it by the adviser . . . Heteronomy and probabilism destroyed the autonomous, self-assured conscience. [19]

Thomas Muentzer, Luther's foe in this matter, claimed the same "light in the soul" resided within each person. "In this way conscience became a source of religious insight and not simply a judge of moral actions."[20] Since this inward light could hardly be distinguished from practical reason, it gave each one the freedom to follow one's own autonomous reason in both ethics and religion. "The 'religion of conscience' and the consequent idea of tolerance are not a result of the Reformation, but of sectarian spiritualism and mysticism.

---

19. Tillich, *Transmoral Conscience*, 71.
20. Tilllich, *Transmoral Conscience*, 72.

Enlightenment philosophers Hume and Adam Smith define conscience in typically human centered fashion by making it mere sympathy with the other. When we identify ourselves with the other and take his approval of disapproval of our action as our own judgment, we presuppose a hidden harmony between all people. In contrast to this rather amorphous conception, Kant "wanted to maintain the unconditional character of the moral demand against all emotional relativism, fear or pleasure motives, as well as against divine and human authorities. But in so doing he is driven to complete formalism. Conscience is the consciousness of the 'categorical imperative' but not the consciousness of a special content of this imperative. 'Conscience is a consciousness which itself is a duty.'"[21] Ritchl seeks to provide that content by using the Lutheran doctrine of vocation while citing special historical time and space. Hegel seeks to find rational contents for the conscience by distinguishing between the formal and the true conscience. "About the first he says, 'Conscience is the infinite formal certainty of oneself—it expresses the absolute right of the subjective self-consciousness—namely, to know within and out of itself what law and duty are, and to acknowledge nothing except what it knows in this way as the good.' But this subjectivity is fallible and may turn into error and guilt. Therefore, it needs content in order to become the true conscience. This content is the reality of family, society and state."[22] And so on until the present day, which is still grappling with the insoluble question of whether an ethic of definable norms for the conscience is even possible. Or to put the question more pointedly, can the problem of conscience be answered at all in moral terms?

Here is Tillich's contribution: "A conscience may be called 'transmoral' if it judges not in obedience to a moral law, but according to its *participation in a reality* that transcends the sphere of moral commands. A transmoral conscience does not deny the moral realm, but is driven beyond it by the unbearable tensions of the sphere of law."[23] (my italics)

But what is this "reality that transcends the sphere of moral commands"? Traditional moral and ethical thinking begins and proceeds almost solely in its consideration of the human deed or act. The Word of God will have none of this. In scripture the consideration of one's being always precedes one's act. As Jesus says in the Sermon on the Mount, Matthew 6, "First make the tree good, and then it will bear good fruit." To repeat, in scripture man's being not only always precedes doing, but absolutely controls all resulting actions or deeds. My Father compared this requirement for a new

---

21. Tilllich, *Transmoral Conscience*, 74.
22. Tilllich, *Transmoral Conscience*, 75.
23. Tilllich, *Transmoral Conscience*, 77.

being to precede absolutely any discussion of action in the "new man" as analogous to a chicken and a duck being led to the edge of a very large body of water. When the command is heard, "Swim!", the chicken hears it as death, while the duck hears it as something it both desires and does naturally. Being absolutely precedes doing!

And so, in order to escape the unbearable tensions of the Law in a fallen world, a new reality, a new *being* must be created, and this new man must be raised from the dead, *ex nihilo*. God needs to change our very ontological definition. This involves both a continuing death of the "old man" and a resurrection of a new person completely unlike the old. The "appeal to God for a clear conscience" that we find in I Peter 3:21 is nothing other than the fact that the conscience of this new person appeals to an alien righteousness which is located not in us, but in Christ. The conscience of a Christian, as well as his or her complete definition as a new person, come from being now incorporated into Christ. Paul, in his long dissertation on the same subject in Romans 6, is emphatic that this is so. So the conflict between faith and unbelief has, from the very beginning, centered upon two completely conflicting definitions of what is *real*, that is, upon the fundamental new ontological definition of "man".

The competing, controlling thought worlds between faith and unbelief come to focus in the world's rejecting as utter nonsense the Christian claim that the venue of our righteousness is located completely exterior to ourselves. The belief in the location of our righteousness residing completely in Christ—a non-demonstrable yet most basic reality concerning our selves— was gradually lost during the middle ages. As evidence, in Thomas Aquinas' theology, the theological virtues of faith, hope, and love are distinguished at least in this: that faith and hope imply a separation from their object (God), while, in contrast to the other two virtues, love unites us to God with the aim of perfecting our nature until *our nature* becomes supernatural. The clear difference between this and Reformation theology rediscovered "as the faith once handed to the saints", is that Luther refuses to talk of such thing as justification happening *within* the believer or of any perfecting of our nature until it becomes supernatural. The justifying verdict from God "can take place in a way appropriate to God and faith through the Word alone. In this way, the basis of salvation remains strictly *outside* the person, as a promise which is believed. Indeed, man himself is drawn out of himself towards the word of Christ. The word must guarantee that faith is *extra nos*;

this is essential if what is said of God is to be certain."[24] Luther says: "Our theology is certain, for it places us outside ourselves."[25]

And so to have the "transmoral conscience" is to experience that a new location for my righteousness is constitutive for any possible affirmative verdict over my life. This location has to be external to the self, in Christ, and separate from all the self's perceptions, feelings, or senses. Moreover, this is an event which only comes by hearing, ever anew, the proclamation of the Gospel. It is an experience which must be believed because there is no other warrant for it other than hearing God's Word that it is so. Faith literally walks in darkness. We hear that we are literally in Christ, that is, inside Christ, incorporated into Christ, into His literal body—and this new *location* constitutes our salvation. But, again, all of the five senses upon which we rely for every other fact of life are helpless to confirm that this is so. Moreover, faith is required because our new verdict has to be "counted to us" by reason of the fact that it does not reside in us, nor is it ours, but is external to us and resides in another. Again, faith is required, because all the evidence of conscience, via which we perceive and feel our sin, cries out against what faith is asserting as the new affirmative verdict that we have from God through Christ. The contest is on over which "voice" to believe—our conscience or the Word of God. To repeat the citation: I John 3:20 is dealing with this anguish of all Christian consciences when he says that "we can reassure our hearts before him whenever our hearts condemn us, for God is greater than our hearts."

Luther's sole aim is "to locate what is said of God at the point where a universal event in the strictest sense takes place, and God and the world, and God and Satan, struggle with one another like two riders struggling to possess their mount. Thus the concentration on the conscience is a concentration upon the process in which the most powerful and most strictly opposed powers that exist are at work, a process which, precisely because it is centered upon the hidden heart of man, gives rise to the most powerful consequences in his outward and visible life."[26] And that is why Luther will not have anything to do with the ice-cold, frigid way Erasmus speaks of God. When it comes to conscience, and our struggles against our own conscience's continuing accusation, God's action to vindicate us must be spoken of decisively or not at all. This is not a time for cool speculation, nor is it a time for philosophical abstractions regarding essences and persona. This is a time for the "here and now" proclamation of God's deliverance.

24. Ebeling, *Luther: An Introduction to His Thought*, 260.
25. WA 40, I; 589 , 8 (1531).
26. Ebeling, *Luther: An Introduction to His Thought*, 262.

For the same reason it is necessary "that whenever anything is said about God, it must be made fully evident that it is *God* who is being discussed. But if God is to be spoken of at all, then it is necessary for God's sake to rely on God alone, on Christ alone, on the scripture alone, on the cross alone and on faith alone; that is, one must exclude everything which prevents God from being God, and which gives an opportunity of speaking of theological matters in an un-theological or pseudo-theological way."[27]

The Word Alone

So how can faith come about? How is the new person resurrected? Or, to ask the same question in still another way, how can one be assured in one's conscience that one has been chosen by God in love, and that "He who began the good work in us will complete it at the day of Christ." (Phil 1:6) Paul answers: "Faith comes by hearing." (Romans 10) Luther agrees: "Through the word alone."

This is not just any word. This resurrection-giving word can only be the sole word which does what is says—the living active Word "pouring forth from the mouth of God" (Matt. 4:4) The content of this word of proclamation always relates to the cross of Jesus Christ where the sins of the world were laid to rest. This word is always characterized by giving the actual gift of absolution through the announcing the forgiveness of sins. Hearing this proclamation is our only our warrant for believing that the incredible news is meant for us. To the objection, "Is not the Word too little?" one simply says, "If it is God's Word, it will not return void but will accomplish that for which God sent it." (Isaiah 55) After all, God's Word is never just a symbol. It is a living active verdict, sent for the singular purpose of creating faith, when and where God pleases.

This finally brings up the preacher's task. Since the conscience of the believer is always under attack in this passing age, and since there is no solution to this anguish for a Christian other than being delivered from this accusation by hearing God's Word ever anew (for example, "Besides me, there is no Savior!" (Isaiah 43:3 and Hosea 13:4), the preacher sent by God has the most vital task of creating the event of the coming of God's kingdom into this world. Yes, she or he is sent to proclaim God's Law to *kill* each fond human hope of relying on personal righteousness and so to create an utter end of hope in ourselves. That always first. The critical distinction between God's two words of Law and Gospel needs to be maintained. Yet God's promise always is primary, even though it arrives second in the order of things. Part

---

27. Ebeling, *Luther: An Introduction to His Thought*, 146.

of the goodness of the Gospel is its defining characteristic as "the last word." In faithfully proclaiming these two words of God in their proper order, the preacher creates, once again God's miracle—the death of the old person and resurrection of the new person. Both events happen in the conscience of the hearer. In this way, the preacher is sent to decisively engage each Christian hearer under God's Word, and to equip them with the promise of Jesus Christ. He or she is sent so that each Christian can hear, yet again, that the verdict of God's love for them in Christ supersedes and has overcome all accusations of conscience to the contrary. This is why preaching is not a teaching hour, nor a speculative hour, nor a "three points and a poem hour." Preaching is mortal conflict, where the most strictly opposed forces in the universe contend. It flows from the preceding event of personal engagement and confrontation under the personal coming of the Word to the preacher. And so in preaching, the preacher testifies. He or she bears witness. The word preached flows from and through that same prior personal engagement and confrontation in the delivery of the proclamation.

The good news proclaimed is the on-going prosecution of God's election, where we hear him say anew, "I have chosen you in love, through Jesus Christ. (Ephesians 1) It is God's Word against the accusation of the devil, against the accusation of the world, and against the accusation of our own conscience. The preacher, through proclamation, *gets to create the very coming of the kingdom of God*, to produce the victory that is on the side of God, and to extend what was won for us at Jesus' cross. That proclamation, alone, is both the coming *and* the victory of the kingdom of God. That proclamation, alone, produces the resurrection which Luther called the established conscience. That proclamation creates the new person, the "transmoral conscience", confident in the righteousness of another, external to themselves. That proclamation, itself, *is* the coming of the kingdom, here on earth—the very kingdom for which we pray in the Lord's Prayer.

CHAPTER NINE

Toward a "Proper Confidence"

"I love to tell the story, because I *know* 'tis true"

NUMBERLESS PASTORAL INTERVIEWS (INCLUDING my first one) have included the question: "Do you, pastor, believe that Jonah was actually swallowed by a fish?" by which question such committees hope to establish one's conservative credentials. In entering the long theological fray concerning whether or not the book of Jonah is based in history or is merely a moral and religious tale designed to teach certain ideas to the Jewish people, thus making it a work of imagination and a spiritual satire, one enters the arena of conflict over the historicity of *every* biblical narrative and the relation of this historicity to the Christian faith. In this sense, such interview committees have a valid concern.

Jacques Ellul in his book, "The Judgment of Jonah" does not avoid the question and begins with an interesting distinction with which Martin Luther would agree. "The prophet is characterized, not by *ideas*, but by the fact that God's word is addressed to him and is to be conveyed by him. The content of this word of God may vary according to situation and the divine decision without affecting faith. Conversely, saying the same things as a divine revelation is not *ipso facto* a word of God. The Jews do not have a rational view of prophecy but a view according to faith. The important thing in recognizing prophecy is to know *from whom the word comes,* not what it contains."[1] (my italics) He goes on to say, "One must take the book of Jonah for what it is: a prophetic book. A commentary must respect this character and indeed takes it as its center. Hence one is not to interpret the text in a moral sense . . . It is by relating the specific revelations of the book to its central revelation that we ourselves shall try to understand it."[2]

A distinction is thus made here between abstracting the content of a prophecy so as to discern "the moral of the story", and, in place of that,

1. Ellul, *Judgment of Jonah*, 14.
2. Ellul, *Judgment of Jonah*, 18.

hearing the address of that prophecy as a living, unique in history, one-time gracious confrontation by God's address *to you*. The present tense preamble of all of the prophets is critical: "Thus *says* the Lord!" Though this exact phrase does not appear in Jonah, the Jewish decision to treat it as a prophetic book in their canon directly implies that they heard its message with that preamble assumed. By "prophetic" the Jews do not, as Christians do, require it to refer to the messiah (which we now know that it does), but rather they require it to refer to God's dealings narrowly to them, the chosen ones. Every Old Testament prophet stakes his very continuing survival upon the careful, literal verbal report that follows. The prophet "bears witness". His word is a "testimony" (to use popular evangelical parlance) of a precise event that has happened to him, something he has heard which relates directly to the here-and-now situation of the people.

All the above raises the urgent question: how is current "preaching" something less or different than "prophecy"? When did preaching become reduced to a teaching hour to elucidate the "timeless truths" of the story or the "moral of the story"—that is to say, limiting exposition or proclamation to the "content"?

To say the same thing in a simpler way, one must make the distinction between "the text", as the biblical critics call it, and "what the text did to you," the hearer/reader of the text. God speaks through the "text" to create an encounter. Yes, it is necessary to use every critical tool at one's disposal to secure the most definitive literal text possible, including making translation decisions where there are textual discrepancies, and including using as your companions of faith the best research commentaries can provide. Yet that remains only the first step in the process. Now, one who is called to be a preacher needs to do some honest reflecting on how God has used this process to personally speak something definitive. In turn this requires the preacher to reflect on *what* this process has newly carved upon his or her mind, and to bear witness to that as the controlling theme in proclaiming the Word, now newly made flesh.

"Bible interpretation could have been spared the agony over demythologizing and related methodologies if it had not succumbed to the idea of the univocal equivalence between the biblical text and the reality to which it referred. What eventuated was a literalist and fundamentalist Biblicism, with calamitous results."[3]

A relative newcomer to biblical criticism is called reader-response criticism. "*Mark and Method: New Approaches in Biblical Studies*" by Anderson and Moore, and "*Let the Reader Understand*" by Robert Fowler

---

3. Harrisville, *Jesus and Man's Hope*, vol 2:204.

are two good examples of this newer biblical critical research. These researchers have demonstrated that much of what is passed off as "objective" biblical criticism is really an unconscious report of what the text has done to the critic.

Martin Luther was at least making the same distinction between biblical content and living address, as well as between text and experience with the text, which both Ellul and reader-response critics make, when he held up a Bible during one of his sermons declaring, "This is not the Word of God. Jesus is the Word of God. This is the manger that holds him." Luther reinforces the same distinction in his prefaces to the books of the Bible by decrying the fact that the Gospel had to be written down at all, thus removing it one step from its original intention of being a living, present tense, I-you, oral address.

Finally, Jesus, himself in Matthew 22:23ff clearly makes the same point. The Sadducees mockingly ask Jesus to prove that resurrection even exists, requiring Jesus to limit the basis of his response to the core witness to Israel, the only definitive authority acknowledged by the Sadducees, themselves— the first five books of the Law. They begin, "*Moses* said." Jesus corrects them by responding, in verse 31, "Have you not read what *God is saying to you*." Jesus asserts three critical things here regarding proper biblical hermeneutics or interpretation in this single sentence:

- First, he corrects their biblical interpretive method by asserting that, more fundamentally, *God* says, not Moses. The Bible always and everywhere has two authors. Behind each prophet's declaration is the Speaker who gave that Word.
- Second, Jesus says, "God *is saying.*" The Greek is clearly present tense— *legontos*. God's Word is a living present tense phenomenon, not some canned "content" or "text" subject to human authority.
- Third, *to you*. God is dealing with them right now.

When Jesus completes his argument, the rest of what he says is just as sobering a corrective for modern biblical interpreters. Jesus hangs his proof of the entire doctrine of resurrection—the most central doctrine of the Bible—upon a single word! And, more narrowly, upon the *tense* of that one word!! It is the Name of God—I AM. The one scriptural word for Jesus' entire proof of the entire doctrine of the resurrection is AM. The logic is: God never says, "I *was* the God of Abraham." God says, "I AM the God of Abraham." Ergo, Abraham still lives! Jesus takes every word of God so seriously that he is able to assert with utter confidence the central truth of scriptural revelation which the Sadducees cannot find anywhere in "the text." He builds faith not only upon a single word, but upon the tense of that single word!

Fighting the Danger of "Subjectivism"

The attempt to evade the danger of hopeless subjectivism in preaching, which this view seems to invite, has always consisted of elevating the "objective" over the "subjective" as the more secure warrant for any claim to the reliability or truthfulness asserted in proclamation. This Enlightenment axiomatic requirement proceeds from its deep distrust of any talk of "the Spirit". Since man must be the measure of all things, (say the Enlightenment philosophers) and since there seemed to be such a clear presenting necessity of being delivered from the shackles of the benighted superstition brought upon Europe by the church—it was necessary, above all, be "objective." But this view is unable even to consider a hermeneutic that the scripture has two authors! Objectivity, in turn, requires that a repeatable event occur, similar to those which serve for provable scientific events, in which all the variables are accounted for and all the variables are subject to human management. (In addition, Enlightenment axiom states that such events must always be limited to what has been experienced by humans and cannot transgress into the area of "the miraculous"). But in proclamation, that requires some constant such as the "moral of the story", or "establishing the text" with some repeatable, verifiable "content," which would deliver it from the hands of "subjectivism" or talk of the "Spirit." Objectivity requires human provenance and mastery of the Word. And this appears to be the foundation for what now passes for the large majority of "biblical criticism" as well as for what is now commonly called "preaching." Ironically, Fundamentalism falls into the very same trap as the historical critics it so despises by claiming that the authority of the Word resides or inheres in its infallibility, a claim nowhere made in scripture, and a fallacy rooted in the same failure to make the distinction between the Word of God as "content" and the Word of God as "spoken encounter." To summarize: *The authority of scripture resides in the simple fact that God speaks it, and nowhere else.*

Soren Kierkegaard was the first to mount a sustained argument against "objective" truth as the sole reliable or possible path to what he called "eternal" truth. In his renewed emphasis upon the importance of the subjective in philosophical inquiry, he has been called the "father of existentialism." His argument does not offer systematic syllogisms, and is characteristically diffuse, devious and difficult to follow, yet it may be formulated in the following way:

1. There are two opposing ways to approach the truth: the objective and the subjective ways.
2. The objective ways fails.
3. Hence the only appropriate way is the subjective way.
4. Christianity is the subjective way of life that meets all conditions for the highest subjectivity.
5. Hence Christianity is the appropriate way to teach/reach the truth.[4]

For him, knowledge is good, but action is the goal. From reading Hamann Kierkegaard concluded that only the anti-speculative approach does justice to the subjective aspect of man's nature. But that meant that reason alone was inadequate for solving the problems of theological matters. He became convinced that bare fact of believing the Christian witness could only be the result of a miracle. "The Christian religion not only was at first attended with miracles, but even at this day cannot be believed by any reasonable person without one. Mere reason is insufficient to convince us of its veracity. And whoever is moved by *faith* to assent to it is conscious of a continued miracle in his own person which subverts all the principles of his understanding and gives him a determination to believe what is most contrary to custom and experience."[5] (his italics) Miracle stands in disjunctive relation to human reason and unexpectedly breaks into the lives of men. "Wonder", not "reason", is the proper response to the wonderful.[6]

The required turn to subjectivity is rooted in the very witness or evidence of two undeniable realities from the existence of every person. They are: that a) our soul and body are related but opposing forces which we are unable to resolve into a unity, resulting inevitably in despair; and b) since we are aware that this is so, we must have been constituted by a superior power, and constituted to be in relation to Him. Therefore, "objective" or disinterested inquiry in this case, is not only inappropriate, but impossible. The famous tortured, yet foundational passage from "Sickness Unto Death" is worth quoting at length here to demonstrate both points.

(Do not despair when you finish this quote with your head spinning. Just consider the herculean mental process it took to write it!)

> A human being is spirit. But what is spirit? Spirit is the self. But what is the self? The self is a relation that relates itself to itself or the relation's relating itself to itself in the relation; the self is not

---

4. Pojman, *Logic of Subjectivity*, p. xi.
5. Kierkegaard, "Papers" I A 100.
6. Pojman, *Logic of Subjectivity*, 8.

> the relation but is the relation's relating itself to itself. A human being is a synthesis of the infinite and the finite, of the temporal and the eternal, of freedom and necessity, in short, a synthesis. A synthesis is a relation between two. Considered in this way, a human being is still not a self.
>
> In the relation between two, the relation is the third as a negative unity, and the two relate to the relation and in the relation to the relation; thus under the qualification of the psychical the relation between the psychical and the physical is a relation. If, however, the relation relates itself to itself, this relation is the positive third, and this is the self. Such a relation that relates itself to itself, a self, must either have been established by itself or by another. If the relation that relates itself to itself has been established by another, then the relation is indeed the third, but this relation, the third, is yet again a relation and relates itself to that which establishes the entire relation.
>
> The human self is such a derived, established relation, a relation that relates itself to itself and in relating itself to itself relates itself to another. This is why there can be two forms of despair in the strict sense. If a human self had itself established itself, then there could be only one form: not to will to be oneself, to will to do away with oneself, but there could not be the form: in despair to will to be oneself. This second formulation is specifically the expression for the complete dependence of the relation (of the self), the expression for the inability of the self to arrive at or to be in equilibrium and rest by itself, but only, in relating itself to itself, by relating itself to that which has established the entire relation ... The misrelation of despair is not a simple misrelation but a misrelation in a relation that relates itself to itself and has been established by another, so that the misrelation in that relation which is for itself also reflects itself infinitely in the relation to the power that established it.
>
> The formula that describes the state of the self when despair is completely rooted out is this: in relating itself to itself and in willing to be itself, the self rests transparently in the power that established it.[7]

Objectivity, which denies the very power that created it, is an imaginary composite of unemotionality, disinterested evaluation, neutrality, and impartial judgment, where the uninvolvement of the subject is paramount. The individual's deepest aspirations are set aside as secondary. It is not necessarily a bad thing in its proper place. But in ethical-religious inquiry, mere

---

7. Kierkegaard. *Sickness Unto Death*, 13f.

objectivity it is both poisonous and obscuring. All existential reflection requires the total involvement of the thinking individual. Anglican Cardinal John Henry Newman (1801-1890) and leader of the Oxford Movement, posed the question which illuminates the critical distinction between subjective and objective 'knowing'. It is apropos here. He asked, "Why is that people will die for a dogma who won't stir for a conclusion?"

But if the validity, in their respective spheres, of two kinds of knowing, objective and subjective, is granted, what remains is to discuss whether inquiry, on a subjective basis, is an adequate approach to epistemology (the theory of knowing) in general. Here Kierkegaard suggests the need for 1) an "adequacy to subject principle" and 2) an "adequacy to object principle". In the first instance what is acknowledged is that "all knowing is perspectival, theory laden, from a particular point of view. It follows that everyone knows what he knows in a unique way and that every instance of coming to know something involves personal interpretation, and that every personally interpreted and appropriated bit of knowledge involves one in a new choice, a personal decision with regard to how one will accept, then use the putative knowledge."[8] Thus, "Adequacy to Subject Principle" requires that whatever is known must be known in a way peculiar to the knower. "Adequacy to Object Principle," by contrast, focuses on the nature of what is known. What is known must be known in a mode appropriate to the thing known. Knowing "that" requires knowing "how", drawing attention to the objective structures in reality. Only the like is understood by the like.

Using this distinction, Kierkegaard sought to protect the concept of subjective inquiry from the accusations of either "subjective madness" or "nonsense." In the case of subjective madness, a subject treats a finite object, which has nothing to do with the spiritual development of the self, as having infinite importance. This is a case of misrelation, according to the "Adequacy to Object Principle." "Nonsense" is similar. It is a misfit of intensity. Minute subjectivity is appropriate for things of minute importance. Infinite subjectivity is appropriate for the proper relationship to God. Here, absolute passion is appropriate.

And so, with Kierkegaard, one must reckon with the rare, uncommon claim that "the truth" inheres or resides in "subjectivity" rather than in "objectivity". The argument here is that the Truth and the Word has chosen to reside in I-you intercourse, and not in abstracts. The Truth and the Word reside in testimony. Its form is "bearing witness" and "testifying". It is present tense. It is personal encounter. Proclamation is created by, and witnesses to, previous encounter.

---

8. Pojman, *Logic of Subjectivity*, 61.

Gerhard Ebeling, in his book "*The Truth of the Gospel*", also argues, this time hermeneutically, that the truth resides in subjectivity, by focusing upon Paul's use of the word *eidotes* (because we know) in Paul's densely packed thesis statement in Galatians 2:16. All biblical interpreters agree that the term "to know" as used biblically in the Old Testament connotes major subjective reference. But when Paul says, "We who know that a man is not justified by works of the law but through the faithfulness of Jesus Christ", Ebeling asserts that Paul is precluding all possibility of deriving a saving knowledge of Christ simply by study of scripture. In 2 Corinthians 3:14 Paul speaks of a veil that still lies over the eyes of those reading the Old Testament—a veil that is only removed through Christ. "Something must therefore have taken place. Faith must have come (Gal. 3:23, 25), Jesus Christ must have appeared (Gal. 4:4-5), the Spirit must have been sent (Gal. 4:6), that people's eyes might be opened to this faith and that it might also be found in Scripture . . . This refers to a knowledge that cannot possibly be achieved through study of the Scriptures alone. It is based rather on an oral message that came to these Jews and changed them. And this oral message, in turn, grew out of *an event* that had taken place not long before. Now the source of this knowledge . . . is not learned by rote but entered into through personal experience, which is itself made possible only by the message of faith . . . Because this knowledge is not learned but lived, it has enormous motivating power."[9] (Ebeling makes exactly the same point regarding the importance of the subjective nature of truth, this time by carefully noting how Paul uses the word *kalon* (call). "Paul's concern is to make explicit *the decisive criterion. He does this by appealing not to principles or ideas, but to an event, to what the Galatians have experienced . . . by deserting this God you are deserting yourselves, you are deserting what you have become through the call of God, your are deserting what you have been called to by this call. By the appeal to experience, the "no" to God is made a self-contradictory denial of the Galatians themselves.*"[10] (my italics)

Humility before the Word

God will not abide human claims to mastery of certain things which he reserves for himself. He alone determines how and when the Kingdom comes. We are not "kingdom builders." That he has removed from human hands. Nor will God have humans claim mastery or control over the Word. The Word will remain sovereign in spite of all human attempts to domesticate

9. Ebeling, *Truth of the Gospel*, 126.
10. Ebeling, *Truth of the Gospel*, 47.

it, to "objectify" it, or to master it by proper criticism or scientific inquiry. How else to understand God's threat in Amos 8:12 of a time when one will suffer "a famine of hearing the words of the Lord; they shall wander from sea to sea, and from north to east; they shall run to and fro, to seek the world of the LORD but they shall not find it"? God will not allow human control over his Word. His Word remains sovereign over us, despite all our attempts to domesticate, control, staple, fold and file it for future reference. And notice it is the "hearing of the Word" that shall be removed, not some written "content". God will remain sovereign over both his kingdom and the Word which creates it.

When Ellul says above that by including Jonah in their canon, the Jews did not proceed from a *rational view of knowledge* but from a view according to faith, one needs to give what constitutes a rational view of knowledge a little more detail. The Roman Catholic theologian Roman Guardini attacked the historical critical method's division of "form criticism" for its rationalistic concept of knowledge. For form critics, all data, whatever is source, essence or value are the same regarding their knowability. But Guardini counters with this observation: "The knowing organ(!) . . . is actuated before what is living other than before what is lifeless, before what is human-spiritual other than before what is biological, before what is personal other than before what is merely sensuous."[11] (my exclamation mark) What Guardini is doing here, without saying the word "Holy Spirit", is directly challenging the viability of the narrowness of such a rationalistic concept of knowledge, whose practitioners define it as residing completely in the province of human reason, while blithely ignoring what we know from personal encounter. To put the matter bluntly, one could ask, "Are some things unknowable apart from divine revelation and God's gracious proclamation to us? And is reason competent to overrule such revelation as it finds inconvenient to its presuppositions? " The answer seems self-evident! One could cite Kierkegaard's requirement of an "Appropriate to Subject Principle" here, as well.

C.S. Lewis ridiculed the same critics for

- not being able to read between the lines, while carefully adhering to the *History of Religion's School's* insistence that "appreciation for the Bible's truth must begin with a preliminary understanding that involves appreciation for the Bible's truth as contained in a 'process'",[12] asserting that holy salvation history is an evolving thing, and

---

11. Guardini, *Das Christusbild der paulinischen and johannesischen Schriften*, 7.
12. Harrisville, *Pandora's Box Opened*, 346.

- their claim that the "real purpose" of the text has now, at last, been discovered by moderns; and
- their claim that the miraculous simply does not occur; and
- for the fact that their "reconstruction of history" is completely unverifiable.[13]

Two quotes are germane to the discussion here. The first is from Adolph Schlatter of Tubingen. "For me, faith and criticism never divided into opposites, so that at one time I would have thought in a Bible-believing way, and at another critically. Rather, I thought in critical fashion because I believed in the Bible, and believed in it because I read it critically."[14] Yet I do not read this as a defense of the Historical Critical Method. I read it as a confession of a Christian describing the excitement which comes from the discoveries made by applying the best historical research to the biblical text. This very thing is what Christians are eager to do.

Roy Harrisville, in his newest book on biblical criticism, "Pandora's Box Opened", includes his summary confession regarding a proper approach to hermeneutics. "There is no understanding, no interpretation of the Bible apart from faith. Faith alone yields understanding, penetrates behind that poor child in the crib to the Savior of the world. This word will have the heart and soul, and if not, it will work despair. For in the last analysis the Bible is a self-effervescing source that does not take its credibility from anything or anyone. Its integrity is not derived; it is its own interpreter. On its own it yields understanding. On its own it gives the Spirit through whom it is understood. On its own it possess the quality of certainty that neither feeling nor experience can equal. What gives to it this great power, this effervescence, this independence and non-derivability is its witness to Jesus Christ, Lord of heaven and earth. He is its content and rules the method of its understanding."[15]

But if Harrisville's entire confession is axiomatic to the proper use of biblical criticism (which I am sure he means it to be), then that paragraph, alone, disqualifies the entire Historical Critical Method project, on its face. Because the Historical Critical Method demands, arrogantly, that reason be prior to faith, and at the most, that faith is irrelevant to its inquiry! But if faith alone yields understanding, one requires a hermeneutic less hostile to faith than the Historical Critical Method.

---

13. Harrisville, *Pandora's Box Opened*, 281.
14. Schlatter, *Ruckblick auf meine Lebensarbeit*, 83.
15. Harrisville, *Pandora's Box Opened*, 349-350.

Going more to the roots of the controversy here, one must enter into the discussion regarding the right relationship between reason and revelation. How one rightly comes "to know" respectively through each avenue of knowledge has been an unending source of controversy since the very beginning of the Christian faith. Already in the Gospel of John, from chapter 7 all the way through the end of chapter 9, the subject is "knowing". During the debate in question, each route to knowing has its own rival evidentiary claims presented, both of which profess sufficient warrant for proper certainty. In this extended three-chapter debate, the theological faculty at Jerusalem claims the sufficient power of reason alone, while Jesus consistently refers to the knowing that comes only by faith and revelation. But revelation does not preclude reason. They should work together. I understand this somewhat simplified characterization of the bitter controversy in these chapters as John's effort to shed light upon the unavoidable future controversy regarding the proper relationship between these two methods of knowing. And just so that one does not miss the point, John uses the verb "to know" an incredible 31 times in these chapters! And this does not include two instances of "to understand" nor the allusions to the critical fact always in question—Jesus identity—nor to the allusions to the Spirit, light, truth, and seeing. Completely unaccounted for (not to say denied) in the historical critical method is a new factor introduced by Jesus toward the end of this controversy—that there exists an agent who can obscure knowing. Jesus introduces him, for the first time in the Gospel of John, calling him the father of lies. Paul, in II Corinthians 4:4 calls him "the god of this world who has blinded the minds of unbelievers." This new factor, alone, requires something beyond and besides arrogant "reason" for any saving "knowing" to happen.

Again citing *"Pandora's Box Opened"*, Harrisville takes the irenic mediate position that the historical critical method, shorn of its arrogance, can be a useful tool of the serious biblical scholar. But his careful (even encyclopedic) argument provides all the fuel for a much less irenic conclusion, only some of which I list here. My argument is that far from being helpful, the historical critical method as presently employed in academia and in theology:

- originated among those intent on undermining its authority"[16]
- has obscured the distinctions among the ways we come to know, and has refused to recognize any knowledge apart from the rational;

---

16. Harrisville, *Pandora's Box Opened*, 348.

- has pitted reason against revelation, or at the least has reason insisting on its priority over revelation regarding any valid warrant for "scientific" knowledge;
- has never acknowledged the distinction between the "content" of the text and the experience which that "content has engendered" in you, the reader/hearer for fear of being "subjective" rather than maintaining a rigid "objectivity";
- refuses to acknowledge that there is any viable warrant or claim for the "truth" residing outside the "objective", all the while ridiculing "subjective" knowledge and avoiding any talk of the "Spirit";
- has not only crippled biblical proclamation, but has actually formally *prevented* it by denying the very bases upon which such valid proclamation vitally depends, such as the assertion that the Word of God is primarily encounter, even before it is "text", or that true preaching is "bearing witness" to this existential event;
- directly attacks the primary objective for which God sends his Word—the creation of certainty or proper Christian confidence—by forcing the proclaimer to begin any biblical criticism with the presupposition of *doubt or suspicion* when encountering the "text";
- refuses to engage in or allow any theological critical discussion that is not "scientific", that is, any discussion that does not begin with its own narrow and confining presuppositions regarding how "knowledge" happens.

Having listed the damages done to biblical interpretive effort by the "historical critical method," one can draw up how it may be more narrowly defined from that very list for the purposes of this argument. By "historical critical method" I mean:

- any biblical interpretive method that proceeds fundamentally from a hermeneutic of suspicion;
- Any biblical interpretive method that proceeds from the axiomatic assumption of the priority of reason in ascertaining the truth;
- Any biblical interpretive method that insists upon the interpreter's authority over the "text", rather than vice versa;
- Any biblical interpretive method that seeks as much as possible empirically demonstrable truth, thus relegating into lower categories all knowing which arrives via revelation, Spirit, or more subjective approaches to knowledge.

Proper biblical criticism, such as the hermeneutic of the theology of the cross, by contrast, invites classification of textual genres, prioritizing the authority of some parts of scripture over others, seeking to find the best translation, seeking to understand properly the original *"sitz-im-leben"* (situation for which it originally functioned), and so on. For example, proper biblical criticism takes the narrative in Acts 19 relating an instance of re-baptism, not as *doctrine* but as a *narrative* of an anomaly which existed in the early church. Doctrine regarding baptism is located in such places as Romans 6, Ephesians 4, and Titus 3, which define and understand themselves as doctrinal teaching. These are not narrative but are clearly written as teachings for the church. A second example of proper biblical criticism is Luther's peculiar method, which led him to assess the *words* of the gospel as more authoritative than the *narrative* of Jesus, thus preferring Romans and Ephesians and Galatians as even more essential than the more narrative Matthew, Mark, and Luke. Clearly, biblical criticism is both commanded by Jesus and is logically necessary given the wide diversity of content in scripture. However, it can be done wonderfully, completely and savingly, absent any claims from the "historical critical method."

Four Important Qualifications for the Preceding Argument

Full disclosure here requires that I confess that I have been grievously attacked by the practitioners of the "historical critical method" not only in college religion courses, but also in later seminary classes, where the disparity of power between student and teacher was used unfairly. Later, as a pastor, I heard that my church youth, brought up in faithful prairie congregations, had been subjected to the same withering criticism of their faith so patiently nurtured in catechism classes. In both cases, the faith that is always so vulnerable, was placed unnecessarily at risk. That is why I take to task the "historical critical method" so severely and categorically. But such vitriol, such vehemence requires that four qualifications to this criticism be clearly enumerated. They are:

- That lumping the "historical critical method" in with criticism of the Bible in general obscures rather than clarifies the description of good interpretive practice;

- That refusing to accept the validity of the "historical critical method" does not require jettisoning the valid, pressing concern for the *historicity* of biblical events;

- That the "tool" for biblical interpretation, which the "historical critical method" represents, is neither benign nor inert. Its required presuppositions rule out any possibility that its user is completely unaffected. The proposition that by its proper use, the user of the "historical critical method" will be so unaffected, that by his or her faith that they would be in any position to ostensibly shear this method of its inherent arrogance, becomes logically indefensible.

- And finally, that all theology which has its direct purpose bent toward proclamation, and thus toward the certainty of the Christian hearer, (a basic requirement of Reformation proclamation) far from being helped, is rather destroyed and rendered categorically impossible by this method.

Expanding each of these arguments, I begin with problematic categorizing of the "historical critical method" (as defined above) as merely one part of biblical criticism in general. Correlating the "historical critical method" with other valid methods of biblical criticism obscures the poisonous effects upon faith which the "historical critical method" uniquely engenders as compared with historical research not similarly constrained. No serious biblical scholar would disagree that the historical question of the biblical witness simply "will not down." Yet that serves neither as a logical excuse nor a defense of the "historical critical method." There are many ways to conduct more defensible historical research than, for example, by beginning with presuppositions requiring doubt or suspicion of the "text" even before one begins; or with presuppositions requiring belief that the complete warrant for the validity of all research is bestowed by some imagined objectivity; or with presuppositions that how one "knows" places reason as the controlling function over revelation (where revelation is even seriously considered). Too often, the way in which practitioners of the "historical critical method" proceed is analogous to the Roman emperor, Nero, who had his own mother disemboweled, so that he could behold the womb which bore him.

Rejecting the validity of the "historical critical method" does not require jettisoning biblical criticism altogether, nor does it demonstrate a cavalier or irresponsible attitude toward the historical question in biblical research. I will demonstrate, at length, an example of such alternative historical biblical research below.

Luther was not alone in rejecting theology done for any other purpose than for proclamation. Kierkegaard weighs in almost three centuries later with his work entitled "Concluding Unscientific Postscript", restating Luther's reason for such an apparently obstinate point of view. He writes, "When Christianity is viewed from the standpoint of its historical documentation, it becomes necessary to secure an entirely trustworthy account of what the Christian doctrine really is. If the inquirer were infinitely interested in behalf of his relationship to the doctrine he would at once despair; for nothing is more readily evident than that the greatest attainable certainty with respect to anything historical is merely an *approximation*. And an approximation, when viewed as the basis for an eternal happiness, is wholly inadequate since the incommensurability makes a result impossible."[17] (his italics) All practitioners of the "historical critical method" readily admit that its highest result can only be a high degree of probability. But mere "high probability" is centrally what is most terrifying to searchers for a foundation for faith or proper certainty. It is thus, by its very definition and structure, disqualified from being anything more than a preliminary to the preparation of proclamation.

An Additional Problem

An additional problem to a false hermeneutic is that the encounter created by proclamation always requires discernment in hearing. False preaching will always be rampant. Therefore, both the Christian preacher, as well as the hearer, are required to practice the primary charisma given to all God's children—the practice of discerning the spirits. This is required and not merely ancillary to the process of proclamation, because the evil spirit also has a word, and, as we have previously mentioned, he is always confusing the two words of God—the Law and the Gospel. To give two common examples: the Law is falsely made into an assignment to be achieved toward salvation, or is preached to create despair in the repentant; likewise, when Paul says that the Gospel is "the end of the Law" in Galatians, this phrase is falsely interpreted to mean a way of living that welcomes license, or excludes all talk of Christian progress, since Jesus has accomplished all that is necessary for justification.

When we say "the Christian's primary charisma" we are talking about two things at once: the use of reason in biblical criticism, and the recognition of the existence of revelation by the Holy Spirit through the "organ of knowing" (which for Luther is the conscience). Every Christian is called upon to be a biblical critic at every instance of the Word's encounter with us. Such criticism is authorized by Jesus himself, when he asks the biblical scholar, "*How* do you read?" Jesus approves of the scribe's hermeneutical method, again authorizing every Christian to have one. The issue is not whether

17. Kierkegaard, *Concluding Unscientific Postscript*, 25.

Christians should jettison reason or all biblical critical methods in dealing with revelation. The issue is whether the *historical critical* method, in its narrow definition, and with its insistent, non-negotiable presuppositions, can ever serve to help a Christian rightly hear the Word of Truth.

Additionally, such requirement of discernment, whenever proclamation is heard, recognizes the reality and power of the evil spirit whose overriding purpose in all his activities is to split us from the Word of God. It has always been thus. The prophets in their Old Testament proclamation always had to work against the testimony of false prophets. Once again, to belabor the obvious, the "historical critical method" would regard these three paragraphs as mere superstition, benighted, and anti-rational.

An Example of Credible Historical Research

I preface this section with a quote from Gotthold Ephraim Lessing (1729-1781) simply because he asserts that credible historical research regarding biblical witness is categorically impossible. Lessing, just like G.W. Leibniz before him, distinguished between the contingent truths of history and the necessary truths of reason and wrote: Since "no historical truth can be demonstrated, then nothing can be demonstrated by means of historical truths." That is, "the accidental truths of history can never become the proof of necessary truths of reason." Someone might object that miracles like the resurrection of Jesus from the dead, are "more than historically certain," because these things are told to us by "inspired historians who cannot make a mistake." But Lessing counters that whether or not we have inspired historians is itself a historical claim, and only as certain as history allows. *This, then, "is the ugly broad ditch which I cannot get across, however often and however earnestly I have tried to make the leap."* "Since the truth of these miracles has completely ceased to be demonstrable by miracles still happening now, since they are no more than reports of miracles, I deny that they should bind me in the least to a faith in the other teachings of Christ."[18] As I understand Kierkegaard's preceding argument, he would respond, "I agree with Lessing's narrow point. Yet, objective reflection (reason together with its "truths") is inappropriate to this object and cannot be expected to make the crossing. A leap of faith is required to traverse this yawning chasm, this ditch." N.T. Wright disagrees with both of them. He seeks to demonstrate that the provenance of strict historical research, unaided by faith, can accomplish more than a little.

---

18. Lessing, *Lessing's Theological Writings*, 51-55.

N. T. Wright, in his massive study entitled "The Resurrection of the Son of God", makes the following arguments to assert what responsible historical research can contribute, regarding actuality of resurrection of Jesus. He begins by clarifying what is meant by "historical", listing five varying uses of the word in modern research. [19]

1. An event—something which happened, whether or not we can know or prove that it happened. The death of the last pterodactyl is in that sense a historical event.

2. A significant event—a "historic event" which carried momentous consequences. Bultmann famously uses the adjective *geschichtlich* to convey this sense, over against *historisch*. (sense one)

3. A provable event—something we can demonstrate as actual on the analogy of mathematics or the so-called hard sciences.

4. Historical as "a written-about-event-in-the-past"—It has a literary record.

5. A combination of the third and fourth—a written-about-event which can be demonstrated as valid only *within the post-Enlightenment worldview*. This is what people have often in mind when they have rejected 'the historical Jesus.'

Confusion among these senses has bedeviled the debate concerning the resurrection. For example, is it only the first, or the second, or only the fourth, and so on? Willi Marxsen in particular denies that we have any access, as historians, to the resurrection itself.[20] "Marxen recognizes that nobody, at least so far as we know wrote about the actual transition of Jesus from death to life (sense 4), deduces from this that nothing can be proved about the event (sense 3), and constantly writes as if this means that we as 'modern historians can say nothing about it (sense 5). Positivists hold roughly the same position, requiring direct access before calling anything "historical". But this is especially inappropriate in historiography.[21] "Ernst Troeltch argues that we can only speak or write, as historians, about things which have some analogy in our own experience; resurrections do not occur in our experience; therefore we cannot, as historians, speak of the resurrection."[22] Pannenberg suggests that the ultimate verification of the resurrection of Jesus Christ (sense 3) will eventually be provided through

---

19. Wright, *Resurrection of the Son of God*, 12-13.
20. Wright, *Resurrection of the Son of God*, 15.
21. Wright, *Resurrection of the Son of God*, 15.
22. Wright, *Resurrection of the Son of God*, 16.

the final resurrection of those in Christ, which will constitute the required analogy.[23] The first of two related "Road Closed" signs to historical research regarding the resurrection are the post-Bultmannian efforts to subject the resurrection stories to form-critical analysis using theories themselves based upon elaborate guesswork.[24] "The second way of explaining away the evidence, notable especially in the work of Crossan, is to apply to the texts a ruthless hermeneutic of suspicion."[25]

A second set of arguments begin not by asserting that such research can't be done, but that it shouldn't be done. Hans Frei, among others, argues "that we should not try to investigate the resurrection historically because the resurrection is itself the ground of a Christian epistemology. [26] But doesn't this beg the question? There is no reason in principle why the question, of what precisely happened at Easter, cannot be raised by any historian of any persuasion. N.T. Wright argues that "Paul's thought moved *from* his Jewish perception of 'the plight' *to* the solution offered in Christ *and thence to a fresh analysis of the problem* . . . In the same way, I suggest, historical knowledge about the resurrection, is of a sort that can be discussed without presupposing Christian faith.[27] (his italics) Moule writes, "A Gospel which cares only for the apostolic proclamation and denies that it either can or should be tested for its historical antecedents, is really on a thinly veiled Gnosticism or Docetism and, however much it may continue to move by a borrowed momentum, will prove ultimately to be no Gospel."[28]

N.T. Wright then arrives at the point of his argument after almost seven hundred tortuous pages of engaging every possible alternative research. He concludes that the two things which emerge, which must be regarded as historically secure when we talk about the first Easter, are these: *the emptiness of the tomb, and the meetings with the risen Jesus.*[29] He lists seven reasons for this:

- The world of second-Temple Judaism supplies the concept of resurrection, but the striking and consistent Christian mutations within Jewish resurrection belief rule out any possibility that the belief could have generated spontaneously from within its Jewish context.

---

23. Wright, *Resurrection of the Son of God*, 17.
24. Wright, *Resurrection of the Son of God*, 18.
25. Wright, *Resurrection of the Son of God*, 19.
26. Wright, *Resurrection of the Son of God*, 21.
27. Wright, *Resurrection of the Son of God*, 22.
28. Moule, *Phenomenon of the New Testament* vol 1:80f.
29. Wright, *Resurrection of the Son of God*, 686.

- Neither the empty tomb by itself, however, nor the appearances by themselves, could have generated the early Christian belief. The empty tomb alone would be a puzzle and a tragedy. Sightings of an alive Jesus, by themselves, would have been classified as visions or hallucinations.
- However, taken together, they would present a powerful reason for the emergence of the belief.
- The meaning of resurrection within second-Temple Judaism makes it impossible to conceive of this reshaped resurrection belief emerging without it being known that a body had disappeared, and the that person had been discovered to be thoroughly alive again. The other explanations sometimes offered for the emergence of the belief do not possess the same explanatory power.
- It is therefore historically highly probable that Jesus' tomb was indeed empty on the third day after his execution, and that the disciples did indeed encounter him truly alive and well.
- Finally, is there *any* alternative explanation that can be given for the powerful explosion of faith in the whole Mediterranean basin in the following century than these two combined phenomena?[30]

He continues his argument by distinguishing between sufficient conditions and necessary conditions to produce a valid conclusion. For instance, a *necessary* condition for the conclusion that a computer could run would be some source of electrical power. Something has to be the case for the conclusion to follow. A *sufficient* condition, however, is something that will, without fail, bring about the conclusion. Someone playing bagpipes out side one's bedroom window will surely prevent sleep. Thus it is a sufficient condition for the conclusion of sleeplessness. "The empty tomb and the appearances, we have seen, are, by themselves, insufficient to generate early Christian belief. Bring them together, however, and they form, in combination, a sufficient condition."[31] But asserting that together they also form a necessary condition involves proving a negative. This involves asking the question: Could anything else have produced the result of such faith?

Two major rival theories are propounded: cognitive dissonance, and resurrection existing only in kerygma and the experience of the hearer. Cognitive dissonance is the theory that when individuals or groups fail to come to terms with reality, they live instead in a fantasy which corresponds to their own deep longings. In this view the disciples wanted so badly to

---

30. Wright, *Resurrection of the Son of God*, 686-687.
31. Wright, *Resurrection of the Son of God*, 692.

believe in Jesus that instead of facing the fact of his death they claimed he was alive.[32] The flaws in this argument, based on a theory by Festinger, followed by Schillebeeckx, and propounded ad nauseam in countless college and seminary classrooms, are enormous and include the glaring problem that whatever it was that the early Christians were expecting, wanting, hoping and praying for, this was *not* what they said, after Easter, had happened.[33] Schillebeeckx's effort is to contrast himself from the reductionism of mainstream German Protestantism, as represented by Bultmann and Marxen. In Bultmann's view, Jesus has risen only 'in the kerygma' or 'in our experience as believers' while he himself lingers on 'in the realm of the dead.'[34] But neither of these are rival theories to the actual resurrection of Jesus are credible historical arguments to describe either a sufficient or a necessary condition for the power of the phenomena before us.

So, if historical research, by itself, can establish the two anchor points of the empty tomb and the appearances, without invoking any external a priori beliefs, the remaining questions for a pious Jew would not be

- *Who* (that would be YHWH),
- *Why* (that would be the creator)
- *Where* (that would be at the temple) or
- *How* (that would be to deliver his people).

But it would be *What* (would happen then) and above all *When*.

Because the resurrection of Jesus recast *How, What,* and *When*, it also recast *Who, Why,* and *Where*. Therefore:

"The actual bodily resurrection of Jesus (not mere resuscitation, but a transforming revivification) clearly provides a *sufficient* condition of the tomb being empty and the 'meetings' taking place. My claim is stronger: that the bodily resurrection of Jesus provides a *necessary* condition for these things; in other words, that no other explanation could or would do. All the efforts to find alternative explanations fail, and they were bound to do so."[35]

I believe that N.T. Wright has demonstrated the right use of historical research regarding the biblical witness. But consider how relatively modest the conclusion is! And after 700 pages of careful historical work! It is certainly is not the stuff from which faith is created. It confesses that its result is only highly probable, and that that is the best that such research is capable of.

---

32. Wright, *Resurrection of the Son of God*, 697.
33. Wright, *Resurrection of the Son of God*, 699.
34. Wright, *Resurrection of the Son of God*, 701.
35. Wright, *Resurrection of the Son of God*, 717.

Having said that, such research is still vital to the church and its proclamation. Historical criticism of this sort demonstrates that faith is not built upon wishful thinking, but upon a historical event. Criticism of this sort demonstrates that reason and revelation are not in opposition to one another, but can work powerfully together. Even though the Christian confession of the resurrection is based upon revelation and only in an ancillary way upon history, the historical witness is much more than nothing.

The Object of all Proper Hermeneutics: Certainty of Faith

Since the central assertion of this book has been that Reformation preaching, according to the pattern espoused by Martin Luther has the non-negotiable goal of creating and establishing assurance of faith; and since the hermeneutic Luther crafted for that purpose (which he called the theology of the cross) is bent to that primary goal; and since that hermeneutic insists, above all, upon describing the vital significance of the Word's encounter with the expositor/preacher as well as with the hearer of the proclamation, as events called Law and Gospel; and since that hermeneutic will tolerate absolutely no rivals; it seems to me that it is incumbent especially upon those biblical critics who claim a Lutheran heritage to give their rationale as to why the theology of the cross should be given only lip service while the historical critical method reigns supreme in the classroom, presumably to win the acceptance of modern academia. It is simply not possible to accommodate the hermeneutic of the theology of the cross to any other hermeneutic—least of all to the "historical critical method"! The two can't even agree upon where to start in the most basic definitions critical to the task.

I take fellow Lutherans to task here because the one central gift Lutherans bring to the table of fellow denominational Christians is their hermeneutic of the theology of the Cross with its emphasis which insists upon dividing all scriptural revelation into two operative words—*Law and Gospel*. These two words simply bear witness to what God *does* to every hearer—to the only two events which happen there—death and life. (Or, more accurately, by going through execution, being brought to resurrection.) Bearing witness to one's own execution and resulting resurrection is the only way for a preacher to rightly exposit the doctrine of our justification. It is an event created solely by Christ, solely by the cross, solely by the Word, solely by the creation of faith, and solely by coming to us of God's grace. (Each of the various referents is to God alone, the one and only sure foundation for proper Christian confidence.) Because of that, Lutheran preaching should have a completely different sound from what now commonly passes for preaching.

But far deeper than the gift of knowing God through a proper hermeneutic, the central issue for Paul in the epistles is not that he "knows", since knowledge "puffs up" (I Cor. 8:1), but rather that he is fully known and understood. "Now I know in part; then I shall understand fully, even as I have been fully understood." (I Corinthians 13:12 also I Corinthians 8:3, II Corinthians, 5:11 Galatians 4:9, Psalm 139:1-16.)What Paul refutes here is the whole object of the historical critical method. Knowledge of God—biblical knowledge—does not inhere or consist in completeness or manageability or creation of a "system" in order to be valid, or become, through that, a warrant for certainty. God's creatures acknowledge that they will always know only in part and that that is part of "walking humbly with your God." (Micah 6:8) Certainty does not inhere in the completeness of our knowing, nor in the construction of a huge monolithic system called "orthodoxy". It inheres in the One, outside ourselves, who creates the miracle of our being known and loved.

More: (or shall I say, less!) A Christian does not even know *how* he knows. Try bearing witness to anyone about *how* you are certain of your salvation. You will be able to bear witness *that* you are certain. But how that came to be will never be known by you. Yes, we know the means by which we came to faith. That is not the 'how' I am referring to. On any kind of empirical or scientific level, the 'how' remains hidden in mystery and miracle. Nor can we predict who will have this gift written on their hearts when many hear the self-same Word. In giving such account, and in bearing witness, a Christian can say only for sure (and this is by faith, as well) that Holy Spirit must have quietly written that faith into our heart by using the means He promised to use: the hearing of the Word and His personal coming in the sacraments.

More: (or, again less!) Proper knowledge of God—biblical knowledge—arrives only through having our own previous personal knowledge stripped away in a kind of death/resurrection. My personal barometer to test whether I have really heard the Gospel, is to assess upon its hearing, the degree to which my previous thoughts have been scrambled, undone and reassembled.

More: Hamaan insisted that any witness to the truth requires that we acknowledge forthrightly the incompleteness that attends all human knowing. He called our knowledge of faith "blowing leaves." It is part of our suffering humanity in this time that awaits the coming of the Truth.

And yet, in spite of not knowing how, in spite of having our previous conceptions to knowledge done in, and in spite of the partiality of all human knowing, we are called to preach and to announce and proclaim that *which is certain*! It doesn't sound possible! And yet it becomes possible by God's ability to create out of nothing. God insists on creating out of nothing in the case of faith especially, because, He insists, "My glory I will give to no other." (Isaiah 42:8)

CHAPTER TEN

Distinguishing Law and Gospel

Certainty Comes by "Going through Hell"

IT IS HUMBLING FOR both theologians and Christians in general to discover and to acknowledge that the incompleteness of our understanding of God simply is not going to end in this age. We continue to live by faith and not by sight. "By faith" includes being content to live in the truth that comes to us in the tension between the God revealed and the God hidden, between the God preached and the God not preached. True theology is practiced in temptation and in this way and for this reason alone it is a theology of certainty, says Luther. Since proper Christian certainty is the goal of Lutheran proclamation, it is necessary to attend carefully to how Luther asserts one achieves that.

"As long as the believer is on the way, he or she lives in the midst of temptation . . . God's promise of life addressed to all creatures is contradicted by daily experience . . . Luther does not play down this situation of temptation in which God withdraws and hides himself. Rather . . . Luther refuses to acknowledge them with finality. By denying them their ultimacy, Luther flees away from the God hiding himself, toward the God who has become man, to the God who in the hiddenness on the cross, has revealed himself. It is necessary to 'make one's way to God, against God, and pray to Him'[1] to the revealed God against the hidden one."

To understand what Luther means by saying that true theology is practiced in temptation, it is necessary to begin by describing what Luther referred to as the "theology of glory", the pseudo-theology he had learned from Scholasticism. Luther objects to the way Scholasticism discusses God and man and their relationship to each other, because the whole discussion in Scholasticism is established upon at least two false major premises. The first is that God and man are related by analogy. This is a non-negotiable

---

1. LW 19:72.

premise if one is going assert that there is any knowledge of God at all with reason as the fundamental source of such knowledge. However, Paul's observation in Romans 1:20 is that while the Gentiles' attempt to perceive the invisible nature of God from the works of creation through reason has some limited validity, in I Corinthians 1:18 he clearly rejects the adequacy of any knowledge of God via reason alone, saying that it stands in contradiction to a *saving* or true knowledge of God. A true and saving knowledge of God is foolishness to reason. God is hidden to reason. If nothing else is revealed at the cross, it is this: God and man are not related by analogy, but by contradiction.

A second Scholastic theological presupposition, based upon the "Physics" of Aristotle, completely ignores the actual broken situation which obtains between God and man and proceeds blithely upon the assertion that one can adequately and usefully describe this relation in terms of "cause." God, regarded by contrast and in relation to all being, is the sole original cause. Man is not the origin of his own being but he is the origin of all his works. Three factors are proposed in this metaphysical view: that man possesses reason, that he has free will, and that he acts to progress and realize himself in the direction of his goal. God and man are already fixed in their causal relationship, which is fundamentally free from contradiction. Again, it needs to be emphasized that all this is made under the illusion that one is describing a "neutral" situation, and not the actual situation of sinful man "in the sight of God."

In turn, these two major presuppositions, adopted by Scholasticism, work to completely transform the definition of grace found in scripture. The non-negotiable criterion now becomes "free will." Grace (it is now supposed) endows man, who has free will, with the ability to achieve a supernatural goal, perfecting his nature, enabling him to lead an existence in accordance with grace, and by the "habit" of carrying out meritorious works, makes him worthy of the goal toward which he is moving. However the *terminus ad quem* of this theological project is never clearly defined. The question regarding when one has ever done enough, is never answered, as Luther discovered, among others. Any proper Christian confidence is impossible in this scheme. However, to somewhat assuage one's anxiety over this, some continuing uncertainty was supposed to denote proper piety.

These philosophical presuppositions also are necessary if one is to achieve the attempt to perceive the invisible nature of God from the works of creation, through reason. Here, one *ascends* from the visible to the invisible, God's metaphysical attributes becoming glorious abstractions such as being omnipresent, omnipotent, the object of our highest desires.

As Forde notes in *Theology is for Proclamation*:

> God is indeed love, but we will not have it . . . The declaration of love—'I will have mercy on whom I will have mercy'—*taken in the abstract* is the most threatening of all because we do not know upon whom, in particular, God desires to have mercy. Everything turns to wrath and such wrath never ends in this age. God, as we have said repeatedly, simply cannot actually have mercy in the abstract. For God actually to have mercy God must die as abstraction and we must die as would-be gods. So Jesus' death engenders the Word that ends the abstraction, the wrath of God, and ends our lives as would-be gods at once. Jesus dies for us and so is the end of the God of wrath and the beginning of actual love when he is proclaimed and received in faith.[2]

An abstract, neutral description of the relationship between God and man accords neither to what Luther found laid out in the New Testament, particularly in Paul and John, nor to one's experience of actual reality. Nor is a description of God with glorious attributes particularly helpful to a sinner. What Luther proposed was not a different theology, but a confrontation regarding what constituted the very definition of what could validly be termed theology. The summary of the Scholastic approach briefly laid out above, Luther called pseudo-theology. Valid talk about God, he asserted, has a different criterion and a vastly different approach. The "theology of the cross," as Luther called it, insisted that the criterion and subject of all true theology is this: "True theology and knowledge of God lies in the crucified Christ." He stoutly held to this core principle in all his treatises and expositions of scripture. It became the hermeneutical principle for all his scriptural interpretation. His doctorate was in the Old Testament, and yet in his teaching of the Old Testament, throughout he was tireless in pointing out how every piece of it, including the psalms and the Genesis stories, pointed to Christ. But that still does not specify clearly enough what Luther insisted upon in his "theology of the cross." Everything is scripture pointed to Christ, yes, but to Christ *crucified*. That was the key.

But the crucified Christ is the *hidden* God, so that the world would not know God through wisdom, says Paul in I Corinthians 1! Yet the whole Scholastic structure is precisely an attempt to know God through wisdom. To attempt to know God in this way is a pretentious and deceiving wisdom, confidently based upon the assumption that an analogy between God and man obtains and that it adequately can arrive at a valid and true knowledge of God. The simple narrative of the crucifixion exposes how ridiculous that claim is. There, the highest and most competent theological faculty on the

---

2. Forde, *Theology is for Proclamation*, 131.

planet, at the foot of the cross, confidently proclaimed that God's own Son could not be God because he did not measure up to our expectations of what a true God would do or would look like. So the cross of Jesus exposes how blind human wisdom is without God's revelation, by showing that, through wisdom alone, we will always make the twin claims that what is not God actually is God, while at the same time denying that what is truly God is not. In the Heidelberg Disputation Luther says that 'the theology of glory calls evil good and good evil. The theologian of the cross says what is true; that is: he gives a true account of reality.' And again, 'without the theology of the cross man misuses the best things in the worst way.' Luther's aim in the theology of the cross is "practical", for its aim is the right use of reality.

The theology of the cross pays close attention to the human experience of the encounter with God's Word, what we now call existential theology. Once again, to be rigorous here, it is helpful to point out that 'theology of the cross' is an abstraction. What Luther is calling for on the part of all Christians requires the experience of "becoming a theologian of the cross." Becoming a theologian of the cross is a lived experience calling for personal witness. The truth arrived at through the cross of Jesus Christ, which puts to death all human wisdom is sure, not speculative. It is concrete, not abstract. It is sensual and historical, completely denying a philosophical world of "ideals". It is a living truth, not a fixed quantity or idea, subject to filing and stapling and shelving. If subjective truth resides in the existential, and if objective truth is strictly defined and confined to human rules regarding what is empirical, then saving knowledge resides in the subjective. Kierkegaard took at least this much from his Lutheran background. But this assertion is offensive in the extreme to human wisdom, because the initiating of saving knowledge would then reside outside ourselves. Once, again we are driven back to the most terrifying prospect imaginable to humans—God's election.

"What is striking is that Luther could speak of the believer's inner conflict (*Anfechtung, tentatio*) as an experience of hell. To contemplate one's condition in the face of the judgment of God meant to experience hell in the full and real sense: 'God saves only the damned, not as some say, that they feel damned and yet are saved, but they are damned, and there's no pretending in that feeling...' Solely to affirm God's will and to be totally free of self, meant to endure hell itself."[3]

Since "true theology is practical while speculative theology belongs in hell with the devil," the difference between them obtains in this: true theology hangs upon God's living, present tense, spoken promise—upon a word. That word commands us to rely not on feelings, nor wisdom, nor

---

3. Holl, *Gesammelte aufsatze zur Kirchengeshchichte*, I: Luther, 18, 27, 146.

intuition, but solely upon the confidence that because God speaks it, the word is true. In addition it commands us to believe that in spite of pressing crises to the contrary, God is in command. It commands us to believe that in the experience of God's absence, He is most present. It commands us to believe that the Gospel, by its very definition is the "last word of all". And, against the argument that this position is hopelessly solipsistic, and lacking in "cosmic" reach, the rejoinder is that what is fundamental here is not the person encountered, but rather the Word that is doing its work. And the Word is cosmic in its claim. *"Verbum Dei Manet in Aeternum."* God's Word endures forever.

The task for preaching is to recognize in proclamation, that for every hearer, this call to hang everything upon God's Word is instantly challenged. And it is challenged not only instantly but constantly. The Word of God is challenged by our opponent, the evil one, who has his own word to throw at us. At Jesus' baptism, Jesus heard the clear unequivocal word from the Father, "You are my beloved Son, with you I am well pleased." The first three Gospels are agreed that first thing in Jesus' ministry resume, his baptism, includes the fundamental word of the Father regarding both his identity, and by extension, his mission. Immediately following that clear Word comes the frontal challenge by the tempter that this Word of God indeed describes reality and the actual facts of the case. "*If* you are the Son of God . . . " begins the first temptation. Luke notes that this is just the beginning of a whole ministry lived in temptation. Any Christian will bear witness that, unlike Jesus, our doubt regarding our standing before God is created by the condition in which sinful man and justifying God are intimate. These two persons come together through a deadly dissociation where sin and its overcoming are both recognized and acknowledged in our experience. Hamann called this the "coincidence of opposites." So our theology is a theology practiced in continuing temptation to see if God's word holds true even in a continuing sinner. And, because it is a theology practiced in temptation, Luther arrives at the surprisingly opposite conclusion than the obvious one expected. What one would expect of a "theology of temptation" would be constant uncertainty. The reverse is the actual case! Because our theology is practiced in temptation, it becomes an existential thing, where we experience, time and again, that God's Word proves true. *The lived-through challenge confirms God's truth and mercy.*

One could go further and assert that this is the *only* way anyone arrives at saving certainty or comes to know God in truth. As an example, just ask any AA member who has experienced the miracle of sobriety for any length of time. Truth arrived at in the anguish of being brought through death to life, compared to the truths of speculation have very little relation to each other. That is why Luther was so appalled at Erasmus' cold, speculative, impassive approach to scripture. Later in life Luther once said at table that if lived longer he would like to write a book about temptations, "for without them man could understand neither the holy scripture, nor faith, nor the fear or love of God. For the only real understanding is that which endures when it is put to the test." "There is only one article and one rule of theology, and this is true faith or trust in Christ. Whoever doesn't hold this article and this rule is not theologian. All the other articles flow into and out of this one; without it the others are meaningless. The devil has tried from the very beginning to deride this article and to put his own wisdom in its place. However, this article has a good savor for all who are afflicted, downcast, troubled, and tempted, and these are the ones who understand the gospel."[4]

The Truth of the Gospel Resides in a *Distinction*

When it came to proclamation, Luther insisted upon a single interpretive criterion which made his preaching distinctive, and which provides, to this very day, his central contribution to the life of the Christian church. Luther's preaching has a distinctive sound, a sound which, as we have already noted in chapter one, created a continent-wide sensation among his students and readers. The absolute certainty, the personal confrontation, the present tense immediacy, the living and non-speculative nature that characterized his proclamation—all these arose from a truth that emerged from deadly conflict in the person of the preacher. This conflict arises from the intensely difficult task required in making the *distinction* between Law and Gospel in the present moment. Since Law and Gospel describe the two active and competing effects of God's Word upon a person's conscience, Luther requires of a preacher that he or she engage in critical reflection about how that Word is impacting him or her. The distinction is *a report from the battlefield*, where the field in contest is one's own person. Such proclamation arises from the midst of a deadly strife, what Luther called temptation, in which death and life literally contend for the victory. Such proclamation cannot be abstract, speculative, dry, or merely regurgitated facts. It is witness. It is bearing witness. And it is instantly recognized as such by those who are being called by the Truth into the Truth. Truth itself emerges as cross-shaped in that it arrives only from a process of going through death to life.

The arrival of the Law-Gospel hermeneutic was an involved process. First, Luther gradually jettisoned the received Scholastic interpretive system

4. LW 54: 157.

called the Quadriga, the fourfold interpretation of a passage which required the interpreter of scripture to consider four levels of meaning—the *literal* (or historical), the *allegorical*, the *tropological* (how it applies morally), and the *anagogical* (how it bears on the future or eschatological life of the church). In his earliest lectures on the Psalms he began his move away from that, to what instead became his insistence upon the Law-Gospel hermeneutic. "In the holy scripture it is best to distinguish the Spirit from the letter; because this is what makes one a true theologian."[5] "Virtually the whole of the scriptures and the understanding of the whole of theology depends upon the true understanding of the law and the gospel."[6] (1530) "Anyone who can properly distinguish the gospel from the law may thank God and know that he is a theologian."[7] In his first dispute with the antinomians he said, "I have often heard before that there is no better way to hand down and to maintain true doctrine than by following this method, that is, of dividing Christian doctrine into two parts, the law and the gospel."[8]

Second, the Quadriga assumed that all scriptural interpretation was confined to the level of signification. It did not even *conceive* of a level that involved a living encounter with the interpreter, which required a report by that interpreter. Luther believed that "God encounters us in the Word, but this Word is an oral Word, a living proclamation."[9] He later wrote this summary of his position: "So it is not all in keeping with the New Testament to write books on Christian doctrine. Rather in all places there should be fine, goodly, learned, spiritual, diligent preachers without books, who extract the living word from the old Scripture and unceasingly inculcate it into the people, just as the apostles did. For before they wrote, they first of all preached to the people by word of mouth and converted them."[10]

Third, the dividing of all scripture into the distinction between what he first termed "letter" and "Spirit," was based upon two previous settled convictions in his interpretive system—first, that as a practical matter all theology consisted solely in the interpretation of scripture,[11] and second, that Christ is the midpoint of scripture.[12] Though he painstakingly avoided advocating a Christological interpretation in any immediate sense, still he

---

5. WA 40, 1; 361, 76ff.
6. WA 30, 2; 300, 4-6.
7. WA 30, 2; 86.
8. WA 30, 1; 39ff.
9. Lohse, *Martin Luther's Theology*, 189.
10. LW 52:206.
11. Ebeling, *Luther: an Introduction to his Thought*, 96.
12. Lohse, *Martin Luther's Theology*, 189.

was able to say to Erasmus in the Bondage of the Will debate, "Take Christ from scriptures and what else will you find in them?"

> *The task was completely identified in his mind with the question, which constantly pursued him, of his standing in the sight of God.* For he never doubted that the will of God was revealed and comprehensible to men solely through the holy scripture . . . Obviously if the scripture alone is valid, everything depends upon how this validity is understood, and how the scripture is interpreted . . . An extraordinary degree of devotion to the scripture is necessary, in order not to do it violence by approaching it from individual and isolated points of view, but trying instead to understand the fundamental message. The less one approaches the scripture from a previously established position, looking for specific answers to specific questions, or in order merely to enrich one's knowledge, *the more radically one accepts the challenge to one's own existential life of an encounter with the scripture, concentrated upon a single fundamental question aimed at human existence itself and touching one's very conscience, the more one looks ultimately for only one thing in the scripture, the word which brings certainty in life and in death* the better will be one's prospects of a real understanding and adequate interpretation of the scripture. For its fundamental theme is clearly *the unique and ultimately valid word, which* is *called the Word of God because it is a decisive utterance about our existence as human beings.*[13] (my italics)

In order to understand the remarkable fact that this distinction between Law and Gospel is presented as the criterion which divides true theology from pseudo theology, as well as the criterion which decides whether or not one has encountered the truth of the gospel, it is necessary to be clear that this is no cut and dried formula. But what precisely does he mean by insisting upon this distinction? Here is a brief but incomplete list of misunderstandings which this distinction of Luther's between Law and Gospel has suffered:

- It does not mean a division or a mere separation between Law and Gospel.
- Nor are they in competition with one another. For example, in the dispute with the antinomians, Luther emphasized that if the Gospel were simply to compete with the Law it would become only another form of law.

13. Ebeling, *Luther: an Introduction to his Thought*, 96-97.

- The distinction is not understood accurately if one considers the two powers as complementary, as though the Law were not sufficient, and the Gospel had to be added to it—a position implicitly assumed by much evangelical American preaching.
- This distinction cannot be carried out at the level of abstraction or by means of theological definition. It requires the personal involvement of the preacher who reports the existential encounter under the address of both powers.
- Nor are the Law and Gospel merely alternatives with proper hierarchy.
- Nor is the distinction properly understood as the Old Testament representing the Law, and the New Testament representing the Gospel.
- Nor are these two words of God. The Word of God is one. The reason it has this dual way of encountering us is because of the Fall. Such a distinction cannot apply to the situation enjoyed by Adam and Eve in paradise.

It is illuminating to consider the origin of this distinction. When Luther finally reduced his struggle to understand God's Word to assigning Christ, the Word, and faith into their proper relationship, the entire scriptural interpretive system which he had been handed by Scholasticism crumbled. Yet it not so simple as that. *It is axiomatic for Luther that the Spirit, not the interpreter, is the one who makes the law-gospel distinction.* "In his commentary on Psalm 45 Luther says of the way in which we should hear and read the word of God, that it is not something we should attempt to do through our own powers, nor should we be content with the letter and with the mere outward hearing of the word, but should make it our concern to listen to the Spirit Himself. It is not by the word as it is uttered outwardly that we are really taught inwardly, for it is merely the tool and instrument of him who writes living words in the heart. What is uttered *vocaliter* by the voice, must be understood *vitaliter* in the heart through the Holy Spirit."[14] While emphasizing the incredible miracle that the truth arrives subjectively, Luther battles opponents such as his older fellow faculty member, Muntzer, and the 'Schwarmer' who took this assertion too far by divorcing the work of the Holy Spirit from the medium through which the Spirit insists upon—the Word. The Holy Spirit, Luther emphasizes, encounters us always *mediately*, through the Word and Sacrament, and not '*immediately*' through our own visions. Thus, God provides the truth of the Gospel with an objective foundation.

14. Ebeling, *Luther: an Introduction to his Thought*, 98.

The Law-Gospel distinction is not concerned with theoretical understanding. It is rather experienced. Nor are parts of scripture law, while other parts are gospel. The whole can be law which kills, or the whole can be gospel which gives life. A 'spiritual' understanding of scripture is that which is yielded by distinguishing between Law and Gospel.

Forde describes how biblical interpretation which believes that preaching actually kills and makes alive differs from every other hermeneutic :

> "Luther's different hermeneutic leads to a different authority structure and thus a different ecclesiology. Where one tries to move from the 'dead letter' to the 'life-giving spirit' in allegorical fashion, one needs assurance as to which 'interpretation' is 'right'. An authoritative office is demanded by the hermeneutic itself. But, where the word actually kills and makes alive, matters are quite different. The one so killed and made alive needs no earthly structure to *guarantee* the 'doctrine'. Where death and resurrection are not reckoned with theologically, however, such 'assurance' can only be misunderstood a 'psychological' egotism and 'subjectivism'. The system which does not entertain the fact of death and life through the word operates only with a kind of antithesis between the ontological and the psychological. Hence Roman Catholics seem able to understand Lutheranism only as a kind of 'psychologism' or 'existentialism' whose main point it to translate abstract ontological language into the language of 'personal experience' and 'assurance of salvation' on a subjective level—the consolation of the 'terrified conscience'. When the theological significance of death-life language is not grasped, one tends only to pit ontology against psychology in the continuum of the 'deathless' being."[15]

> "It now becomes clear what 'spiritual' means. It means everything, in so far as it is understood 'in the sight of God'; that is under the sign of the cross of Christ, and therefore the sense of the concealment of God beneath the contrary. Salvation is 'spiritual' . . . when understood as being crucified with Christ, and so possessing life in the midst of death; . . . The believer is 'spiritual' in so far as he understands that he is hidden in God; . . . the Church is 'spiritual' as long as it regards itself as hidden in this life and realizes that it must be persecuted; . . . even sin is 'spiritual' in so far as it is recognized in the sight of God a self-righteousness. *In short, 'spiritual' is the category of true understanding.*"[16]

---

15. Forde, *Justification by Faith—a Matter of Death and Life*, 100
16. Ebeling, *Luther: an Introduction to his Thought*, 105-106.

For Luther the distinction between law and gospel coheres most intimately with his doctrine of justification, since that doctrine can be developed only on the basis of that distinction. Nevertheless, it would be a misreading and a misunderstanding to take this as his making all of theology concentrate on only one of its facets. Instead, it is Luther's gateway into *all* theology, as was suggested in the preceding paragraph. From a sermon from 1532 he writes that the distinction "between law and faith, commandment and gospel . . . is the highest art in Christendom."[17] And from the first disputation against the Antinomians he wrote, "But now you have often heard that there is no better art of handing on and preserving the pure doctrine than to follow this method, than is, to divide Christian doctrine into two parts, law and gospel. And so there are two things set before us in God's Word, that is, the wrath or the grace of God, sin or righteousness, death or life, hell or heaven."[18] The distinction can only be properly drawn when drawn afresh, when each situation that it addresses is carefully noted. It cannot be passed on to a new situation unchanged. "The law can only fulfill its God-intended function when seen in constant contrast with the gospel, just as the gospel is properly preached only in constant contrast to the law. Both must be preserved in their true nature and authentic function through being continually related to each other."[19] The dangers of failing to properly distinguish law and gospel include losing the gospel, losing the law, falsifying each, or making a new law out of the gospel.

Luther's very dividing the law into its two 'uses' shows that his concern is for what the law *does* to its hearer, demonstrating once again that this distinction resides in the existential and not in the theoretical. He is the first in all the history of dogma to view the law from the standpoint of its "uses," thus in its concrete function. "For Luther, law is an existential category."[20] The law is not the efficient cause of sin, but rather the ostensive cause—it points to sin and reveals it to surprised sinners.[21] The law leads to sin becoming 'great,' striking at the heart so that the wide world becomes too narrow and help is to had nowhere but with Christ.[22]

But, in the process of making this distinction, if the willingness to be a battleground between two mortally opposed powers is daunting enough as a challenge to the scriptural interpreter, it is made exponentially more

---

17. WA 36, 9, 26-29.
18. WA 39 I, 361, 1-6.
19. Lohse, *Martin Luther's Theology*, 269.
20. Ebeling, *Word and Faith*, 65.
21. WA 39 I 529.
22. WA 39 I 456.

difficult by the fact that *the two powers present themselves in a confused fashion*. Personal stress is evident in the heated way Luther describes his suffering under the conflicting claims of God's Word.

> "It's the supreme art of the devil that he can make the law out of the gospel. If I can hold on to the distinction between law and gospel, I can say to him any and every time that he should kiss my backside. Even if I sinned I would say, 'Should I deny the gospel on this account?' It hasn't come to that yet. Once I debate about what I have done and left undone, I am finished. But if I rely on the basis of the gospel—"The forgiveness of sins covers it all'—I have won . . . So don't be too daring. The distinction between law and gospel will do it. The devil turns the Word upside down. If one sticks to the law, one is lost. A good conscience won't set one free, but the distinction (between the law and gospel) will. So you should say, "The Word is twofold, on the one hand terrifying and on the other hand comforting.' Here Satan objects, 'But God says you are damned because you don't keep the law.' I respond, 'God also says that I shall live.' His mercy is greater than sin, and life is stronger than death. Hence if I have left this or that undone, our Lord will tread it under foot with his grace."[23]

As we have already noted, for Luther theology is only done meaningfully when done not for the sake of curiosity or academics, but solely for the purpose of proclamation.[24] Here proclamation is defined narrowly as a word which: a) is *spoken,* and b) *must* be spoken, c) in concrete circumstances, d) for Jesus Christ's sake.

> "Only when we have something to say for Jesus Christ's sake, appealing to him and speaking in his name, which means speaking with an authority we receive from him, is there any point in theology. And the distinction between the law and the gospel is only the central issue of theology because it is concerned with what is the true word of Christian preaching. Christian preaching is the process in which the distinction between the law and the gospel takes place . . . that is to carry on the progress of a battle, in which time and again the distinction between the law and the gospel is newly at issue and is made in practice . . . so that the event of salvation takes place . . . A confusion of the two

---

23. LW 54:106-7.
24. Ebeling, *Word and Faith*, 69-76.

is not a misfortune of little significance, but it evil in the strict sense, the total opposite of salvation[25]."

In his second Galatians commentary he illustrates how this misfortune happens in practice when he exegetes Paul's difficult to understand question in Galatians 2:17, "Is Christ then an agent of sin?" Luther writes,

> "So let us establish the proposition: Everyone who believes in the Lord Jesus Christ is a sinner and is worthy of eternal death; and if he does not have recourse to the Law and do its works, he will not be saved . . . Of course, our opponents do not use these very words; but this is actually what they teach. For they say that 'infused faith,' which they properly call faith in Christ does not free from sin, but that only 'faith formed by love' does so. From this it follows that faith in Christ by itself, without the Law and works does not save. Surely this is to declare that Christ leaves us in our sins and in the wrath of God and makes us worthy of eternal death. On the other hand, if you perform the Law and works, then faith justifies, because it has works, without which faith is useless. Therefore works justify, not faith . . . How deep the abominable blasphemy of this doctrine is!"[26]

Finally, this distinction is vitally a matter of death and life. Late in his life, struggling with ill health, Luther took on the exposition of Psalm 90. In his exposition we find that the law shows us that death is under the wrath of God. Since this is so, humans cannot accept death as a natural phenomenon, but march toward death full of anxiety and fear, since judgment is linked to death. Luther shared the traditional view that death should not exist at all, but that it was imposed as punishment because of sin. As such, there should be no death, "but rather life. And that great fear of death in man means that his death is something quite different than the death of beasts. It means that no beast has such fear of death as man and, of course, as a sign that he is created for life."[27] "Death always appears in the company of sin and the law."[28] These are the triad of enemies that always attack us together. Because Christians know the law and sin, they also sense more strongly than others the horror of death.

But then the gospel makes the horror of death retreat because, hidden under the mask of deserved punishment, is revealed the grace of finally being freed from sin. Additionally, Christians hear the distinction made in

25. Ebeling, *Luther: an Introduction to His Though*, 117.
26. LW 26:146.
27. WA 39 II, 367, 20-24.
28. LW 14:83.

I Thessalonians 4, that because Christ died, we only 'sleep.' Luther writes, "This significance of baptism—the dying or drowning of sin—is not fulfilled completely in this life. Indeed this does not happen until man passes through bodily death and completely decays to dust. As we can plainly see, the sacrament or sign of baptism is quickly over. But the spiritual baptism, the drowning of sin which it signifies, lasts as long as we live and is completed only in death. Then it is that a person is completely sunk in baptism, and that which baptism signifies comes to pass. Therefore, this whole life is nothing else than a spiritual baptism which does not cease till death."[29] The sense of guilt can even be fortunate! "Therefore, we have no greater horror than of sin and death. Yet God can so comfort us in it that we may boast, as St Paul (Romans 5:20-21) says, that sin has even served for this that we should be justified, and that we also gladly would be dead and long to die."[30]

The order in which these two words are spoken is critical because their effect is to kill us and to give us life. Forde opposes Barth's theological position that a preacher should "lead" with the gospel: "The old being will not and cannot *hear* the gospel no matter what one says. The old being will turn *whatever one says* into law. It is impossible, therefore, to set out to preach gospel first, as if there were some sort of methodological key to the matter . . . If justification by faith alone is death and resurrection, then it is the proclamation of that justification itself that does the deed we are looking for. It is the proclamation itself that puts to death and raises up—at one and the same time."[31] (his italics)

The Cross as the Sole Criterion for Truth

In virtually every piece of literature a tale is told in which the whole falls into two parts, a beginning and an ending, but bifurcated and interpreted by a middle event, upon which the whole story turns. In literature class in college we were told to analyze "the change in Emma," which was the whole point of telling the story in the first place. This entailed considering the critical turning point of the story. Just so, our own life story emerges condensed into critical scenes, some so real that they are burned into our memory like slides for detail and color. These scenes have emerged for us as non-negotiable in understanding our story. Among Christians, these events are often crises in which the mystery of God's love became personally operative and clear.

---

29. LW 35:30.
30. WA 12, 410, 31-34 (sermon 1523).
31. Forde, *Justification by Faith–a Matter of Death and Life*, 92-3.

To begin with the obvious, Jesus story is unintelligible without the cross. It is the destination looming ever closer during Jesus' journey of three long years of ministry. While it is the source of all the derision directed at Jesus from every unbeliever, it is the source of all joy for every believer. While the cross obscures God from the unbelieving, it reveals the very heart of God for the believing. The cross reveals both the fierceness of the implacable, terrifying wrath of a holy God against our sin, as well as the world-embracing mercy of the same God who would take upon himself that wrath to remove sin from us. Since the cross of Jesus destroys the power of sin and death, it creates the ensuing resurrection of the body (the new ending to the story), thus validating that crucifixion's power and purpose. The cross is the non-negotiable criterion for understanding the person and ministry of Jesus, the person of the Father who so loved the world, and the person of the sinners he came to rescue. The cross, alone, makes intelligible the saving God to sinners.

The great heroes of the Christian church likewise have lives which fall into two parts, where a crisis is imposed upon them and fundamentally changes them, so that their whole life becomes intelligible only by interpretation from that single event of conversion. That conversion event stamps the whole first part of their story null and void, while disclosing by its presence all the meaning of the new life which follows. Paul is caught at the height of rebellion, with weapons literally in hand, thrown from his horse, confronted by a word of accusation and command from the very person he is persecuting. It takes three days without water or food, experienced in the stygian darkness of total blindness for this titanic personal will to acknowledge the loss of all things, and in thus dying to be raised to God's purposes. Paul forever afterward proclaimed it as the impossible extent of God's mercy toward sinners. His personal change was so enormous that the church itself could not believe he was the same man. His personal change was so enormous that he outstripped even the called disciples who had spent three years of training with Jesus himself. He began to preach a life that he characterized wholly as a continuing death—a death to sin. For Paul, there was no other criterion for knowledge of God than Jesus Christ, and Him crucified. What follows ineluctably, without exception in Paul's proclamation, is that there is no saving knowledge of God without one's attending personal crucifixion. (cf. Romans 6, Galatians 3, II Corinthian 4:8-12)

Saint Augustine is another example of a rich spoiled profligate who literally hears(!) the Word while visiting in Bishop Ambrose' garden, "Come and read." And, finding the book in that place opened to Romans, he is converted by that Word. Later he says of his former existence, "That was my life. Was that life?"

One could adduce countless other examples, including Luther, the Wesley brothers, C.H. Spurgeon, and P.T. Forsythe to show that, without exception, the U-form shape described by Jesus' career in Philippians 2:5-11, bisected by death, after which life appears, is the shape of the career of faith for all Christians. Passing through death, the Christian is brought to life. To say that the whole of a Christian life is a death to sin is to reiterate the same axiom. Each of us may be able to identify critical events which stand out more than others in shaping who we are as persons with a story, but they are not the only operative factors. Cumulatively they stand as witnesses to us of the long but faithful process of God's Word bringing the power of Jesus' cross to bear upon our lives and so to save us by bringing us constantly through death to life.

CHAPTER ELEVEN

On the Work of the Holy Spirit

> "in us who walk not according to the
> Flesh but according to the Spirit."
>
> ROMANS 8:4

THE CHRISTIAN PREACHER ENTERS the public arena, where direct counter claims to his or her testimony regarding what is certainly true, collide with the proclamation of the gospel. Included in this controversy is the stubborn misconception, held by many Christians, that the gospel will somehow be attractive if only preached correctly. But that possibility is absolutely precluded when it is properly recognized that the Bible's whole theme is the conflict between God and the devil. Preaching is how God carries on that conflict. The gospel will never be appreciated by the world.

Thus, the task of a preacher is to do battle. In this combat, human ability will not prevail. The evangelical preacher counts on the power of the Word itself, together with the Holy Spirit's testimony to the hearer (when and where He pleases), that this proclaimed Word is true. Thus, any notion of preaching absent the work of the Holy Sprit is a biblical impossibility. The terminology of the Romans verse quoted above describes the ongoing warfare. *Spirit and Flesh are two Powers*. In reality, we are under the power of the Spirit. But our senses, reason, and experience, because they are fleshly, all tell us otherwise. Therefore Paul says, "We walk by faith and not by sight." (2 Corinthians 5:7) and, "You have died, and now your life lies hidden with Christ in God." (Colossians 3:2)

The sole content of Evangelical preaching

It is absolutely essential to recognize that Luther underwent severe spiritual conflicts not only at the beginning of his monastic career but throughout his life—so severe that he described them almost as spiritual terrors (*Anfechtungen*). At the beginning, their chief cause lay in the anxious question as to how he could appear before God at the last judgment.[1] Contributing to this anxious search were three factors: the unparalleled emphasis in the sixteenth century on the impending apocalypse, Luther's personality, and his training in Occam's theology that "humans on the basis of their natural powers are automatically able to keep the commandments and thus to love God above all things."[2] In addition, the doctrine of predestination, so clear throughout scripture, only intensified his anxiety and seemed to remove any possibility or hope of finding a gracious God. In fact, it seemed to render God both capricious for saving some and not others, at the same time removing any warrant from our hands to make claims upon him. It seemed, as well, to make God hateful in requiring of humans what they could not do. But hating God was blasphemous, which only compounded the problem!

Together, these all worked to sharpen the undying conviction, which Luther held throughout his life, *that theology's first concern was the question of salvation or damnation.* This sole criterion became for him that which distinguished true theology from false theology. Put more narrowly and succinctly it became the question of the forgiveness of sins. In the sixteenth century, the understanding of the forgiveness of sins was intimately related to the question of how to navigate the post-baptismal life of a Christian. Forgiveness of sins had become, after long theological battles, a whole medieval industry. It had become a stop-gap system filled with such things as indulgences, purgatory, masses for the dead, and monastic estates, in which one could escape a wicked world. Did there exist any possible theological warrant in such a system, anywhere, even in monastic estates, for certainty regarding a sinner's current or future standing before a holy God? No one could give Luther an answer.

This could all be dismissed by moderns as a past historical situation which does not at all relate to our current situation, and it has been so treated in many popular expositions of Luther's theology. Among these theologians it is commonly stated that we moderns are no longer interested in "how to find a gracious God." However, one salient problem remains in our fallen humanity, which is never a past historical situation—the question: how shall we "love ourselves", given the undeniable fact that, looking in the mirror, we cannot escape our sinfulness, even with our best efforts? The whole industry of modern psychotherapy is built to address that question. And, can one "love oneself" without regard to the judgment of the One before whom we

---

1. Lohse, *Martin Luther's Theology*, 33.
2. Lohse, *Martin Luther's Theology*, 33.

stand, whether the verdict over us is positive and not negative? Try as we might, we can never convincingly tell ourselves that the verdict rests with ourselves. I raise the question because one can use the question of "self-love", or even the question of its possibility, as an introit into Luther's understanding of the person and work of the Holy Spirit, which for him was closely connected with the very heart of his whole conception of Christianity.

"The concept of the Holy Spirit completely dominates Luther's theology. In every decisive matter, whether it be the study of Luther's doctrine of justification, of his doctrine of the sacraments, or his ethics, or of any other fundamental teaching, we are forced to take into consideration this concept of the Holy Spirit."[3] Lohse agrees. "For Luther, there was not a single doctrine in all of theology where the activity of the Spirit would not be fundamental. All activity in which God engages the world and humankind is mediated through the Spirit."[4] For example, sin, in its actual essence, cannot be perceived except through revelation of the Holy Spirit. So also, without the Holy Spirit, God is a hidden God. To trace the work of the Holy Spirit in Luther's work, and how that work relates to preaching, one could divide the office of the Holy Spirit it into following headings.

1. The Essential Work of the Holy Spirit: to Create Conflict in the Sinner

What young Luther had been taught was based first upon the theology of Augustine and only then upon the synthesis of idealistic Greek philosophy and biblical revelation created by Thomas Aquinas, known as scholasticism. In Augustine's theology, "amor boni", the good love, was infused into the human through the work of the Holy Spirit. If this love is understood in the right way, it also is possible to describe it as the proper love of oneself. "For to love means to hate oneself, to condemn oneself, and wish ill to oneself according to the words of Christ: 'He who hates his life in this world shall keep it unto life eternal.' Whoever loves himself in this way loves himself truly, for his love of self is not of himself but of God, that is according to the will of God which hates and condemns and wishes evil to all sin, that is to us all."[5] But as Luther struggled to understand scripture rightly, it became no longer possible to understand "amor boni" as a natural idealistic striving of man elevated to the highest point. Rather, it became a love which had been made congruent, or "conformed," to God's love toward the sinner. But this love al-

---

3. Prenter, *Spiritus Creator*, ix.
4. Lohse, *Martin Luther's Theology*, 235.
5. WA 56, 392, 20 (1515-16).

ways carried judgment with it. The attending hatred toward oneself, *odium sui*, became, biblically, not just hatred toward "the old man" but toward the whole of man. No part of man was unsaturated with concupiscence. Even the highest aspirations of mankind were under this judgment. But these changes required an entire new understanding of the Holy Spirit's work to be described as "conforming the sinner's will to the will of God." (In this work of God, who conforms an always rebellious sinful will, are the seeds of his later treatise on the captivation of the will.) The contrast of this "conforming by God" to the scholastic system's "human striving" is so immense that the entire received structure had to crumble.

In the scholastic system the Holy Spirit was the transcendent cause of infused grace. (In fact, Thomas sought to literally flood the whole with grace, in an attempt to avoid Pelagianism.) Grace in the scholastic system is certainly anti-Pelagian, that is, it does seek to have God as the sole agent in salvation. However, because of the primacy given to the Greek philosophy called idealism, where man, by exercise of rational thought, can understand the higher world of ideals and thus bring them into the world of reality, God becomes the distant goal of human striving. Objective satisfaction also is held at a remote historical distance. The Spirit is moved back into metaphysical distance as a transcendent cause. All this remoteness demonstrates that the idealistic system has been given primacy over biblical revelation. The final demonstration that this is a system controlled by idealism and not by biblical revelation is that, in this system, a man moves from "lower" to "higher" rather than God coming to man. In the entire process, man's nature is optimistically judged or assumed to be essentially fitted for God. Man himself is divided into "higher and "lower" strata and "infused grace" perfects the "higher man's" love of the good. Without the axiomatic presupposition that God's Spirit and man's spirit *together* strive toward grace and perfection, which is to say that God and man are related by analogy rather than contradiction, the whole structure collapses. One cannot leave this thumbnail sketch of scholasticism without also noting that by attempting to be the "grand unifying theory of all reality", similar to what current physicists are now attempting, scholastic theology was also the quest for certainty. However, as Luther was discovering, put into practice, it had ironically achieved the direct opposite of certainty, by making such certainty impossible. For Luther, the lack of such certainty made faith, at least at the existential level, impossible. Contrast this to what one instantly sees in "The Bondage of the Will", that, at the existential level, faith is the rock-solid, unshakeable certainty and confidence, for which anyone would unhesitatingly die, and without which there is no Christian good news.

The theology of infused grace, which was to produce *amor boni*, gave Luther unspeakable agonies. The reverse was happening in him. He hated God. Now he was guilty of blasphemy as well as guilty of every other lower crime against God. The Reformation discovery was prepared for by the witness of his conscience against him that the whole received system was not only unworkable and untenable in actual practice, but actually exacerbated the already terrifying situation of the sinner.

The breakthrough came with the effort to understand the concept of "conformity to God's will." Only when this conformity became not a human effort or "striving", but a miraculous gift of God, did things begin to make sense. It worked on the existential level, as well! When conformity became a gift and not a requirement, then all of theology changed, together with all of scriptural interpretation. His 1545 witness is that this breakthrough came in finally having the truth revealed to him that the "righteousness of God" (Romans 1:16-17) is not a *requirement*, but a *gift* of God. Further, this righteousness is no longer partial, but God's total claim upon the total man. Now "odium sui", the proper hatred toward oneself, became not just a hatred of the "lower" man" but of the whole of oneself. Conformity was achieved not by "imitation of Christ", as in the old system, but via a completely passive transformation where one was made to conform by the work of the Holy Spirit. Just as Jesus was conceived by the Holy Spirit in his mother Mary, so the Holy Spirit caused the same real and present person of Christ to be born in every believer.

But this gift engenders a real strife and real suffering within the sinner because the conforming done by the Holy Spirit will always be against our own will. Here is what Luther had to say about The Holy Spirit's conforming work with its necessary component—*Anfechtung*:

> "When God begins his work in men, those who are dominated by 'the spirit of bondage again unto fear' (Romans 8:15) will say, 'God acts as a tyrant, he is not a father but an opponent.' And it is true that God is our opponent. But these people do not know that we must agree with this opponent, for then he becomes kind and fatherly—otherwise he never will. The relation to God does not mean that he agrees with us and changes himself according to our desires so that we may become his friends and sons. No, God is our opponent in the sense that, to our dismay, he lets everything happen contrary to our wishes and desires in spite of our prayer. When God begins to do his will, he exposes everything in man, what he has of both inward and outward glory, makes him completely perplexed, and leads him into the darkness of inner conflict, where it is impossible either to know

or to love God. In this darkness he finally takes away from him even the word of comfort, which in the time of inner conflict can assure him that God only for a season has forsaken him. The words of Christ can be used about this darkness: that except that Lord had shortened the days, no flesh would have been saved."[6]

I would emphasize three things regarding this passage. First, what is described by Luther here is not mere conflict, but terror, because it involves the absence of God. God actually does withdraw from us when He withdraws His Word! Second, we sinners absolutely depend upon one thing, and one thing only—God's coming to us graciously. But this saving event is entirely outside our control. The coming and the saving presence of Jesus Christ, himself, in his Word, happens where and when he pleases, and only when he feels that the time of *Anfechtung* has achieved its ordained purpose. Third, this order of things, this description of actual reality, is the reality of the walk of *every* believer, an ongoing repeated process we never "graduate from." "Thus it is, to be made to conform to the will of God in the crucified Christ; thus it is, to be under the work and operation of God. This is the theology of the cross which also is a theology of inner conflict."[7]

In other words, the Holy Spirit's central office is to create what we could rightly call an ongoing "spiritual warfare" in the life of every Christian. Paul agrees. "But I say, walk by the Spirit, and you will not gratify the desires of the flesh. For the desires of the flesh are against the Spirit, and the desire of the Spirit are against the flesh, for these are opposed to each other to keep you from doing what you would." (Galatians 5:16-17) Many, maybe most, Christians are living in some sort of denial of this most salutary work within them, afraid to either look at or deal with what the Spirit is necessarily revealing to them regarding the sin that dwells there.

Late in his life Luther is recorded as saying, "If I should still live a while, I would write a book about inner conflicts (*Anfechtungen*), without which no man can either understand the scripture nor the fear and love of God; in fact he cannot know what Spirit is."[8] He also said, "Everyone who has begun to serve God must yield to the fact that he must suffer much inner conflict and offense. No Christian person on earth will be without inner conflict. God leads us toward inner conflict." (!) Although such emphasis is found throughout his writings, nowhere is it more concentrated than in his exegesis of the Psalms in 1519-21. And no wonder. Luther did not invent this concept. He found it throughout the Psalmists' prayers. "How long O Lord?

---

6. WA 57, Heb. 186, 16.
7. Prenter, *Spiritus Creator*, 13.
8. BR, 4, 477.

Wilt Thou forget me forever??" And, "Out of the depths do I cry to thee O Lord!" to cite just two examples familiar to every serious Bible reader.

The central cause of inner conflict is unpardonable guilt in which one knows the irrevocable condemnation of God, and becomes convinced that one is stricken from the book of life forever. "There is in reality no difference between death and hell and the reality of the wrath of God in one's conscience . . . In this pass, terrible temptations beset the troubled soul. Ultimately the result is blasphemy, the desire that God were someone else, or that he did not exist . . . But these inner conflicts are the work of God, although as long as this is hidden from the anxious soul, it is Satan who dominates in the conflict and who tries to separate the sinner from God. But God pursues his own aim in the conflict. God is not really (*vere*) angry, and he does not desire that man's sin should be unpardonable. But through the cross of inner conflict God wants to teach us to hope only in his pure mercy."[9] *Anfechtungen* are not psychologically abnormal, but they are the means of God to reveal the truth of our current situation. This provides yet another contrast with the Scholastic theology. In that system, through imitation, the believer is related to Christ as an idea. Luther is proposing something far different. Biblically, he asserts, the believer is conformed to Christ by the person-in-person struggle of the Holy Spirit.

In his exegesis of Romans 8:15 and 23 Luther finds the comfort that he is not the first, nor the only one experiencing this. He finds there that Paul expresses this whole process as the Holy Spirit's *groanings* with us. And with this, *Anfechtungen* become God's alien work, not his proper work. In fact, the groanings are the Holy Spirit's own sufferings in His vital effort to save us. With this, the Holy Spirit is the real presence of God in the believer. When our eyes are opened to see that God is truly present as we undergo this death, and more: that God himself struggles for us in this unavoidable anguish—this is what signifies the end of the Law and the coming of the Gospel. "Luther sternly and firmly contends that everything outside of God himself in the inner conflict allies itself with wrath against the sinner. No form of divine power other than that of God's own presence is available for the sinner in his conflict. No infused grace can groan for man with unutterable groanings. No one but God himself is able to do that."[10]

So, in Luther, the Holy Spirit can no longer be a remote transcendental cause of infused grace for the upwardly striving candidate for salvation. Whenever Luther speaks of God's remoteness, it is only to express His hiddenness during temptation and spiritual conflict, not as a goal toward which

---

9. Prenter, *Spiritus Creator*, 15-16.
10. Prenter, *Spiritus Creator*, 18.

one strives. Most characteristically, the Holy Spirit is the very near one, the very tender one, literally God's personal presence, who works confidence in the saving act of Jesus Christ by stripping our confidence away from anything else at all. But that tenderness is preceded by God's merciful severity of conforming the sinner.

2. Preaching by the Holy Spirit: a Matter of Death and Life

"For Paul, the beginning of the new walk is closely related to baptism. Baptism makes us participators in the death and resurrection of Jesus. It puts an end to the walk in sins."[11] Baptism is the source and the "*a priori*" of the new walk (conduct or behavior) in Christ's Spirit. "Did you not die with Christ and pass beyond the reach of the elemental spirits of the universe?" (Colossians 2:20) "If anyone is in Christ he is a new creation." (2 Corinthians 5:17) These verses express Paul's radical preaching of the effect of baptism on our Christian life. Baptism ended our slavery to the power of sin and set us in the new realm of Christ only through our death to sin in baptism in "walking according to the Spirit" possible. Luther puts it well:

"The meaning is that not only have you been washed and cleansed in soul through the forgiveness of sins, but your flesh and blood have been condemned, given over unto death, to be drowned, and your life on earth to be a daily dying to sin . . . therefore, if you let yourselves be baptized, you give yourself over to gracious drowning and merciful slaying at the hands of your God and say to him: 'Drown and overwhelm me, dear Lord, for gladly would I henceforth, with thy Son be dead to sin, that I may with him, also live through grace.'"[12]

Gerhard Forde would say that the work of the Holy Spirit, which is called sanctification, is simply "being salvationed"—the new life arising from the catastrophe suffered by the death of the old. Ernest Becker, a favorite author of Forde's and no Lutheran, writes, "The hardest thing is not even the death, but the rebirth, no longer as gods, but as human beings, shorn of all our defenses, projects and claims."[13] When Paul said that God's justifying act in Christ must be in faith, apart from the Law, it is a mighty attack on the old being. The entire universe of the old being was constituted by the "if-then" paradigm. But that conditional shape of all existence only made things worse. In absolute contrast, what comes by the preaching of

---

11. Bietenhard, Hans. "Onoma," 944.
12. Luther. *Epistle Sermons*, vol 8:23.
13. Becker, *Denial of Death*, 58.

the Holy Spirit is the conviction engendered in the heart of the believer that we live in a "because-therefore" form of existence, freed from the Law. The Gospel is therefore not an "offer," but a complete execution of the old together with the resurrection of the new. Forde notes that Paul does not say "now get busy and die," but startlingly "You have died." The very fact that there is nothing left to do, *is* the execution of the old being. It puts to death two things that belong to the old: our *morality* together with our *immorality*. Grace explodes any ideas of progress or morality based upon the conditions of the Law. All notions of human progress toward righteousness die under the total assault of Christ's completed Righteousness in the believer. We are baptized into Christ.

"Luther's different hermeneutic leads to a different authority structure and thus a different ecclesiology . . . Where the word actually kills and makes alive, matters are quite different. The one so killed and made alive needs no earthly structure to *guarantee* the "doctrine." Where death and resurrection are not reckoned with theologically, however, such assurance can only be misunderstood as "psychological" egotism and "subjectivism." . . . When the theological significance of death-life language is not grasped, one tends only to pit ontology against psychology in the continuum of the "deathless" being."[14] (his italics)

So the two sequential works of the Holy Spirit regarding our salvation involve the killing of the whole old being, together with the comforting and assuring of the resurrected new creature. Life comes through death. Resurrection does not come without a grave. The resurrected ones can describe that grave in withering detail. With Paul, Luther directs us not to the "higher man" of idealism, but to the place where the whole of man is at his very lowest point. Here all our powers are stripped away in a death and dying where all idealistic striving becomes impossible. There is no human hope in the midst of damnation and death. But something else is there—God himself, with the hope found only in his Son. Death/Resurrection becomes a present reality when the Holy Spirit conforms us to Jesus Christ. This is the work of God. It is a work wholly alien to us. "Grace is the real presence of God himself. Where God is, there the whole salvation is already present. This does not mean that it is finished, but it does mean that it is certain."[15] To preach the gospel includes personally bearing witness that this strange work of the Spirit is not to be feared, but welcomed.

---

14. Forde, *Justification—a Matter of Death and Life*, 100.
15. Luther. *Epistle Sermons*, vol 8 p. 25.

3. Faith, from the Perspective of the Holy Spirit, is Suffering

Faith in Christ is the medium in which the Holy Spirit does His work of creating and destroying. The faith created by the Holy Spirit specifically consists in believing that Christ and the Christian "are one." In faith, the believer is united more closely to Christ than a man and a woman are united in marriage. This union is so close that whatever belongs to one, belongs to the other as well. Thus, the totality of my sins becomes Jesus' sin, and His perfect righteousness becomes totally mine. This is the necessary basis for the fact, claimed throughout Paul's writings, that the righteousness of Christ is truly reckoned to me together with my sin being truly reckoned to Christ. The proof, that faith makes Christ's righteousness currently effective for me, is that Christ would not be with me if he had not taken sin from me.

A few preliminary observations need to be made in order to rightly understand Luther's vital contribution to the understanding of faith under the work of the Holy Spirit. First, *this faith cannot be understood as a work of man!* (a most pernicious notion, often in pietistic garb, that simply will not die, even among those who declare their allegiance to the Reformation.) Faith understood in any sense as an act of human will, which alone validates God's "offer of salvation", inevitably leads to a semi-Pelagian theology together with the loss of any hope of certainty regarding God's election, as we have argued in the chapter on the captivation of the will.

Second, our only help is the righteousness of God given as a gift to the sinner, who now becomes wholly justified yet wholly sinner *at the same time*. It is essential that God's assault upon our sin be an assault on the totality of sin. It follows that proper Christian certainty is located and anchored in the fact that our salvation thus also becomes a totality. This "*simul*" (at the same time) is experienced as a mortal combat, and the person of the believer is the war zone. The suffering that this entails will be more fully discussed below.

Third, in the fight for "totality" in our salvation, Luther distinguishes between the terms "grace" and "gift". One finds this most clearly in his *Magnificat*, where he notices that Mary first praises God for his *favor*, and only after that, for his gifts. For Luther, grace is God's evaluation, his favor, his regard—that which unifies man's life and makes him a personality, that which makes him perfect. "Mary confesses that the foremost work God did for her was that He regarded her, which is indeed the greatest of His works, on which all the rest depend and from which they all derive. For where it comes to pass that God turns His face toward one to regard him, there is nothing but grace and salvation, and all gifts and works must follow."[16] And again, "His good things are merely gifts, which last for a season; but His grace and regard are the inheritance, which lasts forever, as St. Paul says in Romans 6:23:'The grace of God is eternal life.' In giving us the gifts He gives only what is His, but in His grace and His regard of us He gives His very self. In the gifts we touch His hand; but in His gracious regard we receive His heart, spirit, mind and will. Hence the Blessed Virgin puts His regard in the first and highest place."[17] This Grace or Regard is the opposite of God's Wrath. Therefore, the Aaronic benediction becomes a pronouncement of total salvation toward the sinner in that it proclaims God's face turned in blessing toward the hearers. Gift, in contrast, is faith in Christ together with the forgiveness of sins.

Fourth, besides this distinction between God's grace and gift, the believer must also distinguish between what is active and what is passive in our salvation. Since the Grace and favor of God—his positive regard and evaluation—reside completely outside our purview or ability, this "Grace" is always something external, which we receive passively. It is necessary to clearly acknowledge this externality, if proper Christian confidence that our salvation as a total conception is ever to exist, because nothing within us is total, yet. Faith, the gift, however, while it believes the externality and totality of Grace toward the sinner, resides *in* humankind and is active as repentance. Via repentance, the good war is declared where the sinner acknowledges complete agreement with God's judgment. But this is only is possible by faith. Without faith in the gift of Christ's forgiveness, the sinner has no option but to protect himself from judgment by making excuses and disagreeing with God's judgment. (cf. Matthew 25:44ff) So the acknowledgement, on the part of a sinner, that God's judgment is right becomes the most basic, objective, empirical, inarguable evidence of faith. Luther makes this argument extensively in his Romans commentary.

Having made these preliminary observations, when Luther defines faith in relation to the work of the Holy Spirit, one could summarize it in one phrase by saying that *the Holy Spirit must always lead the sinner into conflict*. With regard to the Holy Spirit's work, faith is:

strenuous;

it is *suffering*;

it is *struggle*;

it is *stressful*; and

16. LW 21:321.
17. LW 21:324-5.

it *participates in the Spirit's groanings for us.*
(Romans 8:15, 23, Galatians 4:6-7)

There are at least five reasons for this. The first reason that faith is both a strenuous struggle and suffering, is that for faith to continue to exist, it *must continually live by making ever anew the distinction between the two Words that God speaks to the sinner—Law and Gospel.* Such distinction cannot be demonstrated psychologically or experimentally. It is not open to observation nor to feeling. These two Words must not only be heard in proper order, Law then Gospel, but the believer must not let the Law prevail for too long. But this distinction resides in the Holy Spirit's coming and revelation, and not in the highly trained acuity of the interpreter's perception or rational thought, nor is it mastered in the theological academy.

Here one enters a gray area in Luther's thought. Is this distinction determined in an active or passive capacity? The distinction seems to reside in both areas. For example, in the later Galatians commentary, Luther calls this distinction between the Words of Law and Gospel "an art" at which he, even as a long-term doctor of theology is not very adept. Here the implication seems to be that such a distinction resides in the activity of the faith of a believer. However, the urgent question also arises: can one realistically call this an "active" role by the believer when such a distinction can only be achieved "by faith", which as a gift of God through the coming of the Holy Spirit therefore resides in the "passive" realm of things? To say that it is in preaching where this distinction is made ever anew, only begs the question. The preacher must suffer as he or she prepares to announce that distinction. In any case, (that is, experienced either as an active or as a passive event) the believer must *suffer* not knowing the border between these two Words until God comes. And without knowing that border, the judgment of the Law always prevails against the sinner. To deliver us from this crushing total judgment of God's Wrath, and to help us make the right distinction between His two Words, *God, the Holy Spirit, mercifully comes to the sinner.* This event, a deliverance marked in the conscience, is called preaching, and it is what finally distinguishes the two Words. When the angels at Christmas proclaim to the shepherds (not great candidates for spirituality) "To *you* is born this day a Savior"—that is the specific content of what is here called "the coming of God."

The distinction, this "coming" in the event of preaching, is where the sinner hears the delivering proclamation of absolution. We can expect God to come to us most reliably in His authorized and commanded preaching, where, after the Law is announced, Jesus Christ and His work on behalf of the sinner is proclaimed, in a "here and now", "I-you" declaration. God also comes in the "here and now", "I-you" pronouncement of the sacrament, at the Lord's table or at baptism, that this touchable element *is* God's gracious coming "to you" to remove your sin. But rightly distributed sacraments depend upon the word of preaching. Gerhard Forde's helpful contribution here, is that by emphasizing the actual fact of God's coming in the event of proclamation, the distinction between Law and Gospel is removed from the terrifying realm of the abstract where human ability to determine that distinction with any certainty always meets with shipwreck. And, as Luther would insist, the event of proclamation also removes making the distinction between Law and Gospel from the troublesome venue of human *rational* jurisdiction and places it instead in the jurisdiction of the Holy Spirit. So faith is a suffering because of the necessity of making the distinction between Law and Gospel ever anew. But this entails awaiting the coming of the Holy Spirit, whose coming resides outside our control and strictly within the mercy of God, and whose coming alone makes this distinction apparent to the sinner. This coming of the Holy Spirit, personally to the sinner, is the only foundation upon which faith itself can be built.

Second, faith is suffering because, as continuing sinners, it is necessary to believe that our salvation is a total gift. As such *we can possess nothing whatsoever*. But if it is not ours, it must be alien and completely outside ourselves. The Holy Spirit directs us solely to Christ, away from ourselves. The person of Jesus Christ unites both the "Grace" of God toward sinners and the "gift" of God for sinners. Additionally, a believer's suffering inheres in that which faith believes is totally non-intuitive. We would expect something more "empirical" that could be visibly confirmed by methods of science, or something "analog" like measurable progress, or something that would address our "feelings." We are "unmanned" by a rescue that directs us instead to something completely different. We are commanded in preaching, with the Israelites in the desert, to look at the new location which God has made for what is killing us. Our sin is no longer on us, but it is hung on the cross in Jesus. "Faith in Christ is the real presence of Christ in us as a redeeming reality, which as an invisible and incomprehensible but divine reality, tears us away from, and places us in contrast, to all other reality."[18]

Third, faith is suffering and strenuous because *faith works completely with the non-apparent*. Hebrews 11 is the most concentrated meditation upon this suffering form of faith in the entire scriptural revelation. Instead of being confirmed by either feeling or sight, or any of the other senses, faith hangs solely upon a word that is spoken. What is more, faith hangs upon a word of promise that must be spoken again and again in order to overcome

---

18. Prenter, *Spiritus Creator*, 50.

our threatening doubts. It is no fun—in fact it feels like dying—for a mature person to be reduced to such helplessness. Yet that is the essence of the struggle into which the Holy Spirit constantly leads us. The man who said to Jesus, "I believe. Help my unbelief!" is both a personal witness to this struggle, and an encouragement to absolutely every believer that this struggle is no cause for despair but rather is the most objective evidence of the presence of the Holy Spirit, without whom we would not know this desire. Paul roots our assurance of faith, not in spiritual ecstasies or heights of feeling, but precisely in the opposite, in the anguished cries from the depths of need, in the struggle and groaning of the believer's regress from self-confidence into faith in Christ. (Romans 8:16-17, Galatians 4:6-7)

Fourth, faith is a suffering *because the success of God's total assault upon our sin has to be believed, that is, God's total triumph is not yet apparent to us.* Being under God's Grace and Wrath are both total and comprehensive states for a believer, just as pregnancy is total state for a woman. Neither can the believer be partially under God's Grace. When a sinner is under Grace, he or she is totally so. When a sinner is under God's Wrath, he or she is totally so. But, here is the problem: until the resurrection, believers still have sin. This means that they are, *at the same time,* completely righteous (that is, totally under God's Grace, having His positive regard) while at the same time being completely sinful, and thus, subject to God's total Wrath under the Law. There can be no partly-partly here.

Romans 7, perhaps the most fought over chapter of the New Testament regarding its correct interpretation, weighs in precisely at this point. On one side are the interpreters who, because they believe in the analog or "progress" form of sanctification, have to insist that what Paul describes in verses 15-24 are his experience *previous* to becoming a Christian. They argue that Romans 7 cannot be autobiographical in view of his self-description of his life previous to his conversion in Philippians 3:6, "as to righteousness under the law—blameless." On the other side are the interpreters, who believe that everything included in the very same verses is Paul's description of the *present* radical situation of a believer's suffering faith. These latter interpreters take that position because they emphasize the truth that no un-resurrected sinner has yet been delivered fully from the presence and activity of sin in their lives. Believers, instead of being "sinless", are rather "free from sin", in that for the first time, they can wage war against the remaining sin in their lives. Interpreters who hold this position are convinced that Paul here calls sinners to believe more firmly still, in spite of the pressing and obvious evidence of continuing sin, that we are in a new location, and that new location "in Christ", alone, is the total rescue from the continuing predations of the sin within us all. Freedom from sin comes directly from the announcement of forgiveness, which assures us that we are released from the enslaving power of its guilt. Only the Holy Spirit can impart this confidence.

Finally, faith is suffering because *through this faith the Holy Spirit is conforming us to the person of Christ*. But this conforming is, by definition, a painful process. I Peter 1:6-7 likens it to being put into a forge. The pain is non-negotiable. The believer is guaranteed only two things by the Apostle Paul in Romans 5:1-5—peace with God and suffering. As Christ suffered, so everyone who follows him enters into the same forge of suffering by which one learns both dependence upon and confidence in God. To truly pray "thy will be done" is to pray against ourselves, against our fondest hopes and dreams, and against our very life itself, so that we can have true life for the first time. This is suffering. Conformity becomes just another word for faith in Christ. The reason for this is that such conformity can never be created by imitation, nor by aspiring toward what we think such conformity might look like. Conformity to Christ always leads to the opposite of what we desire, think, or dream. Thus, it always involves our death. True conformity is always a surprise, a resurrection to brand new life, and is not infected with the piety of imitation. In conforming the sinner, Christ overpowers the sinner and enters into an active relation with him in the event of hearing his Word. This conformity is in direct contrast to the paradigm of scholasticism where the sinner is the active one and tries to approach God as a "timeless truth", and as an idea. It is the work of the Spirit to accomplish the miracle of conforming the believer to Christ. His groanings within this work are the most elementary manifestation of faith, which flees from all its own to Christ alone.[19] This conformity is intimately related to the next key concept in Luther's understanding of the Holy Spirit's work.

4. The Work of the Holy Spirit is to Create "Experience" in the Believer

Only the Holy Spirit can create personal "experience", which serves as the criterion for the certainly true. The experience of faith is opposed to all natural experience. Yet it is still experience—experience born from inner conflict. The experience of faith is concerned with reality. The "knowing" which arises from this experience is not about, or from, ideas or human imagination. It is a growing and miraculous confidence that the work of Christ for the believing sinner is going on apace, in the events of our own life. In Luther's Magnificat, from 1521, Luther gives his definition of how the

---

19. Prenter, *Spiritus Creator*, 54.

Holy Spirit creates this "experience" and shows how vital it is to both faith and to the understanding of God and His Word. In virtually the opening sentence of this treatise Luther writes, "Mary is speaking on the basis of her own experience, in which she was enlightened and instructed by the Holy Spirit. No one can correctly understand God or His Word unless he has received such understanding immediately from the Holy Spirit. But no one can receive it from the Holy Spirit without experiencing, proving, and feeling it. In such experience the Holy Spirit instructs us as in His own school, outside of which nothing is learned but empty words and prattle."[20] But this "experience" involves a literal death/resurrection. "(God) lets the godly become powerless and to be brought low, until everyone supposes their end is near whereas in these very things He is present to them with all His power, yet so hidden and in secret that even those who suffer the oppression do not feel it but only believe. There is the fullness of God's power and His outstretched arm. For where man's strength ends, God's strength begins, provided faith is present and waits on Him. And when the oppression comes to an end, it becomes manifest what great strength was hidden underneath the weakness."[21] The entire purpose in God making us undergo it, is to build a level of confidence that God is faithful, a confidence that ideas and syllogisms can never produce. One "knows" in this experience at a level that far surpasses the cognitive. It is a knowing that comes from a person to person interaction and relation. It is a knowing where "guessing" that something is possible or true is rendered ridiculous and inane. It is a knowing where we are literally introduced to the person who indwells every believer. It is a knowing which convinces the believer who has experienced it, that "the truth", that is, saving truth, resides not in objective, detached, observational data, but in subjective, passionately involved experience.

In the Gospel of John chapters 6-9 such "knowing" is center stage. The First letter of John picks this up again where from chapter 2 through 5 this "knowing" appears at least 27 more times. In First John, literally every instance of this "knowing" is connected intimately with the work of the Holy Spirit. "This, then, is the first work of God—that He is merciful to all who are ready to do without their own opinion, right, wisdom, and all spiritual goods, and willing to be poor in spirit. These are the ones who truly fear God, who count themselves not worthy of anything, be it ever so small, and are glad to be naked and bare before God and man; who ascribe whatever they have to His pure grace, bestowed on the unworthy; who use it with praise

---

20. LW 21:299.
21. LW 21:340.

and fear and thanksgiving, as though it belonged to another, and who seek not their own will, desire, or honor, but His alone to whom it belongs."[22]

> "The content of Luther's concept of experience is very clear. Experience means a proof of reality in opposition to a dream, word, or fancy. Thus when Christ by the witness of the Spirit is proven to be reality as apart from a mere idea (thought, word, fancy), this is the experience of faith. But since the object of faith is Christ as God's revelation in the flesh, the experience of faith must necessarily appear as a contrast to all other experience. In the experience of faith the witness of God's Spirit struggles with our own reason and senses. But the experience of faith is a true *experience*. In the man in whom the experience of faith by the witness of the Spirit is produced, there is no doubt that he is face to face with reality, yes, face to face with a reality which is over and above all other reality. Therefore Luther does not hesitate to say that he who believes in Christ shall feel the Holy Spirit in himself. For the feeling of the Holy Spirit is nothing else than to hear his groanings that cannot be uttered and to have part in them."[23]

Only the Holy Spirit is able to take us from faith as an idea, to the conviction that the witness of scripture is most certainly true. Without this testimony of the Holy Spirit the whole Gospel witness becomes mere history or ideal. Only the Holy Spirit can take the word of the Gospel and lift it from the level of signification to the level of event, where the Word happens to us and acts upon us, literally resurrecting dead people. This original distinction between "letter" and "Spirit" of the young Luther grew into the more complex and developed Law and Gospel that became his non-negotiable hermeneutical plow to understand anything he expounded from scripture. As we have already noted, it is a hermeneutic which is polemical to absolutely any other hermeneutic or interpretive system. As Mary herself found, no biblical interpreter, in the process of using it, can avoid the experience of the cross and the resurrection, of "dying" and "being made alive again." I take this "dying" to mean acknowledging our ignorance and complete blindness before God and His Word, no matter how many academic degrees we hold, and our waiting to be made alive again, through the Spirit's ever new revelation, in which God impresses upon us whatever, in God's opinion, needs emphasis for that specific occasion. The Spirit, "the miraculous power which gives man knowledge of the saving

---

22. LW 21:339.
23. Prenter, *Spiritus Creator*, 57.

work which God has accomplished for him, demands of him the renunciation of his own wisdom (I Corinthians 2:1-5), and indeed any verification by human standards." [24] This attacks Greek philosophy's identification of "spirit" and "mind." It also departs from Judaism, by placing "Spirit" and "wisdom" in dialectic opposition.

Two simple examples of this humility before the Word come to mind. Raedar Daehlin, was district president of Montana when I first became a pastor. He was not only respected, but deeply loved by the pastors he served. He would say to us things such as this at pastors' retreats: "Since you are going to preach on an assigned text on Sunday, why don't you open it up and read it the previous Monday so that the Word can "work on you" all week. And, by the way, why don't you memorize it, so that over the course of your whole ministry you furnish your thinking with that same Word." Another example was my doctoral advisor, Jim Nestingen, who would ask me during a week when we were assigned to preach, "Don't you feel that Word working on you?" The Word is not only active. It is both prior to our understanding as well as necessary to our understanding. Its "work" delivers what we are called to proclaim in the current situation.

5. The Work of the Holy Spirit Shapes the New Life of the Believer

There is no adequate word in the English language to convey properly the mixture of what resides in the passive nature of faith in relation to what resides in its active nature. "Piety" has had such a long history understood primarily as the believer's "active" or "validating" accepting of God's grace, as to render it immediately suspicious for any positive role in a more "evangelical" understanding of "new life." Nevertheless, the word "piety" will have to do for purposes of this argument to cover or define *wherever there is faith that is active in love.*

At the outset, let it be emphasized that, for Luther, while faith is unceasingly and inherently active, the *works* of faith are empirically ambiguous. In Luther's teaching regarding vocation, human works are not separated into those which are categorized as holy, as distinguished from works which are more profane or every-day. Rather, the character of each work is determined solely by the presence or absence of faith. As such, the very mundane works required by, for instance, being mother or father can be holy works, provided that those parents believe *that they have God's command to do them.* "Apart from these Ten Commandments no deed, no conduct can be good or

---

24. Kleinknecht, "Pneuma and Pneumatikos," 428.

pleasing to God no matter how great or precious it may be in the eyes of the world."[25] It is God's Word of command together with a believer's faith in that Word which transforms what is, for everyone else a "mundane" work into a holy work. Thus the ambiguity. It is simply not possible to judge empirically or to determine by human classification what works are pleasing to God. It is the faith of the believer that they have God's Word of command to do something which, alone, determines whether any work is a "good work", that is, faith active.

But what is this new life of active faith created by the work of the Spirit? Surely it is more than the groaning of inner conflict, more than "odium sui" (hatred of oneself), more than taking refuge in an alien righteousness. And it is. This life is nothing else than the living, indwelling presence of Christ Himself who, as our complete and alien righteousness, is in the process of reclassifying the entire old man. Here there is no clear distinction between justification/conversion and sanctification/growth in holiness. They happen together. When sanctification is no longer understood in an analog fashion as a "progress" (as one would expect it to be if it were an exodus from vice into virtue), but rather as the total assault of God upon our sin where the exodus from personal virtue into an undeserved and alien grace entails the sinner being literally relocated into Christ, then it is an event which the believer experiences as personal "regress" more than a "progress". Yet it is a progress, but it is one completely hidden from the sinner in whom it is being performed.

We *have* died with Christ. Sin no longer has us in its power. This is the first premise of the Christ life. Yet this is far from self-evident! "Our life is *hid* with Christ in God." (Colossians 3:3) Luther condenses it into pithy Latin, "*Proficere, hos est semper a novo incipere.*" (To advance: this is always to begin anew.) "The saints are inwardly always sinners, therefore they are always being justified outwardly . . . Inwardly, I say, as we are in ourselves, in our own eyes, in our own opinion—outwardly, however, as we are with God and as we stand in his judgment. Thus we are outwardly justified not from within ourselves, not from our own works, but solely through the power of divine imputation . . . Within yourself is nothing but perdition, but your salvation is without."[26] Since we are always sinners in ourselves and always believe that our only hope is in an alien righteousness, the "progress" in our Christian life is a constant beginning anew. In sermons Luther compares a believer's "progress" to being in the hands of a good physician. We are not well yet, but we are in recovery. Our recovery depends upon three things, in

---

25. Tappert, *Book of Concord*, 407.
26. WA 56, 268, 27.

this order: the promise of the physician, our faith in that promise, and our consequent obedience to what he tells us to do.

Nevertheless, a believer's new location "in Christ", and not any "progress", is the sole warrant for a sinner's safety from the accusations of our opponent, the devil. But this new location must be believed. And so a Christian constantly goes back to the beginning, which is the pronouncement of the forgiveness of sins. It is this justifying event of forgiveness which creates the regress from trusting in personal virtue as well as reaffirming our confidence in our new location. The constant and daily regress from believing that our growth in holiness must be defined by our own exodus from vice to virtue, forces the believer into the only alternative left—the daily exodus into the grace of the new location "in Christ". The apostle Paul literally wears out this two-word phrase "in Christ", trying to tattoo onto our brain and into our consciousness that we are saved by location, location, location. But this insistence that our new location is the only proper warrant for certainty of faith, produces this delicious irony: *Real piety can only exist in flight from "piety", into Grace.*

The Shape of Exiting from Virtue into Grace

Returning to the opening verse of this chapter, *"who walk not according to the flesh but according to the Spirit,"* it seems that the church has always squirmed out of, or modified the radicality of Paul's message. Notice the variety of efforts in the following list:

- The synergism (cooperation between man and God) of classical Catholic theology has no place in Paul.

- Methodism also stumbles at verse 4. According to Barrett, "this means that it is now *open* to men to live 'after the flesh' or 'after the Spirit' . . . Perhaps some of us need to recover the personal and evangelistic urgency that grips men when they see that life after the flesh can lead only to death"[27] But choice and free will introduced as possibility after justification separates sanctification from justification and places the emphasis on man's action once again. Paul, however, sees the walk as a process controlled by God *alone* (according to the Spirit).

- Enthusiasts stumble here because the Spirit is not connected with baptism and our daily death to sin and reliance on God's grace. They don't

---

27. Barrett, *Reading Through Romans*, 48.

recognize the inner conflict that the Spirit works in us, which teaches us to pray.

- Calvin stumbles by making grace or the Spirit irresistible and not placing predestination and responsibility side by side.
- Barth stumbles here because of the radical discontinuity he postulates between the "Unmensch" (literally, the monster) and the man in Christ. He writes, "How can we, who walk after the Spirit and in whom has occurred so incomprehensible, irresistible, and irrevocable a transformation, fail to stand completely above the life we lived in the flesh—before this transformation?"[28] This can only be heard as law.
- Lutheran orthodoxy stumbles here because of its "third use of the law." (The "first use" is to drive us to Christ. The "second use" is to maintain earthly order and safety. The contested "third use" asserts the continued necessity of the Law's directives to inform Christian behavior.) But to assert a third use would be to say that the Holy Spirit doesn't know His office.
- Closely related to the preceding, Pietism stumbles here because "walking" becomes a new moralism. Flesh and Spirit are not understood in their true power.

This very incomplete list demonstrates how the church has traditionally made loopholes were there were none, or tried to explain the paradox of predestination with responsibility by logic alone, without relying on the experience of faith. Or, it has omitted the concept of baptism with its daily suffering and death as part of the work of the Spirit.

Romans 8:4 is in the indicative verbal mood, describing a fact, and not in the subjunctive or hortatory mood. These verbal moods are never mixed in Paul's theology. The contemporary Christian must have this radical Word preached to him more so now than ever in the face of the inroads of enthusiasm, skepticism and scientism. The Gospel of God's unmixed grace is as needed now as in any age, to address the anxieties cause by our helplessness in the face of God's absolute.

Regarding the sinner's exodus from virtue into Grace, Luther writes in the meaning of the Third Article of the Apostle's Creed on the work of the Holy Spirit: "In this church, day after day, he fully forgives the my sins and the sins of all believers and keeps me united with Christ in the

---

28. Barth, *The Epistle to the Romans*, 282.

one true faith."²⁹ In the Large Catechism, on the same subject of the Holy Spirit he writes,

> "How does this sanctifying take place? Answer: Just as the Son obtains dominion by purchasing us through his birth, death, and resurrection, so the Holy Spirit effects our sanctification through the following: the communion of saints or Christian church, the forgiveness of sins, the resurrection of the body, and the life everlasting. In other words, he first leads us into his holy *community*, placing us upon the bosom of the church, where he preaches to us and brings us to Christ . . . Therefore to sanctify is nothing else than to bring us to the Lord Christ and receive this blessing, which we could not obtain by ourselves . . . Where he does not cause the Word to be preached and does not awaken understanding in the heart, all is lost."³⁰

Luther's idea of the relation between faith and love is this: where God is the lover and the sinner is the object of his love, that describes faith; but, where flowing from being yourself beloved, you become the lover, and your neighbor is the object of your love, that describes love. That miraculous work of the Holy Spirit, entails twin reversals: turning our eyes from being *curvatus in se* (curved in upon ourselves) toward those outside ourselves; and, at the same time turning our eyes from always looking upward for the "glorious" and instead looking "downward", along with God's eyes, to where our neighbor lives and where he needs our service. This reversal of direction is not the result of human achievement, but is the result of the Holy Spirit working the promise into the believer's heart.

One more thing needs to be said about the Law as it relates to a Christian's new "walk", as Paul calls it. For the first time Luther gives the Law a resoundingly positive assessment, but again, not as one would expect. For him the Law is not a "to do list" by which one measures one's suitability for salvation nor is it a tool to measure any sort of "progress" in holiness. Rather, it now becomes the warrant for knowing that one is living under God's blessing! For instance, a Christian mother and father know that in the routine of diapers, school schedules, dentist appointments, feeding, clothing, and modeling proper behaviors for their children—that in all these myriad tasks God is pleased with their efforts. The reason is this: they know that they have God's command to do these things from the Ten Commandments where He both commands and protects the human family.

---

29 Tappert, *Book of Concord*. 345.
30. Tappert, *Book of Concord*. 415-16.

Again, the ambiguity of "good works" is instantly evident. Doesn't everyone do the very same things? Yes they do. But not all believe that they have God's warrant to do them. It is the knowing and believing that warrant which creates the blessing. In fact Luther goes so far as to say that if you do not have God's warrant or command, which blesses what you are doing, quit doing it. "Here, then, we have the Ten Commandments, a summary of divine teaching on what we are to do to make our whole life pleasing to God. They are the true fountain from which all good works must spring, the true channel through which all good works must flow. Apart from the Ten Commandments no deed, no conduct can be good or pleasing to God, no matter how great or precious it may be in the eyes of the world."[31] In short, the Law is not restricted to being an accusing voice. In the new life of the Holy Spirit, the Law resumes its original function of describing for a believer what is blessed.

Gerhard Forde makes a greatly needed contribution to the discussion of sanctification by questioning the adequacy of the dominant view of Christian life as a "progress." His essay in "Christian Spirituality: Five Views of Sanctification"[32] bases his exposition on Romans 6:1-11. He writes that if we do need to speak of such a things as progress in sanctification, we should do so with great care. If it is a growth, "It is a growth in grace, a growth in coming to be captivated more and more, by the totality, the unconditionality of the grace of God."[33] He notes that Paul does not say, "Now get busy and die!" but startling says, "You have died!" This total assault is what ends the old being's dream of moral progress and moves all conceptions of human performance from under the "if-then" paradigm of the Law, into the "because-therefore" promise of Grace.

This total assault of God absolutely undoes the analog system of morality. All notions of progress are now contrasted to the simultaneity of sin and righteousness in the believer. "In this life we never get over grace, we never entirely grasp it, we never really learn it. It always takes us by surprise . . . .It is rather more like an oscillation between beginning and end in which both are always equally near . . . It is not that we are somehow moving toward the goal, but rather that the goal is moving closer to us. That is why it is a growth *in grace*, not a growth of our virtue or morality."[34]

For Luther, faith is not a supernatural substance of which the Holy Spirit is the supernatural cause. It is the personal gift of God which is

---

31. Tappert, *Book of Concord*, 407.
32. Alexander, *Christian Spirituality: Five Views of Sanctification*," 13-33.
33. Alexander, *Christian Spirituality: Five Views of Sanctification*," 27.
34. Alexander, *Christian Spirituality: Five Views of Sanctification*," 28-29.

constantly depending on God's renewing and gracious giving. Faith never becomes a possession, and the Spirit never becomes a divine cause. Faith is the life which is brought about by the really present reality of Christ mediated by the Spirit, which is simultaneously a escape from one's own empirical piety.[35] Now I am in the power of the Spirit. All that is left is continue to recognize that the very struggle and the conflict that mark my life Christ, is the most vital sign of the Holy Spirit's work, and thus my source of assurance. Already righteous, we offer our bodies as a living sacrifice in all the specific areas that are shown to us. This is the response to God's grace. This response IS God's grace.

Something about Joy

The walk according to the Spirit is to live in ambiguity. Like Abraham, we don't know where God has called us to go. Like Paul we don't know if we will be permitted to go to Rome or not. Our flesh constantly fights with that ambiguity seeking something more "certain." We are always uncomfortable to be dependent on faith alone. Like the Jew, we want to "remove the veil." (2 Corinthians 3) But if that is our attempt, all certainty is removed and we are once again striving against God. To reaffirm God's leading, to rely on His grace alone, to trust Him completely—in that lies suffering, freedom, and joy. But does this ambiguity prevent any structured attempt to systematize Christian behavior into an ethic? The answer is: not if systematics takes as its task description only, and stays in narrative form.

According to Luther, the Holy Spirit leads us completely to fulfill the law in every specific through creating love for our neighbor and 'merry hearts' within us. Thus the new ethic of "accomplishedness" fulfills the requirements of the old ethic. No Christian can prescribe for their brother or sister—only admonish. Christian ethics is always done in community where there is proclamation which supports the faith on which it rests.

Christian ethics is a dance where we respond to God's music. No longer are we in lock step with the Ten Commandments, but we become graceful dancers, able to respond thoroughly and spontaneously to our partners and to the music. Life is now a creative dance where the freedom is not alarming but natural and joyful. Every experience we can affirm in God. God's grace in Christ receives a new expression in these words of Sam Keen, "Inevitably graceful action, whether it be that of a gymnast performing of the parallel bars, or a patient coming to a creative acceptance of his illness, elicits the response, 'He make is look so easy, even I could do it!'

---

35. Prenter, *Spiritus Creator*, 87.

... Grace appears so simple it should be common, so natural it should be normal. Yet, in fact it represents a triumph over awkwardness and disease, which is so rare that its occurrence is always something of a miracle ... Description reveals a similarity between athletic, social, and theological meanings of grace which cannot be overlooked ... the foundations of gracefulness are trust and confidence."[36]

Faith and love correspond to prayer and work. Faith and love can't be separated at all. "Progress" in faith entails a regress from any confidence based upon personal virtue. "Progress" in faith, instead, is the growing acknowledgement of our weakness, together with our growing confidence in God's Grace and Regard toward us in Christ Jesus. Salvation consists not in becoming better and better, but rather in being led by the Holy Spirit more and more into the sphere of the power of Christ, that is: having His death and resurrection conform us into his image. Faith is a movement which never stops, which moves us always away from ourselves and always into Jesus Christ. If this is the case, such an understanding interprets Luther's strange last words before he died and reveal them as one of his finest testaments: "*Wir sind Bettler. Hoc est verum.*" (We are beggars. That is true.)[37]

At the end of all this one could rightly ask, "You make clear what the Holy Spirit *does*, but who *is* the Holy Spirit?" My answer entails another question. "How can one know the Holy Spirit *apart* from experiencing what the Spirit does?" I am convinced that our children, our friends and family, together with our surrounding community of saints need to hear our varied narrative answers to that single question. I am also convinced that the valid answers to the question "Who is the Holy Spirit" can only be given in personal testimony, in witness, in story.

---

36. Keen, *Apology for Wonder*, 201-203.

37. WA 48; 241, 2ff.

Epilogue: Bearing Witness

It was one of those gorgeous Alabama Sunday afternoons in late April of 2005. The sun was shining upon the oak and hickory tree canopy over our house on the banks of the Tennessee River, and all was well with the world. My wife Sheila and I were unwinding from the normal stress of the morning worship and Bible study when the telephone rang. The policeman on the other end was calling from Scottsdale Arizona, and at that very moment the world, as we had known it, ended. He told us that our daughter had been involved in a serious motorcycle accident and had been helicoptered to emergency at Scottsdale North Hospital. Friends raced us to the airport in Nashville where we caught the last flight to Phoenix, to get to Jennifer's side. On the way to the airport, my physician brother, Tim, delivered to us the truth which the policeman had avoided—that there was no hope of recovery for our daughter from this type of brain injury. The only hope was to get to her side before she died. Southwest Airlines seated us in the front row so that together we could process the shock in some sort of privacy. We raced the setting sun across the long miles. On the other end, a group of friends from the church we had formerly pastored in Scottsdale met us at the hospital and we formed a prayer circle around Jennifer's bed. They embraced us in our weeping. Jennifer was taken off life support the next day. The funeral and the sad packing up of her things from her apartment consumed the next few days. And again we were aided by our old church members who helped us pack and hosted the reception following the funeral. The critical moment for me, though, came later, as we paused, just our little family, at Jennifer's front door when the whole apartment was empty. Our son, Adam, Sheila and I shared a moment of prayer and then we went through that door and closed it forever. That simple act marked the character of a world we had never known before. I can only say that the beginning of our grief was like looking in on a bubble of a world where everyone else lived and we were on the outside.

The loss each of us suffered differed, but the theme of our loss was the place that Jennifer had uniquely occupied in our family. She had always been, from the day she entered our lives, this little ray of sunshine, filling every day with her cheer and beauty. She would call literally every day and prattle on about work and traffic and the neighbor's kids she babysat. Always there was laughter. Always we would end the conversation by saying, "I love you." Her last call, the previous Saturday, had been just the same, but since I was not particularly interested when the call became "girl talk", I signed off early and we said our "I love you's". On the one hand, I am so very glad that those were our last words. I can't think of better ones. On the other hand, they just underline the depth of our loss. Adam has since tried to be the cheer bringer to his mother, but it's not the same. He has the more melancholy streak of his father.

The long process of healing called grieving set in. I experienced a first—tears into my ears as I lay on our bed. Sheila and I began experimenting on ways to forge a new relationship between ourselves that included this mutual pain suffered so differently. God became an issue, as well. Why had he done this to our family?

Part of grieving is anger, and one day in my church study, I just had to get up and have it out with God. So I went out the church door to march around the Florence city park not far from the church office. It is about a forty-five minute total distance. It became a forty-five minute conversation, day after day, for the next several months. This is something I had never ever done in my previous ministry. It was a completely new experience. I began to experience it as a revelation. After awhile, I did not want to miss it.

I had grown up as a missionary kid in Madagascar where at some point in my teenage years we had had to learn sixty psalms by heart—one psalm per day for several months. It was pretty challenging. Consider learning Psalm 37 some morning! However, on these walks I began living in Psalm 130. The old words came back. "Out of the depths I cry to thee O Lord! Lord, hear my voice!" And I got up to the line "I wait for the Lord, my soul waits", and then I drew a blank. What was the next line? I was in the middle of my walk and I just could not remember what was next. Finally getting back to the office, I got right to my Bible and opened it up to the passage in question. There was the answer: "And in His Word do I hope."

Here I need to back up and tell you that I had been noticing two things occurring on each an every one of these walks. First, there was always a time for tears. At the beginning they marked a time of sorrow. Sometimes the sorrow was so wordless that I became convinced that some healing was going on there too deep for description. Imperceptibly the tears also sometimes became tears of joy. The second phenomenon, which caught me by surprise, is that I was becoming aware that after each walk I had learned something new. Not "new" in the sense that I had never known it before, but new in the old having a brand new impact, or new in making a connection I had never seen before. I had done doctoral work in theology. I have bookcases stuffed. Still, I was learning something new every day! But that should not have been a surprise either, since prayer is a two-way conversation where the Holy Spirit uses that connecting time to teach, encourage, rebuke, or comfort, as the case is needed. On the day I had the memory lapse, I am convinced that it was the Holy Spirit's way of impressing upon my heart the simple truth of those words, "And in his Word do I hope". He was preaching to me. First, so that I would never forget those words again, but more importantly, those words were the proper rock upon which I could anchor my grief.

Not long after this, as I was reaching the end of my ministry in Florence, a brother pastor and I were praying in my office. He looked up at me when we finished and asked me, out of the blue, "Are you supposed to be writing a book?" I said, "Yes." But how did he know that I had been putting this off, and putting this off, for the last several years? With his question, the pressure was on, and now it clearly became a matter of conscience. This book is the result. Writing it has been very much like a childbirth, full of trauma, and long pauses, and lots of questions about how to end it.

As each of us gets nearer and nearer to the finish line, the questions we once thought were critical get winnowed away until there is just about one question left. *Do we really trust the Word, and nothing else at all?* It has taken two painful deaths in my experience to teach me that this Word is a living Word. The severe mercy of going through such trauma is surely what Jesus taught us to pray about when he included the petition, "Deliver us from strong testing." Because it is precisely there when one must push all the chips to the middle and declare, "I'm all in." If God does not come through there and then, all is darkness and despair. But God does come through, most precisely and most personally, and most tenderly right there and then. I bear witness that he did for me.

Part of my anger at God on those walks was focused on the beatitude "How blessed are those who mourn!" "There is simply nothing blessed about mourning!" I literally shouted. Later on, it just became a more simmering, abrasive question. Still, there Jesus' words remained—"How blessed are those who mourn." Notice that Jesus does not say that it is blessed to mourn, but rather that *they who mourn* are blessed ones. Yet that significant distinction did not satisfy. Finally I was driven to the conclusion, or, more accurately, God revealed the truth, which I hope these few paragraphs have suggested, that the blessedness to which Jesus refers *is simply his presence*. That is what He means when He completes this beatitude with the words, "For they, (especially they), shall be comforted. He promises to be especially, intimately present to those who mourn. I bear witness that this is true. He also promises that "In His Word is our hope." I bear witness that this is also true. So I am glad to preach to all who will hear: Trust His Word, and nothing else at all.

Bibliography

Alexander, Donald ed., Gerhard Forde contributor. *Christian Spirituality: Five Views of Sanctification*. Westmont, Illinois: Intervarsity Press, 1989.
Althaus, Paul. *Theology of Martin Luther*. Translated by Robert C. Schultz. Philadelphia: Fortress, 1966.
Barrett, C.K. *Reading Through Romans*. London: Epworth, 1963.
Barth, Karl. *Epistle to the Romans*. from the 6th edition Translated by Edwin C. Hoskyns. New York: Oxford University Press, 1968.
Bayer, Oswald. quoting Luther's Table Talk # 5106, from his essay "Preaching the Word" in *Justification is for Preaching*. edited by Virgil Thompson, 196-216, Eugene OR: Wipf and Stock, 2012.
Bayer, Oswald. "Luther's Relevance for Today's Rupture of Times". in *Lutheran Quarterly* volume XIII, number 1, (1999) 35-50.
Becker, Ernest. *Denial of Death*. New York: Free Press, 1973.
Beitenhard, Hans. "Onoma" In *Theological Dictionary of the New Testament,* edited by Gerhard Kittel and Gerhard Friedrich. V:944. Grand Rapids: Eerdmans, 1981.
Bornkamm, Heinrich. *Luthers Vorreden zur Bibel*. hrsg. Hamburg: Furche Verlag, 1967.
Bruner, Frederick Dale. *Matthew: a Commentary*. vol. 2, Dallas: Word, 1990.
D. Martin Luthers Werke: Kristische Gesamtausgabe; BR, for D. Martin Luthers Werke: Kristische Gesamtausgabe. Birefweschsel; (cited as WA).
D. Martin Luthers Werke: Kristische Gesamtausgabe. Trischreden. (cited as WA TR).
Ebeling, Gerhard. *Luther: An Introduction To His Thought*. Translated by R.A. Wilson. Philadephia: Fortress, 1970.
———. "Luther's Understanding of Reality" in *Lutheran Quarterly,* vol. XXVII number 1, 56-75 (2013).
———. "On the Doctrine of the 'Triplex Usus Legis' in the Theology of the Reformation" in *Word and Faith* Translated by James Leitch. Philadelphia: Fortress, 1963.
———. *Truth of the Gospel*. Translated by David Green. Philadelphia: Fortress, 1985.
Ellul, Jacques. *Judgment of Jonah*. Translated by Geoffrey Bromiley. Grand Rapids: Eerdmans, 1971.
———. *To Will and To Do*. Translated by Edward Hopkins. Philadelphia: Pilgrim, 1969.
Forde, Gerhard. "Exodus from Virtue to Grace: Justification by Faith Today" in *Interpretation* vol 34 number 1 (1973) 32-44.
———.*Justification by Faith—a Matter of Death and Life*. Philadelphia: Fortress, 1982.
———. *On being a Theologian of the Cross*. Grand Rapids: Eerdmans, 1997.
———. *Theology is for Proclamation*. Minneapolis: Fortress, 1990.

———. notes from his lectures.

Guardini, Roman. *Das Christusbild der paulinischen and johannesischen Schriften.* Wurzburg: Werkbund-Verlag, 1961.

Harrisville, Roy Jr. *Pandora's Box Opened.* Grand Rapids: Eerdmans, 2014.

———. citing Roland Mushat Frye, "A Literary Perspective for the Criticism of the Gospel," in., *Jesus and Man's Hope.* Edited by Miller and Hadidian, vol 2 Pittsburg: Pittsburg Theological Seminary, 1970.

Holl, Karl. *Gesammelte aufsatze zur Kirchengeshchichte.* I: *Luther.* Tubingen: J.C.B. Mohr, 1932.

Iwand, Hans. *Righteousness of Faith According to Luther.* Translated by Randi Harrisville. Eugene OR: Wipf and Stock, 2008.

Jedin, Hubert. *History of the Council of Trent.* London: Thomas Nelson, 1961.

Keen, Sam. *Apology for Wonder,* New York: Harper and Row, 1969.

Kierkegaard, Soren. *Concluding Unscientific Postscript.* Translated by Walter Lowrie. Princeton: Princeton University Press, 1941.

———. *Papers and Journals: a Selection.* Translated by Alastair Hannay. London: Penguin, 1996.

———. *Sickness Unto Death.* Translated by Howard and Edna Hong. Princeton: Princeton University Press 1980.

Kleinknecht, Hermann et.al. "Pneuma/Pneumatikos" in *Theological Dictionary of the New Testament,* edited by Gerhard Kittel and Gerhard Friedrich. VI:332-451. Grand Rapids: Eerdmans, 1981.

Lessing, Gotthold Ephraim. "On the Proof of the Spirit and of Power" in *Lessing's Theological Writings,* Redwood City, CA: Stanford University Press, 1956.

Lohse, Bernhard. *Martin Luther's Theology.* Translated by Roy Harrisville, Minneapolis: Fortress, 1999.

Lowenich, Walther von. *Luther als Ausleger der Synoptiker.* Munchen Chr Kaiser Verlag, 1954 Stephenson, Bjarne W. Tiegen, Lake Mills Iowa: Graphic Publishing, 1985.

Luther and Erasmus: Free will and Salvation. Translated by E. Gordon Rupp and Phillip Watson. LCC 17 Philadelphia: Westminster 1969.

Luther, Martin. *Epistle Sermons.* Translated by John Lenker. Minneapolis: Luther Press, 1909.

Luther's Works, American Edition. 55 vols. edited by Pelikan, Jaroslav and Helmut T. Lehman. Philadelphia: Fortress, 1955-86 (cited as LW).

Marquart, Kurt et. al. eds. *A Lively Legacy: Essays in Honor of Robert Preus.* Lake Mills Iowa: Graphic Publishing, 1985.

Mauer, Christian. "Synoida and Syneidesis." in *Theological Dictionary of the New Testament,* edited by Gerhard Kittel and Gerhard Friedrich. VII:898-919. Grand Rapids: Eerdmans, 1981.

Moule, C.F.D. *The Phenomenon of the New Testament: an Inquiry into the Implications of Certain Features of the New Testament.* SBT 2nd series, vol. 1, London: SCM Press 1967.

Nichol, Todd. *Called and Ordained: Lutheran Perspectives on the Office of the Ministry.* Minneapolis: Fortress, 1990.

Nispel, Mark. "De Servo Arbitro and the Patristic Discussion of Freedom, Fate, and Grace," in *Logia, A Journal of Lutheran Theology.* Luther Academy, vol VII no. 4, (1998) 13-22.

O'Daly, Gerard. "Predestination and Freedom in Augustine's Ethics." in *Philosophy in Christianity*, edited by Godfrey Vesey. Cambridge: Cambridge University Press, 1989.
Pelikan, Jaroslav. *Growth of Medieval Theology*. Chicago: University of Chicago Press, 1978.
Pojman, Louis. *Logic of Subjectivity*. Tuscaloosa: University of Alabama Press, 1984.
Prenter, Regin. *Spiritus Creator*. Translated by John M. Jensen. Philadelphia: Muhlenberg, 1953.
Schaff, Philip, ed. *Nicene and Post Nicene Fathers*. Grand Rapids: Eerdmans, vol 4, 1952-1957.
Schlatter, Adolph. *Ruckblick auf meine Lebensarbeit*. Stuttgart: Calwer Verlag, 1977.
Schmidt, Karl Ludwig. "Kaleo/Klysis." In *Theological Dictionary of the New Testament*, edited by Gerhard Kittel and Gerhard Friedrich. III:487-536. Grand Rapids: Eerdmans, 1981.
Schrenk, Gerhard. "Eklogomai" in *Theological Dictionary of the New Testament*, edited by Gerhard Kittel and Gerhard Friedrich. IV:144-176. Grand Rapids: Eerdmans, 1981.
Spurgeon, C.H. edited by Begg, Alistar. *Morning and Evening: Daily Readings by C.H. Spurgeon*. Peabody, Massachusetts: Hendrickson, 1995.
Schweitzer, Eduard. *The Good News According to Mark*. Louisville, Kentucky: John Knox, 1970.
Schlegel, Fr. *Geschichte der alten un neuen Literatur*. 1812, Samtliche Werke 2, 17.
Sundberg, Walter. *Worship as Repentance*. Grand Rapids: Eerdmans, 1999.
Tappert, Theodore. ed. *Book of Concord*, Philadelphia: Muhlenberg, 1965.
Thielicke, Helmut. *Modern Faith and Thought*. Translated by Geoffrey W. Bromiley. Grand Rapids: Eerdmans, 1990.
Thompson, Virgil. ed. *Justification is for Preaching*. Eugene OR: Wipf and Stock, 2012.
Tillich, Paul. *Morality and Beyond*. Chicago: University of Chicago Press, 1963.
Waugh, Evelyn. *Brideshead Revisited*. Boston: Little Brown and Company, 1972.
Wingren, Gustav. *Living Word*. Philadelphia: Muhlenberg, 1949.
Wright, N.T. *Paul In Fresh Perspective*. Minneapolis: Fortress, 2005.
———. *Resurrection of the Son of God*. Minneapolis: Fortress, 2003.

www.ingramcontent.com/pod-product-compliance
Lightning Source LLC
Chambersburg PA
CBHW051738230426
43670CB00012B/2071